Erich Fromm and Critical Criminology

Erich Fromm
and Critical Criminology

BEYOND THE PUNITIVE SOCIETY

Edited by Kevin Anderson and Richard Quinney

With Two Essays by Erich Fromm,
Translated from the German and Annotated by Heinz D. Osterle
and Kevin Anderson

University of Illinois Press

Urbana and Chicago

Library of Congress Cataloging-in-Publication Data
Erich Fromm and critical criminology : beyond the punitive society / edited by Kevin Anderson and Richard Quinney ; with two
essays by Erich Fromm ; translated from the German and annotated
by Heinze D. Osterle and Kevin Anderson.
p. cm.
Includes bibliographical references (p.) and index.
ISBN 0-252-02514-8 (cloth : acid-free paper)
ISBN 0-252-06830-0 (pbk. : acid-free paper)
1. Fromm, Erich, 1900–   . 2. Criminal psychology. 3. Alienation
(Social psychology) 4. Criminal justice, Administration of. I. Anderson, Kevin, 1948–   . II. Quinney, Richard. III. Fromm, Erich,
1900–   . Staat als Erzieher. English. IV. Fromm, Erich, 1900–   .
Zur Psychologie des Verbrechers und der strafenden Gesellschaft.
English.
HV6080.F77E7   2000
364—dc21   99-6327
CIP

1 2 3 4 5 C P 5 4 3 2 1

Contents

Preface

Erich Fromm's name is not often connected to the field of criminology. Yet, as each of the contributors to this collection will argue, his work has important implications for criminology today, whether for critical, peacemaking, or feminist approaches to the field. At one level, Fromm's overall work in social theory offers important general grounding for a critical/peacemaking criminology. At a time when American society seems bent, to an unprecedented degree, on imprisonment, executions, and other violent responses to the problem of crime, Fromm's humanist critique of the existing social system offers a unique vantage point from which to renew and develop a critical criminology. At another level, Fromm's early writings on the problem of crime in modern capitalist society constitute an important if neglected contribution to criminology proper. Published on the eve of Hitler's coming to power in Germany, they appear in English for the first time as part 3 of this volume.

In the first chapter of the present volume, on Fromm's life and work, Rainer Funk outlines the overall critical and humanist foundations of Fromm's social psychology. Funk explores the varying roots of Fromm's thought—in Jewish theology, Freudian psychoanalysis, Marxism, and Buddhism—and how Fromm developed from these a wide-ranging critical vision. Richard Quinney then explores the ways in which Fromm's writings on socialist humanism, peace, and Buddhism offer us perspectives from which to move toward a society free of crime and violence, drawing on works by Fromm such as *Socialist Humanism* (1965) and *To Have or to Be?* (1976). Fromm's critique of modern Western society's stress on having rather than being is used as a vantage point from which to take up the distinction between positive peace, based on humanism and mutual understanding, and negative peace, the mere absence of conflict.

In her contribution, Lynn S. Chancer looks at Fromm's concept of sadomasochism as developed in his *Escape from Freedom* (1941) and other works as a key to understanding the pervasiveness of social violence in America today. Individuals often acquiesce to the powerful in a masochistic fashion and then act in a sadistic fashion toward the powerless. This helps explain how popular anger against social and economic conditions has been channeled away from the powerful, emerging instead in alienated forms, such as extreme hostility toward those convicted even of minor offenses, or domestic violence. In his chapter, John F. Wozniak directs attention to Fromm's work on the alienated, objectified nature of modern social life. Wozniak argues that Fromm's concept of alienation as advanced in *The Sane Society* (1955) sheds much light on common types of crime today—from ordinary street crime to white collar crime and crimes of government. Often, a common feature cutting across these varying types of crime is the perpetrator's having reduced the victim to a mere object.

Next, Polly F. Radosh draws on works by Fromm such as *The Art of Loving* (1956) and *The Crisis of Psychoanalysis* (1970), where he develops a distinction between patriarchal and matriarchal value systems. Connecting this to the writings of contemporary feminist theorists such as Carol Gilligan, Radosh analyzes the sharp differences between the type and frequency of crimes committed by men and by women in American society today. In the final chapter, Kevin Anderson examines Fromm's early work on the criminal justice system, written in 1930 and 1931. Anderson argues that some parts of this work exhibit problematic features common to the psychoanalytic criminology of the period, such as the notion that most criminals are neurotic. More importantly, however, Fromm in these essays used the insights of Marx and Freud to work out a Freudian Marxist critique of the role of the criminal justice system in a class society. He saw the workings of criminal justice as largely ineffective in combating crime, but as an important social and psychological legitimator of the existing social order. Fromm's early work on crime is viewed alongside that of liberal psychoanalytic criminologists of the period, that of his fellow Frankfurt School members Georg Rusche and Otto Kirchheimer, and that of the poststructuralist Michel Foucault.

Part 3 contains two of Fromm's early articles on criminal justice, published in English here for the first time. Fromm originally wrote these articles in German in 1930 and 1931, during the same period as his other early writings on Marxism and psychoanalysis. In *The Crisis of Psychoanalysis,* Fromm published English versions of some of his early work, but did not include any of his early writings on crime. He apparently never returned to the topic of crime and criminology after 1931.

Part 3 begins with "The State as Educator," published in 1930. Here, Fromm set out for the first time his Freudian Marxist critique of the criminal justice system, the central purpose of which he concluded is not its stated function of fighting crime or securing public safety but rather the legitimation of the existing social order in the minds of the population. In "On the Psychology of the Criminal and the Punitive Society," a lengthier article published in 1931, Fromm surveyed and critiqued literature on crime both by mainstream progressive criminologists of the day, such as Gustav Aschaffenburg, and by liberal psychoanalytic criminologists such as Franz Alexander. Then he developed his radical critique of the functions of the criminal justice system once again.

In publishing these two early articles by Fromm on crime, we are not attempting to revive the psychoanalytic school of criminology. However, we do believe that Fromm's important analysis of the mass psychology of criminal justice offers many insights for critical, humanist, and peacemaking criminology today. These early articles also constitute an important and largely unknown part of the history of both radical criminology and Critical Theory.

In part, this book is an outgrowth of an earlier volume, Harold E. Pepinsky and Richard Quinney, eds., *Criminology as Peacemaking* (1991), for which the editors of the present volume each wrote essays. This book also developed out of two sessions on Fromm and criminal criminology organized by the editors at the 1994 and 1995 annual meetings of the American Society of Criminology. All of the chapters in this volume, with the exception of Rainer Funk's, were initially presented as papers in those sessions. The authors contributing to the present volume have for many years been interested in Fromm's writings, and most have used them in their work on criminology. This volume has offered us an opportunity to develop our work on Fromm and criminology in a more focused manner, and, we hope, to bring these concerns to a broader public within the field.

Richard Quinney's chapter appeared previously in *Crime, Law, and Social Change* 23:2 (1995): 147–56. An earlier, abbreviated version of Kevin Anderson's chapter appeared in *Justice Quarterly* 15:4 (1998): 667–96. We would like to thank the editors of these journals for permission to reprint this material. We wish to acknowledge advice and support we have received from Rainer Funk, literary executor and overseer of the Erich Fromm Archives in Tübingen, Germany. We want to thank the contributors to the book, and to acknowledge their part in the overall project from the beginning. Our book has benefited from the comments and suggestions of David Friedrichs and Harold Pepinsky, and we express our appreciation for their help. Our editor at the University of Illinois Press,

Richard Martin, has provided valuable guidance throughout the project. We acknowledge the important contribution that Heinz Osterle has made to this book, as primary translator of Fromm's two essays. To all, including an even wider circle of participants in the book's preparation, we give our thanks. The efforts of all are for a more humanist—and a less punitive—society.

Erich Fromm and Critical Criminology

Part 1

Introduction to Fromm

1

Erich Fromm's Life and Work

Rainer Funk

Erich Fromm was born on March 23, 1900, in Frankfurt am Main, the only child of Orthodox Jewish parents. He died on March 18, 1980, in Locarno, Switzerland. The Judaism practiced by his parents (his father, a wine merchant, and his mother each came from old rabbinical families), and by Fromm himself up to his twenty-sixth birthday, had a profound influence on his life and work. The religious way of life in which Fromm was raised was different not only from the liberal Christianity of the turn of the century, but also from Reform Judaism, which was receptive to the liberal capitalistic spirit of the Christian bourgeoisie. Orthodox Judaism stressed rejection of the majority culture rather than conformity and assimilation.

Fromm always stood opposed to the social majority, was separated from it, and this formed and affected his existential sense of the relation of the individual to society. Fromm was always on the opposing side, the side of the minority. This deeply rooted religious background influenced his subsequent social and critical application of psychoanalysis and also his special interest in law and criminology as a young man. The "spirit" in which Fromm grew up is quite different from the "spirit" of the beginning of this century, and also from that of our culture today.

The world in which Fromm was brought up was directed toward traditional learning, the perfection of humanity, and spiritual values—goals that were opposed to the cliché of a successful Jew at that time. In an interview given shortly before his death, Fromm confessed that as a child: "I found it . . . very strange that people devote their life to making money, and I was very embarrassed when a man had to admit in my presence that he was a businessman, in other words, that he spent his whole time making money. . . . While I went to a German school, took part in German culture as every other boy or student did who lived in Germany, nevertheless I was—not a complete—stranger but I was a stranger very definitely so and I never regretted that" (1979:xv).[1]

When Fromm was sixteen, he joined a group of students around Nehemia Nobel, the rabbi of the synagogue at Boerneplatz in Frankfurt. Nobel was a gifted preacher and also a mystic. He lived a conservative, religious life, and yet at the same time he was a humanist and philosopher in the Enlightenment tradition, as exemplified by Goethe and Kant. When Fromm graduated from the Woehler Gymnasium in Frankfurt he had a strong desire to become a religious scholar and go to a Talmudic university in Lithuania, far away from his parents:

> But that evoked such a fierce reaction on my father's side that I couldn't do it with-out hurting him so deeply, that I had not the courage or maybe the wish to do so. Thus I gave up this project—I would say today fortunately—to become a Talmu-dic scholar, and I began to study law. I had always—and still I have—great interest in law and I love law. For me law is, so to speak, the frozen minimum of ethics, which exists in a society. I am accustomed if I have to make a decision to first ask myself what would be the answer from the legal standpoint, then I try to go beyond the legal standpoint to [the] human standpoint, but I want to make sure that I, at least, fulfill the legal standpoint and do not operate in an empty room in which I may imagine myself all sorts of things to my advantage; first of all comes the legal mini-mum, then comes whatever addition love can make. (1979:xv)

In 1920 Fromm started to study law at the University of Frankfurt, but law did not really satisfy him because he did not want to become a lawyer. In 1920 he went to the University of Heidelberg to study sociology (in these years still a subdivision of political economy) with Alfred Weber (Max Weber's brother), philosophy with Heinrich Rickert, and psychology with Karl Jaspers.

In addition to these teachers at the University of Heidelberg, Fromm was deeply influenced between 1920 and 1925 by another Talmudic teacher, Salmon Baruch Rabinkov. "Herr Rabinkov," as he was referred to by everybody, was a Russian-born Talmudic teacher, an adherent of Habad Hasidism from Lithuania. Although Rabinkov saw his principal task to be the study of the Talmud, he also took a considerable interest in legal and sociological issues. He had close contacts with Alfred Weber, who supervised Fromm's doctoral dissertation. What stood out about Rabinkov was his deep and thorough knowledge of Jewish history and intellec-tual traditions. "Rabinkov influenced my life perhaps more than any other single person," Fromm wrote in his "Reminiscences of Shlomo Barukh Rabinkow," "and his ideas have remained alive in me, although expressed in different forms and concepts. . . . Perhaps Rabinkov's attitude to life could be described as that of 'radi-cal humanism.' It was characteristic of his teaching approach that he both sought for and found this radical humanistic stance anchored in the Jewish tradition, whether in the prophets, the Talmud, Maimonides, or in a Hasidic tale. . . . [He] interpreted Judaism as a system attaching a high value to equality, justice, and the dignity of the individual" (1987 [1971]: 103). Although Rabinkov impressed him much more than his teachers at the university, Fromm admired Alfred Weber as "a man of great intellectual power, of great integrity," and of strong political convictions in support of political freedom (Fromm 1979:xv). From the very beginning, Fromm's sociological interest was a sociopsychological one, addressed to the question of what causes people to think, feel, and behave in a uniform way. This was also the focus of his 1922 dissertation under Alfred Weber, in which he examined the social and psychological functions of Jewish law in the community life of the diaspora Jews—among the Karaites, in Reform Judaism, and in Hasidism. In these diaspora communities no national or religious institution externally ensured the cohesion of the faithful.

In his dissertation, Fromm's main interest was already sociopsychological, although at the time he did not have a developed psychological concept with which he could grasp the psychic function of the religious ethos and other forms of solidarity within the Jewish community. What he said here with regard to the function of Jewish law (in the sense of the religious ethos) he also said later with regard to "libidinous forces in the social process" of modern society as a whole (1970b [1932]: 130). Besides his Talmudic and university teachers, Fromm's thinking was influenced by the prophets of the Old Testament: "More than anything else, I was moved by the prophetic writings, by Isaiah, Amos, Hosea; not so much by their warnings and their announcement of disaster, but by their promise of the 'end of days,' when nations 'shall beat their swords into plowshares and their spears into pruning hooks: nation shall not lift sword against nation, neither shall they learn war any more' (Is 2:4); when all nations will be friends, and when 'the earth shall be full of the knowledge of the Lord, as the waters cover the sea' (Is 11:9)" (Fromm 1962:5). It was not only their messianic message that impressed Fromm, but also the fact that the prophets announce ideas and at the same time they live them—they practice what they are preaching (see Fromm 1967:67–68). Fromm always tried to follow this prophetic tradition. He tried it first in his Orthodox Jewish religious practice and later in his view of humanism as the practice of reason and love.

Of course nonreligious sources also influenced Fromm's intellectual life. Landis and Tauber write that his political interests deepened when he became acquainted with the work of Karl Marx, for in Marx he saw "the key to the understanding of history and the manifestation, in secular terms, of the radical humanism which was expressed in the messianic vision of the Old Testament prophets" (1971:ix). Around 1926, Fromm had become acquainted with Buddhism, an important event in his intellectual development. "For the first time he saw a spiritual system, a way of life, based on pure rationality and without irrational mystification or appeal to revelation or authority" (Landis and Tauber 1971:xii). Fromm's acquaintance with Buddhism was followed, decades later, by his intensive study of Daisetz T. Suzuki's works on Zen Buddhism. Fromm's estimate of religion, his critique of all appeals to irrational revelation and authority, and his preference for combining rational insight with mysticism, were significantly molded by this experience. Another important event in Fromm's intellectual life before 1930 was his reading of the work of Johann Jakob Bachofen (1815–87). Bachofen's *Mother Right* provided insights into the link between matriarchal or patriarchal social structures on the one hand, and cultural and psychic phenomena on the other hand. This influenced Fromm's ideas on the reciprocal influence of social and psychic structures, ideas that went beyond those of Freud.

Very early on, Fromm developed another major interest, expressed in the psychologically oriented question, "How is it possible?" Fromm mentions the suicide of a twenty-year-old woman painter who was a friend of the family as the childhood experience that was responsible for his later interest in Sigmund Freud and psychoanalysis:

> I heard the shocking news: her father had died, and immediately afterwards she had killed herself and left a will which stipulated that she wanted to be buried together with her father. I had never heard of an Oedipus complex or of incestuous fixations between daughter and father. But I was deeply touched. I had been quite attracted to the young woman; I had loathed the unattractive father; never before had I known anyone to commit suicide. I was hit by the thought "How is it possible?" How is it possible that a beautiful young woman should be so in love with her father, that she prefers to be buried with him to being alive to the pleasures of life and of painting? (Fromm 1962:4)

Two years later he was confronted with another "How is it possible?" His sympathy for the prophets and their messianic vision of the harmonious coexistence of all nations was profoundly shaken by the First World War:

> When the war started during the summer of 1914, I was a fourteen-year-old boy for whom the excitement of war, the celebration of victories, the tragedy of the death of individual soldiers I knew, were uppermost in my experience. I was not concerned with the problem of war as such; I was not struck by its senseless inhumanity. But soon all this changed. . . . When the war ended in 1918, I was a deeply troubled young man who was obsessed by the question of how war was possible, by the wish to understand the irrationality of human mass behavior, by a passionate desire for peace and international understanding. More, I had become deeply suspicious of all official

ideologies and declarations, and filled with the conviction "of all one must doubt."
(1962:6–7)

Six years later, psychoanalysis offered Fromm an answer to the question "How is
it possible?"

Fromm was introduced to psychoanalysis by his friend Frieda Reichmann, with
whom he opened a psychoanalytically oriented sanatorium in Heidelberg in 1924.
She conducted his first didactic analysis, and in 1926 they were married. He had
further analyses with Wilhelm Wittenberg in Munich, with Karl Landauer in
Frankfurt, and with Hanns Sachs in Berlin, where Fromm also finished training
in 1930 and opened his own practice. His interest in a social approach to psychology continued and brought him into contact with the Freudian Marxists
Siegfried Bernfeld and Wilhelm Reich at the Berlin Institute. Between 1926 and
1931 Erich Fromm and Frieda Fromm-Reichmann frequented the home of the
Baden-Baden doctor Georg Groddeck, where they also met Karen Horney and
Sándor Ferenczi. They all agreed that Freud's theory of the Oedipus complex was
untenable and that cultural and social factors should be given much more weight
with regard to the formation of psychic impulses.

At the same time that Fromm opened his practice in Berlin, he was appointed
by Max Horkheimer to the Institute for Social Research in Frankfurt, later known
as the "Frankfurt School," as its chief expert in all questions of psychology and social
psychology. Here Fromm became intensively involved with Marxist theory and
worked for years—in addition to his practice as a therapist—on a sociopsychological
field-research project on the unconscious attitudes of working people professing
to be politically leftist (Fromm 1984). That Fromm's sociopsychological interest
originated in his religious upbringing is evident from his Talmudic teachers as well
as from his studies in sociology and his dissertation on Jewish law. But seven years
after he had finished his dissertation, Freudian psychoanalysis permitted him a new
formulation of his sociopsychological interest in the language of Freud's theory of
the formation of psychic impulses. Fromm's attempt to combine sociological and
psychoanalytic theory has hardly received serious attention. One of the main reasons for this is the fact that there are few sociologists who have had training in
psychoanalysis, and also that psychologists, because of their metapsychological
theories, are not usually capable of sociological thinking.

If one takes seriously the basic sociological premise that there are forces and
patterns rooted in society itself—a premise that is difficult for most psychoanalysts to accept—then the extremely fertile question as to whether or not
there is something like a social unconscious can be raised. If a social unconscious exists, according to what patterns does it develop? Can it be investigated

similarly to the unconscious of an individual? If one first accepts the possibility that society has an unconscious, which can be called the social unconscious, then the next step is to free oneself from a misguided understanding of society. Fromm emphasizes in his short but important work, "Psychoanalysis and Sociology," that "the subject of sociology, society, in reality consists of individuals, and that it is these human beings, rather than an abstract society as such, whose actions, thoughts, and feelings are the object of sociological research. Human beings do not have one 'individual psyche,' which functions when a person performs as an individual and so becomes the object of psychoanalysis, contrasted to a completely separate 'mass psyche' with all sorts of mass instincts, as well as vague feelings of community and solidarity, which springs into action whenever a person performs as part of the mass" (1989b [1929]: 37). Rather, the individual must be understood as socialized a priori, and thus the psyche is to be understood as being "developed and determined through the relationship of the individual to society" (1989b [1929]: 39).

As the basis for his approach, Fromm refers to Freud's *Group Psychology and the Analysis of the Ego* (1955 [1921]), grounding his hypothesis of the socialized individual in Freud himself, who wrote: "In the individual's mental life someone else is invariably involved, as a model, as an object, as a helper, as an opponent; and so from the very first, individual psychology, in this extended but entirely justifiable sense of the word, is at the same time social psychology as well" (1955 [1921]: 69). For this reason, the difference between individual psychology and social psychology can only be quantitative. Social psychology, just as individual psychology, tries to comprehend psychic structure from the individual's life experiences. Thus, wrote Fromm, it proceeds according to the same methods: "Social psychology wishes to investigate how certain psychic attitudes common to members of a group are related to their common life experiences" (1963 [1930]: 9).

Fromm distinguishes the concept of the "common life experience" from that of the "individual life experience." In the latter, it is important to know the sibling order or if someone is an only child; sicknesses and "chance" occurrences of an individual sort also are significant because of their strong influence on libidinal structure. On the other hand, the "common life experience" of a group means mainly the economic, social, and political conditions that to a great extent determine the group's way of life. Still completely within the metapsychological conceptions of Freud's instinct theory, Fromm explained in what is probably his best-known psychoanalytic essay, "The Method and Function of an Analytic Social Psychology," that the phenomena of social psychology are to be understood as processes involving the active and passive adaptation of the instinctual apparatus to the socio-economic situation. In certain fundamental respects, the instinctual apparatus itself is a biological given; but it is highly modifiable. The role of primary formative factors goes to the economic conditions. The family is the essential medium through which the economic situation exerts its formative influence on the individual's psyche. The task of social psychology is to explain the shared, socially relevant, psychic attitudes and ideologies—and their unconscious roots in particular—in terms of the influence of economic conditions on libido strivings. (1970b [1932]: 121)

Fromm's main interest is in the libidinal structure of the human being as a socialized being. Thus it is mainly a question of those passionate strivings and the unconscious of the socialized individual, as these factors make themselves evident when the unconscious of society is itself the object of study. Then there is the libidinal structure of society, which can be recognized as independent from the socioeconomic situation, since the life experience of the group is determined by the economic, social, and political conditions. This means that society has not only a certain economic, social, political, and intellectual-cultural structure, but also a libidinal one specific to it. When Fromm embraced the idea of a socially molded unconscious or an unconscious of society by which each individual is to a large extent predetermined, he defined the correlation of individual and society anew. It was no longer valid to say "here I am and there is society," but rather, "I am primarily a reflection of society, in that my unconscious is socially determined and I therefore reflect and realize the secret expectations, requirements, wishes, fears, and strivings of society in my own passionate strivings." In reality, none of the following—not the apparent separation of society and individual, not the apparent separation of conscious and unconscious, not the apparent separation of society and unconscious—actually exist. All of these dimensions are in the social unconscious of every single human being.

Fromm applies the insights of psychoanalysis to the dynamics of the unconscious and to the phenomena of defense and resistance on a social scale. But he does so from a genuinely sociological standpoint, in which the individual is understood as primarily a reflection of society, so that an individual's social traits are not additional aspects of himself or herself, but rather the opposite: the individual can only be properly understood as a product of society. The identification of psychoanalytic instinct theory with libido theory shifts the perspective to the recognition of the dynamics of the unconscious on a social scale. This leads Fromm to downplay Freudian instinct theory in order to avoid giving a predominant position to insights into this single libidinal structure, which is not very relevant to the dynamics of the social unconscious. Fromm took up a number of specific questions about libido theory in the thirties. He was concerned above all with the significance of the Oedipus complex and the patriarchally oriented determinism of Freudian libido theory. What occasioned such criticism was mainly Fromm's interest in the issue of "mother right," as interpreted by Morgan, Briffault, and above all Bachofen. It is precisely the social determinism of the Oedipus complex in Freud's interpretation—namely as a typical product of a patriarchal society—that made evident the necessity of an alternative instinct theory, one that took the individual as a social being seriously and regarded libidinal structure as independent from the individual's socioeconomic situation.

Fromm's critique and new formulation of psychoanalytic theory did not come about without the influence of others. In the group surrounding Georg Groddeck there was broad agreement as early as the late twenties that the Freudian formulation of the Oedipus complex was untenable. The work of Harry Stack Sullivan, with whom Fromm formed a friendship in 1935, proved especially helpful to his formulation of psychoanalytic theory. Fromm's attempt to view human beings as influenced not only by their individual unconscious, but also as a reflection of society, was similar to Sullivan's theory of interpersonal relationships. Here psychological development takes on the same significance as the change from the forms found in primary ties to those in subjective and independent relationships. At the end of *Escape from Freedom,* Fromm summarized his new formulation: "We believe that man is primarily a social being, and not, as Freud assumes, primarily self-sufficient and only secondarily in need of others in order to satisfy his instinctual needs. In this sense, we believe that individual psychology is fundamentally social psychology or, in Sullivan's terms, the psychology of interpersonal relationships; the key problem of psychology is that of the particular kind of relatedness of the individual toward the world, not that of satisfaction or frustration of single instinctual desires" (1941:290).

It may appear that Fromm was rejecting Freudian instinct theory as a whole, but that is not his point. To be sure, the closer psychoanalytic theory came to being identical to libido theory, the more Fromm tended to formulate his critique of libido theory as encompassing Freudian instinct theory in general. However, Fromm's primary interest was in drives and those factors that motivate the thoughts, feelings, and behavior of humans as social beings. The application of Freud's instinct theory to social groups permitted Fromm to recognize the limited validity of the libido theory and in 1935 brought him to the recognition that basically two kinds of drives must be distinguished. He was aware that this distinction introduced a principal disagreement with Freud's instinct theory.

In an unpublished letter of December 18, 1936, to Karl August Wittfogel, the central idea of Fromm's revision of Freudian instinct theory can be clearly discerned. He writes:

> The central point of this fundamental disagreement is that I try to show that the drives which motivate social behavior are not, as Freud assumes, sublimations of sexual instincts. Rather, they are the products of social processes, or, more precisely, reactions to certain constellations under which the individual has to satisfy his/her instincts. These drives, which I divide into those having to do with human relations (love, hate, sadomasochism) and those having to do with methods of acquisition (instincts of receiving, taking away, saving, gathering, producing), are fundamentally different from natural factors, namely the instincts of hunger, thirst, sexuality. Whereas these are common to all human beings and animals, the former are specifically human products and not biological; they are to be understood in the context of the social way of life.[2]

Fromm attempts to connect his concept of a social unconscious to Freud's insight that libidinal structure is molded by life experience. In other words, Fromm thinks of the human being as primarily a reflection of society. Here, however, he runs up against the inadequacy of Freud's libido theory. His adherence to Freud's perception that libidinal structure results from adaptation to life experience led him to a new conceptualization of the drive theory. In Fromm's new conceptualization, psychological phenomena are separated somewhat from their physical source, the sex drive, and acquire independence as psychological drives rather than merely physiological ones, among which Fromm includes the drives of self-preservation as well as sexuality.

Fromm's revision of psychoanalysis also manifested itself in new terminology. Since Fromm used the concept of character for his sociopsychological insights, he called drive theory "characterology"; drive structure became "character structure," instinctual impulses became "character traits" or simply "passionate strivings"; drive itself was conceptualized as "psychological need," libidinal instinct was now called "psychological" or "existential need" (in contrast to instinctive or physiological needs); the libidinal structure of society became the "social character," and instead of libido, Fromm, similarly to Jung, now spoke of "psychic energy." From 1930 onward, Fromm directed his research toward a synthesis of these various insights and revisions: "I wanted to understand the laws that govern the life of the individual man, and the laws of society—that is, of men in their social existence. I tried to see the lasting truth in Freud's concepts as against those assumptions which were in need of revision. I tried to do the same with Marx's theory, and finally I tried to arrive at a synthesis which followed from the understanding and the criticism of both thinkers" (1962:9).

When one surveys Fromm's numerous subsequent writings, one notices that all of his later works are far-reaching explications and modifications of these spiritual and intellectual antecedents. They illustrate his very specific approach to the individual as a social being. This holds true for Fromm's concept in the thirties of the authoritarian character (developed ten years before Adorno et al. published *Authoritarian Personality*) and also for his later discoveries. In the forties and fifties he described the "marketing character" and the "organization man" (as Fromm's analysand David Riesman did in sociological terms), and in the sixties he discovered a new orientation of social character: necrophilia, the passion to be attracted by all that is dead and without life (Fromm 1973). The foundation for these discoveries was laid in the early thirties when Fromm developed his own sociopsychological approach to man and society.

The coming of the Nazis to power in 1933 forced the Frankfurt Institute for Social Research to emigrate, first to Geneva, Switzerland, and then, in 1934, to Columbia University in New York. After a rather long illness, during which he stayed at Davos, Switzerland, Fromm accepted an invitation from the Chicago Psychoanalytic Institute to give a series of lectures in 1933. When the Institute for Social Research found its new home in New York, Fromm moved there and resumed work at the institute while also continuing his psychoanalytic practice. In New York, he met Clara Thompson, Harry Stack Sullivan, and William Silverberg. From 1935 to 1939, he was a visiting professor at Columbia. His connection with the Institute for Social Research continued into the late thirties, when Max Horkheimer and Herbert Marcuse came out against his reformulation of the Freudian theory of drives, the latter eventually denouncing him as a "neo-Freudian revisionist" (Marcuse 1955:238). Fromm continued to develop his thought, which—though bearing some kinship with that of the so-called neo-Freudians Karen Horney, Harry Stack Sullivan, and Abram Kardiner—in its emphasis on culture did not prevent him from clearly distancing himself from these thinkers: "In spite of the fact that we were friends, worked together, and had certain views in common—particularly a critical attitude toward the libido theory—the differences between us were greater than the similarities, especially in the 'cultural' viewpoint. Horney and Sullivan thought of cultural patterns in the traditional anthropological sense, while my approach looked toward a dynamic analysis of the economic, political, and psycho-logical forces that form the basis of society" (1970c:21).

During the Second World War, Fromm tried to enlighten the American public concerning the real intentions of Nazism. In 1943, he and others founded the William Alanson White Institute of Psychiatry, Psychoanalysis, and Psychology, and from 1946 to 1950 he was chairman of the faculty and chairman of the institute's training committee. Throughout the forties Fromm taught extensively. From 1945 to 1947, he was a professor of psychology at the University of Michigan, and in 1948–49, he was a visiting professor at Yale. From 1941 to 1949, he also was a member of the faculty of Bennington College in Vermont, and in 1948 he became an adjunct professor of psychoanalysis at New York University. Fromm was married a second time in 1944, to Henny Gurland, a German photographer who witnessed Frankfurt School–member Walter Benjamin's suicide while fleeing from Nazi-occupied France to Spain in 1940. In 1940 Fromm became an American citizen. On the advice of a physician, who stated that his ailing wife would benefit from a more favorable climate, they moved from Bennington to Mexico in 1950. Fromm became a professor at the National Autonomous University in Mexico City, where he established the psychoanalytic section at the medical school. He taught there until 1965, when he became a professor emeritus. Henny died in 1952, and Fromm married Annis Freeman in 1953. Annis was two years younger than Fromm. She was born in Pittsburgh and grew up in Alabama. Trained in anthropology, she was most interested in his social approach to psychology. She planned their house in Cuernavaca, Mexico, where they lived from 1957 to 1974, when they moved to Switzerland. In addition to his teaching duties in Mexico, Fromm attended to his responsibilities at the William Alanson White Institute in New York, held a position as a professor of psychology at Michigan State University from 1957 to 1961, and was an adjunct professor of psychology at the Graduate School of Arts and Sciences at New York University after 1962. Despite his extensive teaching activities, he kept up his psychoanalytic practice for more than forty-five years, remained active as a supervisor and teacher of psychoanalysis, and participated in social psychological fieldwork in Mexico.

Since childhood, Fromm had been passionately interested in politics, and in the middle fifties he joined the American Socialist Party and attempted (fruitlessly, as it turned out) to provide it with a new program. Although he recognized that he was temperamentally unsuited to practical politics, he did considerable work to enlighten the American people about the current possibilities and intentions of the Soviet Union. Fromm taught a socialist humanism that rejected both Western capitalism and Soviet Communist socialism and sympathized with the the Yugoslav "Praxis" group's interpretation of socialism. His strongest political interest was the international peace movement. In this, he was motivated by the insight that the present historical situation will decide whether humanity will take rational hold of its destiny or fall victim to destruction through nuclear war. As Schultz notes, Fromm was a cofounder of SANE, the Committee for a Sane Nuclear Policy, "the most important American peace movement, which not only fought against the atomic arms race but also against the war in Vietnam" (1976:37). His last important political activity was his work on behalf of antiwar candidate Eugene McCarthy during the 1968 campaign for the Democratic presidential nomination (see Fromm 1994b). After 1965, Fromm increasingly concentrated on his writing. Beginning in 1968, he spent the summer months in the exceptionally benign climate of the Tessin, Switzerland, where he moved permanently in 1974. He and Annis took up residence in Muralto, far from the hectic pace of modern life, and it was there that Fromm died on March 18, 1980. Solitude and retirement on the Lago Maggiore did not lessen Fromm's interest in contemporary problems, a fact that is evidenced clearly by his literary productivity during the last years of his life.

Fromm has been called "one of the most influential and popular psychoanalysts in America" (Glen 1966:11). Friedenberg wrote: "Of all the psychoanalytic theorists who have tried to formulate a system better suited than Freud's to problems of contemporary life, none has been more productive or influential than Erich Fromm" (1962:305). Even one of his sharpest critics, John Homer Schaar, had to admit that Fromm's writings "make his name a prominent one in any serious discussion of modern social problems" (1961:3). The increasing number of doctoral dissertations on Fromm all over the world testifies to the ongoing scientific discussion of his thought and discoveries. The bibliography of literature on Erich Fromm comprises some 3,850 titles (Funk 1997). As one surveys Fromm's literary output, one is struck by the variety and breadth of his interests and research. The sociologically oriented dissertation he wrote as a twenty-two-year-old doctoral candidate examines the "correlation between social structure and the [religious] idea entrusted to its charge among the Jews of the Diaspora" (Fromm 1989a). A number of shorter essays written between 1927 and 1930 reveal Fromm as an orthodox Freudian. The treatise originally entitled "The Development of the Dogma of Christ: A Psychoanalytical Study on the Sociopsychological Function of Religion" demonstrates his interest in the relevance of religion and the religious idea to social and cultural reality (Fromm 1963 [1930]). This essay represents the first instance of Fromm's particular type of sociopsychological analysis of these phenomena. His method differs from both the vulgar Marxist base-superstructure theory and the psychologizing cultural analysis à la Freud. Besides religion, Fromm in these years focused on criminology (see the essays published in English for the first time in this volume).

Next, Fromm explicated his theory and method of "analytic social psychology" (1970b [1932], 1970d [1932], 1992). Bachofen's and Robert Briffault's theories of matriarchy play a particular role here, and the subsequent studies on authority and family that utilized this sociopsychological method represented a kind of testing of it (Fromm 1933, 1936, 1970e [1934]). In 1941 Fromm published his first important monograph in social psychology, *Escape from Freedom*. Based on an analysis of the relation between Protestantism and the development of early capitalism, the work demonstrates the modern individual's incapacity to value his "freedom from" as a "freedom to." Instead, Fromm wrote, the modern individual attempts to escape from freedom by placing himself in authoritarian relations of dependency, becoming in the process destructive and conformist. The book's insights into the contemporary situation in Nazi Germany made a considerable impression on the American public. Fromm also devoted a number of years to an intensive effort to shed light on the connections between socioeconomic structures on the one hand, and human needs as psychic necessities in the process of orientation of assimilation and socialization on the other hand. In this effort, Fromm developed a characterology that widens the perspective of Freudian libido theory and its narrow human image, while simultaneously indicating the ethical relevance of the various character orientations. The results of this research found expression in Fromm's important work, *Man for Himself—An Inquiry into the Psychology of Ethics* (1947).

The Sane Society, published in 1955, develops further the themes of *Escape from Freedom* (1941) and *Man for Himself* (1947). Written from the viewpoint of a humanistic ethic, the book points to the socioeconomic reasons that prevent the realization of the human project. His analysis of the modern capitalist and bureaucratic social structure lays bare the universal phenomenon of alienation that can be overcome only if economic, political, and cultural conditions are fundamentally changed in the direction of a democratic and humanist socialism. In addition to these three works, with their abundant observations and discoveries, Fromm wrote a number of monographs during the fifties and sixties in which the horizons of his thought emerge more clearly. In 1950, he published a shorter work, *Psychoanalysis and Religion,* in which he discusses his understanding of a humanistic religion as influenced by psychoanalysis and Buddhism in greater detail. *The Forgotten Language,* a discussion of fairy tales, myths, and dreams as universal and revelatory phenomena of human existence, appeared the following year, in 1951. Fromm's best-seller was the short book, *The Art of Loving.* First published in 1956 and translated into thirty-five languages, it has sold more than 25 million copies worldwide. Using the concept of "productive love," Fromm shows the consequences of a humanistic ethics for the understanding of self-love, love of one's neighbor, and love of one's fellow human being. Fromm paid tribute to Freud and Marx in three further books (1959, 1961b, 1962), while at the same time attempting to define his position in relation to these seminal modern thinkers. *Marx's Concept of Man* (1961b) is of special significance because it drew the attention of the American public to Marx's early writings, which were published in this book in English for the first time.

The importance of religion for a successful human existence and the future of man is clarified in two works, the essay "Psychoanalysis and Zen Buddhism"

(1960a) and *You Shall Be As Gods* (1966), a "radical interpretation of the Old Testament and its tradition" that pleads the cause of a nontheistic religion. Fromm develops a historical-philosophical perspective that views the Old Testament account of God and man as a process in the course of which man comes increasingly into his own. Thus God as an idea becomes identical with man's complete "being at home with himself," and belief in a revealed God is understood as a stage on the path toward a "humanistic religion" that develops in and through itself.

Subsequently, Fromm focused on two problems, one of which is the historically decisive question of whether man will once again become the master of his creations, or whether he will perish in an overly technological industrial world. Fromm's writings on politics, especially on nuclear weapons and the peace movement (1960b, 1961a), and his *Revolution of Hope: Toward a Humanized Technology* (1968), which can be considered a continuation of *The Sane Society* (1955), address this question. The second problem relates to the decay of the individual and of humanity as a species. Using the types of nonproductive life he had previously explicated (1947, 1964), Fromm presents a systematic treatment of the polarity of possible orientations on the basis of character. The related questions concerning the antithesis of instinct and character, the inherent human destructive instinct postulated by behavioral research, and the skepticism concerning the human being's potential goodness that this view entails (and the doubt this skepticism casts on humanism) guided Fromm's research for five years. The results of his work over this period are summarized in *The Anatomy of Human Destructiveness* (1973).

His last major publication, *To Have or to Be?* (1976), attempts to synthesize the insights of social psychology with those of humanistic religion and ethics. Fromm identifies two fundamentally antithetical orientations of human existence—having and being—and links his abundant insights into the individual and social psyche to the tradition of humanistic religion and of significant historical figures. Fromm believed that responsible scientific work could not ignore the ends of its activity or refuse to synthesize insights from a variety of disciplines. Neither could it be neutral toward the ethical relevance of its findings. Science therefore requires a frame of orientation that is ultimately not deducible from the insights of any single discipline.

Notes

1. Although I refer to a published interview, I am quoting from the transcript of the interview, which was conducted in English and is held by the Fromm-Archiv in Tübingen, Germany.

2. This letter is held by the Fromm-Archiv in Tübingen.

References Cited

Freud, S. 1955 [1921]. *Group Psychology and the Analysis of the Ego*. In *Complete Psychological Works, Standard Edition*. 24 vols. 18:65–143. London: Hogarth Press.

Friedenberg, E. Z. 1962. "Neo-Freudianism and Erich Fromm." *Commentary* 34 (October): 305–13.

Fromm, E. 1933. "Robert Briffaults Werk über das Mutterrecht." *Zeitschrift für Sozialforschung* 2:382–87.

———. 1936. "Sozialpsychologischer Teil." In *Studien über Autorität und Familie (Schriften des Instituts für Sozialforschung*, vol. 5). Ed. M. Horkheimer. 77–135. Paris: Librairie Félix Alcan.

———. 1941. *Escape from Freedom*. New York: Holt, Rinehart and Winston.

———. 1947. *Man for Himself: An Inquiry into the Psychology of Ethics*. New York: Rinehart and Co.

———. 1950. *Psychoanalysis and Religion*. New Haven, Conn.: Yale University Press.

———. 1951. *The Forgotten Language: An Introduction to the Understanding of Dreams, Fairy Tales, and Myths*. New York: Rinehart and Co.

———. 1955. *The Sane Society*. New York: Holt, Rinehart and Winston.

———. 1956. *The Art of Loving: An Inquiry into the Nature of Love*. New York: Harper and Row.

———. 1959. *Sigmund Freud's Mission: An Analysis of His Personality and Influence*. New York: Harper and Row.

———. 1960a. "Psychoanalysis and Zen Buddhism." In *Zen Buddhism and Psychoanalysis*. Ed. D. T. Suzuki and E. Fromm. 77–141. New York: Harper and Row.

———. 1960b. "The Case for Unilateral Disarmament." *Daedalus* 89(4): 1015–1028.

———. 1961a. *May Man Prevail? An Inquiry into the Facts and Fictions of Foreign Policy*. New York: Doubleday.

———. 1961b. *Marx's Concept of Man*. New York: F. Ungar.

———. 1962. *Beyond the Chains of Illusion: My Encounter with Marx and Freud*. New York: Simon and Schuster.

———. 1963 [1930]. "The Dogma of Christ." In *The Dogma of Christ and Other Essays on Religion, Psychology, and Culture* 3–91. New York: Holt, Rinehart and Winston.

———. 1964. *The Heart of Man: Its Genius for Good and Evil*. New York: Harper and Row.

———. 1966. *You Shall Be as Gods: A Radical Interpretation of the Old Testament and Its Tradition*. New York: Holt, Rinehart and Winston.

———. 1967. "Prophets and Priests." In *Bertrand Russell, Philosopher of the Century: Essays in His Honor*. Ed. R. Schoenman. 67–79. London: George Allen and Unwin.

———. 1968. *The Revolution of Hope: Toward a Humanized Technology*. New York: Harper and Row.

———. 1970a. *The Crisis of Psychoanalysis: Essays on Freud, Marx, and Social Psychology*. New York: Holt, Rinehart and Winston.

———. 1970b [1932]. "The Method and Function of an Analytic Social Psychology." In Fromm 1970a:135–62.

———. 1970c. "The Crisis of Psychoanalysis." In Fromm 1970a:9–41.

———. 1970d [1932]. "Psychoanalytic Characterology and Its Relevance for Social Psychology." In Fromm 1970a:163–89.

———. 1970e [1934]. "The Theory of Mother Right and Its Relevance for Social Psychology." In Fromm 1970a:106–34.

———. 1973. *The Anatomy of Human Destructiveness.* New York: Holt, Rinehart and Winston.

———. 1976. *To Have or to Be?* New York: Harper and Row.

———. 1979. "Erich Fromm: Du Talmud à Freud." Interview with Gérard Khoury in *Le Monde Dimanche* (Paris), October 21, xv.

———. 1984. *The Working Class in Weimar Germany: A Psychological and Sociological Study.* Ed. Wolfgang Bonss. Cambridge, Mass.: Harvard University Press.

———. 1987 [1971]. "Reminiscences of Shlomo Barukh Rabinkow." In *Sages and Saints.* Ed. L. Jung. 99–105. Hoboken: Ktav Publishing House.

———. 1989a. *Das jüdische Gesetz: Ein Beitrag zur Soziologie des Diasporajudentums.* Weinheim und Basel: Beltz-Verlag.

———. 1989b [1929]. "Psychoanalysis and Sociology." In *Critical Theory and Society: A Reader.* Ed. S. E. Bronner and D. M. Kellner. 37–39. New York: Routledge.

———. 1992. "Die Determiniertheit der psychischen Struktur durch die Gesellschaft. Zur Methode und Aufgabe einer Analytischen Sozialpsychologie." In *Gesellschaft und Seele. Beiträge zur Sozialpsychologie und zur psychoanalytischen Praxis* (*Schriften aus dem Nachlaß,* vol. 7). 23–97. Weinheim and Basel: Beltz-Verlag.

———. 1994a. *On Being Human.* New York: Continuum.

———. 1994b. "Campaign for Eugene McCarthy." In Fromm 1994a:89–95.

Funk, R. 1997. *Bibliography of the Literature about Erich Fromm.* Tübingen: Private Printing of the Erich Fromm Archives (Ursrainer Ring 24, D-72076 Tübingen, Germany).

Glen, J. S. 1966. *Erich Fromm: A Protestant Critique.* Philadelphia: Westminster Press.

Landis, B., and Tauber, E. S. 1971. "On Erich Fromm." In *In the Name of Life: Essays in Honor of Erich Fromm.* Ed. B. Landis and E. S. Tauber. i–xi. New York: Holt, Rinehart and Winston.

Marcuse, H. 1955. *Eros and Civilization.* Boston: Beacon Press.

Schaar, J. H. 1961. *Escape from Authority: The Perspectives of Erich Fromm.* New York: Harper and Row.

Schultz, H. J. 1976. "Humanist ohne Illusionen: Zu Werk und Person von Erich Fromm." *Evangelische Kommentare* (Stuttgart) 9:36–38.

Part 2

Fromm and Contemporary Criminology

2

Socialist Humanism and the Problem of Crime: Thinking about Erich Fromm in the Development of Critical/Peacemaking Criminology

Richard Quinney

What is important in the study of crime is everything that happens before crime occurs. The question of what precedes crime is far more significant to our understanding than the act of crime itself. Crime is the reflection of something larger and deeper.

As a critical criminologist, I find it ever more difficult to witness crime or to think about crime. Instead, I envision a world without crime, and that vision comes from imagining a world that would not produce crime. To be critical, to be a critical criminologist, is to imagine what might be possible in this human existence.

The ground upon which we stand may be named. As with all naming, words simplify the complexity of reality but indicate the direction of our attentions. I now use these words to describe my grounding: humanist, existentialist, Buddhist, pacifist, and socialist. I assume the intersubjectivity of social reality, and my approach is interdisciplinary and integrative. Thus my recent turn, in search of support and elaboration, to the life and work of Erich Fromm. Our thoughts about crime, and our actions of peacemaking, are furthered by Fromm's socialist humanism.

My central assumption throughout is the interconnection between the inner peace of the individual and the outer peace of the world. The two develop and occur together. The struggle is to create a humane existence, and such an existence comes only as we act peacefully toward ourselves and one another.

Great care, then, must be taken in our response to crime. Our actions—our social policies—must be consistent with our understanding of crime, and let it be maintained that the realization of peace in our everyday lives is the best social policy. This is positive peacemaking in criminology and criminal justice.

The Relativity of Things Human

We begin necessarily with an understanding of human existence. All things human (and otherwise) change. Nothing remains the same; nothing has permanent substance. In the flux of change and impermanence, in this human world, we mortals can cling to nothing. Cling to naught is our earthly imperative.

What then is real? What can be perceived as real? Simply to ask is to understand reality as ontologically existential. All human perception is intersubjective, a creation of the lived experience. At the beginning of my book *The Social Reality of Crime,* I had written that "we have no reason to believe in the objective existence of anything" (1970:4). To this day I am happy to be counted among the existentialists.

The problem of what is real and how reality may be known goes far beyond the traditional debate over the objective and the subjective. It has to do, rather, with the human mind's inability to think and see beyond its own innate construction. How can we know for certain of the existence of anything, including existence itself? The mind is the grand piano that provides the space for the mice—*our thoughts*—to play. We humans cannot step outside of our existence, and we cannot know, in the larger scheme of things, or non-things, if the grand piano is other than a dream. The dream of a cosmic dreamer. Why not?

It is not for us to know what cannot be known. To have such knowledge is not to be human. The simple teaching of Buddhism: "Only don't know" (Seung 1982). We have the mind to question the reality of our existence, universal and otherwise, but we do not have the capacity to answer with objectivity and certainty. As Albert Camus noted, the absurd is the essential concept of our lives (1955). Entirely reasonable, then, is our perpetual ambivalence, or uncertainty, and our fear of life and death. Humility, mixed with wonder, makes more sense than the continuous pursuit of scientific knowledge.

We stand before the mystery of existence. Our understanding is in the recognition of our common inability to know for certain. Our fate, and our saving grace, is to be compassionate beings in all humility. Whatever may be known is known in love. Not in manipulation and control, not in the advancement of a separate self and a career, but in the care for one another. That is reality enough.

In these times, the only approach to reality—and to truth—that makes sense is one that is existentially grounded. We remind ourselves, again and again, that any construction—as with all knowledge and understanding—occurs only in the context of personal experience. Jean-Paul Sartre observed that any notion of truth that is abstract and removed from the struggle of everyday life is but a form of ignorance and bad faith (1992 [1948]: 58). The truth that comes from our intersubjective struggle to be human—a truth however relative and lacking of the absolute—is the real truth. As critical criminologists, our thinking and our writing are an intimate part of the struggle for existence.

But this is not to say that we humans do not desire certainty, do not seek the absolute. The absurdity of our human condition is that we have the mind to ask about reality and truth, but we do not have the capacity to answer the questions. Existentialism offers us the courage to entertain the ambiguity of our existence, to have what the novelist Milan Kundera calls "the wisdom of uncertainty" (1988:7). Without such wisdom, we humans create worlds that are cruel and oppressive. Kundera observes: "Man desires a world where good and evil can be clearly distinguished, for he has an innate and irrepressible desire to judge before he understands. Religions and ideologies are founded on this desire." We humans have, as Kundera notes again, "an inability to tolerate the essential relativity of things human, an inability to look squarely at the absence of the Supreme Judge" (1988:7). To this I would add that in our time (in our epoch) the law, the modern legal system with its criminal justice apparatus, is a result of our inability to tolerate the essential relativity of things human. In the absence of God, the law has become Supreme Judge. There must be another way to live, but first we would have to accept the human condition. To accept what Kundera referred to on another occasion, in the very title of his novel, as *The Unbearable Lightness of Being* (1984). As existentialists, we are learning—and living—the nature of our being.

To Have or to Be?

An understanding of our being, and how we might realize that being, is enhanced by exploring once again the writings of Erich Fromm. Although several books of Fromm's writings have been published posthumously (1992, 1994), Fromm's last book, *To Have or to Be?* was published in 1976. Before he died in 1980, Fromm noted that he was working on a sequel, a book on "a godless religion" (1978:220). It was to be a study of religious experience in which the concept of a supreme being, a god, is "unnecessary and undesirable." The pursuit of a nontheistic perspective is reflected also in Fromm's study of Zen Buddhism in the 1960s (see Funk 1982; Fromm 1992). Throughout his life of eighty years, Fromm proclaimed the central importance of the human being—and the human spirit—in the creation of a better world.

In 1965, Fromm edited a collection of international essays, titled *Socialist Humanism*. Introducing the book, Fromm outlined his basic vision (1965:vii–xiii). Humanism, he said, is in simplest terms the belief in the unity of the human race and the potential of human beings to be perfected by their own efforts. Socialist humanism is human development in relation to the full development of society. It is the ending of the epoch of prehistory, as Karl Marx had noted, and the opening of the epoch of human history. For Fromm, as well as for Marx, human history goes beyond a theistic belief in the existence of God, and beyond the ethic of consumption that dominates capitalism. The other premise common to the essays in *Socialist Humanism* is the "conviction that the urgent task for mankind today is the establishment of peace" (xii). Peace and the realization of the human project go together; they are one and the same.

In the introduction of *To Have or to Be?* Fromm discusses the two main premises of capitalism, in addition to its economic contradictions, as the sources for the failure of the great promise of unlimited progress. First, there is *radical hedonism,* seeking the maximum pleasure, trying to satisfy the desire to possess; second is *egotism,* selfishness and greed. The remainder of the book is a rich, erudite, and compassionate examination of our contemporary human condition.

The crucial problem, Fromm observes, is that capitalism promotes the *having* mode of existence over the *being* mode. He writes: "In a culture in which the supreme goal is to have—and to have more and more—and in which one can speak of someone as 'being worth a million dollars,' how can there be an alternative between having and being? On the contrary, it would seem that the very essence of being is having; that if one *has* nothing, one *is* nothing" (3). The imperative is to create individuals and societies based on the being mode of existence.

For Fromm, ultimately, love is the essence of being human. His most popular book is *The Art of Loving,* published in 1956 and reprinted several times since. Love opens us to the fullness of our being: "Love is an activity, not a passive affect; it is 'standing in,' not 'falling for.' In the most general way, the active character of love can be described by stating that love is primarily *giving,* not receiving" (Fromm 1989 [1956]: 20).

Fromm then observes that love is difficult to find and to practice in contemporary society. Love disintegrates in such a world. He opens his chapter "Love and Its Disintegration in Contemporary Western Society" with the following observation:

> If love is a capacity of the mature, productive character, it follows that the capacity to love in an individual living in any given culture depends on the influence this culture has on the character of the average person. If we speak about love in contemporary Western culture, we mean to ask whether the social structure of Western civilization and the spirit resulting from it are conducive to the development of love. To raise the question is to answer it in the negative. No objective observer of our Western life can doubt that love—brotherly love, motherly love, and erotic love—

is a relatively rare phenomenon, and that its place is taken by a number of forms of pseudo-love which are in reality so many forms of the disintegration of love. (75)

The basis of peacemaking criminology is compassion and love. A love that not only allows us to identify ourselves with others, but allows us to know that we are one with another, that we are one. Such love makes a different world, a world without crime.

Everything Is Everything Else

Erich Fromm's interest in Buddhism began as early as the mid-1920s. Decades later, at the end of the 1950s and in the early 1960s, Fromm studied intensively the works of D. T. Suzuki. His contact with Suzuki resulted in several writings and collaborations (1960a, 1960b). Fromm's critique of irrational authority and his preference for rational insight combined with mysticism were significantly shaped by his experience with Zen Buddhism (see Funk 1982:88–128).

Zen Buddhism is essentially existential and humanistic. In the moment, here and now, we humans experience the wonder of our existence. The ultimate, even the very notion of the ultimate, cannot be known by discursive thought. We are left with living our lives daily. Awareness, found in the practice of meditation, a concentration in the moment, is the focus of life (see Fromm 1992:31–54). There is a sense of the interconnectedness of all things, and a compassion for all that exists.

We are interrelated—"not just people, but animals too, and stones, clouds, trees" (Aitken 1984:10). We are an integral part of everything. Nothing exists by itself; nothing has a separate existence, a separate self. As Thich Nhat Hanh writes: "In the light of emptiness, everything is everything else, we inter-are, everyone is responsible for everything that happens in life" (1988:51–52). As human beings we are intimately connected to one another, in all the joy and all the suffering of the world. As human beings we are of nature, we are nature, one with the world. The truth is our interbeing, beyond the dualistic thinking of the Western mind.

Thus, we are aware of the impermanence, the emptiness, of the world, and peace comes in the awareness of impermanence—and interrelatedness. One of my favorite observations on such awareness, and the relation of this awareness to peace, is from Stephen Batchelor's book *Alone with Others: An Existential Approach to Buddhism:* "Lasting and stable peace of mind is achieved not through discovering the permanence of anything, but through fully accepting the impermanent *as* impermanent and ceasing to insist that it is otherwise. Likewise, genuine contentment is found in realizing that what one previously assumed to be capable of providing satisfaction is actually unable to do so. . . . As the new vision unfolds, our basic anxiety and our sense of meaninglessness are dissolved in the growing awareness of the profound mystery of interrelatedness that permeates all phenomena" (1983:105–6).

Such awareness is not merely another form of *having,* a having of more knowledge. Rather, it is in the sphere of *knowing.* Fromm writes in *To Have or to Be?:*

> Our understanding of the quality of knowing in the being mode of existence can be enhanced by the insights of such thinkers as the Buddha, the Hebrew prophets, Jesus, Master Eckhart, Sigmund Freud, and Karl Marx. In their view, knowing begins with the awareness of the deceptiveness of our common sense perceptions, in the sense that our picture of physical reality does not correspond to what is "really real" and, mainly, in the sense that most people are half-awake, half-dreaming, and are unaware that most of what they hold to be true and self-evident is illusion produced by the suggestive influence of the social world in which they live. Knowing, then, begins with the shattering of illusions, with *dis*illusionment (*Ent-täuschung*). Knowing means to penetrate through the surface, in order to arrive at the roots, and hence the causes; knowing means to "see" reality in its nakedness. Knowing does not mean to be in possession of the truth; it means to penetrate the surface and to strive critically and actively in order to approach truth ever more closely. (1976:28)

The being mode of knowing allows us, as Fromm also observed, to go beyond ourselves, outside the ego (1992:117–20). We turn to others.

The implications for peacemaking are evident. Directly following Thich Nhat Hanh's line that "everything is everything else" and that "everyone is responsible for everything that happens in life" is the following, simple observation: "When you produce peace and happiness in yourself, you begin to realize peace for the whole world" (1988:51–52).

Where does this lead in our criminology? The objective is clear: to be kind to one another, to transcend the barriers that separate us from one another, and to live everyday life with a sense of interdependence. Returning to the source, as in the Zen search for the ox (see Sekida 1975:223–37), we go to town, enter the marketplace, with helping hands. Criminology is our service.

Peace Is the Way

Social action—our service—comes out of the informed heart, out of the clear and enlightened mind. We act with an understanding of our own suffering and the suffering of others. If human actions are not rooted in compassion, these actions will not contribute to a compassionate and peaceful world. "If we cannot move beyond inner discord, how can we help find a way to social harmony? If we ourselves cannot know peace, be peaceful, how will our acts disarm hatred and violence?" (Dass and Gorman 1985:185). The means cannot be different from the ends; peace can come only out of peace. As A. J. Muste (1942) noted, there is no way to peace; rather, peace *is* the way.

As in Mahatma Gandhi's *satyagraha,* the truth is revealed in the course of action. And, in turn, it is truth as presently conceived that guides our action. Gandhi's Hindu and Jainist based concept of *satyagraha* was derived from the Sanskrit word *Sat* for "it is" or "what is," things as they are. *Graha* is to grasp, to be firm. "Truth force" is the common translation of *satyagraha*. Gandhi often spoke of his inner voice, a still small voice that would be revealed in the preparedness of silence (see Erikson 1969:410–23).

Truthful action, for Gandhi, was guided by the idea of *ahimsa.* In *An Autobiography: The Story of My Experiments with Truth,* Gandhi describes *ahimsa* as the refusal to do harm (1957:349). Oppression of all kinds is to be actively resisted, but without causing harm to others. Moreover, compassion and self-restraint grow in the effort not to harm.

Gandhi's insistence upon the truth is firmly within the tradition of socialist humanism. As Kevin Anderson has shown in his essay on Gandhian and Marxian humanism, both are a radical rejection of Western capitalist civilization (1991:14–29). Both posit a future society free of alienation, and both share a confidence that human liberation is on the immediate historical agenda. In reconstructing criminology, we are informed by a socialist humanism.

Erich Fromm included in his 1965 collection of essays, *Socialist Humanism,* an essay by the Gandhian scholar and former secretary to Gandhi N. K. Bose. In "Gandhi: Humanist and Socialist," Bose describes the *satyagrahi,* the one who practices *satyagraha,* as a person who lives "according to his own lights," one who opposes (does not cooperate with) what seems wrong, but also one who "attempts to accept whatever may be right and just" in the view of the opponent. Bose continues: "There is neither victory nor defeat, but an agreement to which both parties willingly subscribe, while institutions or practices proven wrong are destroyed during the conflict" (1965:99). A humane society is created in the course of individual and collective struggle.

To be remembered, all the while, is the single objective of peace. Whatever the technique, whatever the philosophy or theory, the movement toward peace is the proof of any thought or action. Erich Fromm spent a lifetime working in the movements for peace. He was a cofounder of SANE, an organization that sought to end the nuclear race and the war in Vietnam. Late in his life, Fromm worked on behalf of the 1968 presidential nomination campaign of Senator Eugene McCarthy. During the campaign, Fromm wrote: "America stands today at the crossroads: It can go in the direction of continued war and violence, and further bureaucratization and automatization of man, or it can go in the direction of life, peace, and political and spiritual renewal" (1994:96). His call was to "walk the way toward life."

Our response to all that is human is for life, not death. What would a Gandhian philosophy of existence offer a criminologist, or any member of society, in reaction to crime? To work for the creation of a new society, certainly. But, immediately, the reaction would not be one of hate for the offender, nor a cry for punishment and death. In a reading of Gandhi and a commentary on punishment, Erik Erikson writes the following:

> Gandhi reminds us that, since we can not possibly know the absolute truth, we are "therefore not competent to punish"—a most essential reminder, since man when tempted to violence always parades as another's policeman, convincing himself that whatever he is doing to another, that other "has it coming to him." Whoever acts on such righteousness, however, implicates himself in a mixture of pride and guilt which undermines his position psychologically and ethically. Against this typical cycle, Gandhi claimed that only the voluntary acceptance of self-suffering can reveal the truth latent in a conflict—and in the opponent. (1969:412–13)

Punishment is not the way of peace.

Responses to crime that are fueled by hate, rather than generated by love, are necessarily punitive. Such responses are a form of violence, a violence that can only beget further violence. Much of what is called "criminal justice" is a violent reaction to, or anticipation of, crime. The criminal justice system, with all of its procedures, is a form of *negative peace*, its purpose being to deter or process acts of crime through the threat and application of force.

Positive peace, on the other hand, is something other than the deterrence or punishment of crime. Positive peace is more than merely the absence of crime and violence—and of war. "It refers to a condition of society in which exploitation is minimized or eliminated altogether, and in which there is neither overt violence nor the more subtle phenomenon of structural violence" (Barash 1991:8). Positive peace is the attention given to all those things, most of them structured in the society, that cause crime, that happen before crime occurs. Positive peace exists when the sources of crime—including poverty, inequality, racism, and alienation—are not present. There can be no peace—no positive peace—without social justice. Without social justice and without peace (personal and social), there is crime. And there is, as well, the violence of criminal justice.

The negative peacemaking of criminal justice keeps things as they are. Social policies and programs that are positive in nature—that focus on positive peacemaking—create something new. They eliminate the structural sources of violence and crime. Positive peace is the objective of a critical, peacemaking criminology.

Thus our socialist humanism attends to everyday existence, love and compassion, and social justice. Our efforts are not so much out of resistance, as they are an affirmation of what we know about human existence. The way is simply that of peace in everyday life.

References Cited

Aitken, Robert. 1984. *The Mind of Clover: Essays in Zen Buddhist Ethics.* San Francisco: North Point Press.

Anderson, Kevin. 1991. "Radical Criminology and the Overcoming of Alienation: Perspectives from Marxian and Gandhian Humanism." In *Criminology as Peacemaking.* Ed. Harold E. Pepinsky and Richard Quinney. 14–29. Bloomington: Indiana University Press.

Barash, David P. 1991. *Introduction to Peace Studies.* Belmont, Calif.: Wadsworth.

Batchelor, Stephen. 1983. *Alone with Others: An Existential Approach to Buddhism.* New York: Grove Press.

Bose, Nirmal Kumar. 1965. "Gandhi: Humanist and Socialist." In *Socialist Humanism.* Ed. Erich Fromm. 98–106. Garden City, N.Y.: Doubleday.

Camus, Albert. 1955. *The Myth of Sisyphus and Other Essays.* Trans. Justin O'Brien. New York: Alfred A. Knopf.

Dass, Ram, and Paul Gorman. 1985. *How Can I Help? Stories and Reflections on Service.* New York: Alfred A. Knopf.

Erikson, Erik H. 1969. *Gandhi's Truth: On the Origins of Militant Nonviolence.* New York: W. W. Norton.

Fromm, Erich. 1960a. "Psychoanalysis and Zen Buddhism." In *Zen Buddhism and Psychoanalysis.* Ed. D. T. Suzuki, E. Fromm, and R. de Martino. 77–141. New York: Harper and Row.

———. 1960b. "The Prophetic Concept of Peace." In *Buddhism and Culture: A Festschrift in Honor of D. T. Suzuki.* Ed. Susumu Yamaguchi. 163–69. Kyoto: Nakano Press.

———. 1976. *To Have or to Be?* New York: Harper and Row.

———. 1978. "Erich Fromm." In *Contemporary Authors,* vols. 73–76. Ed. Frances Carol Locher. 219–20. Detroit: Gale Research.

———. 1989 [1956]. *The Art of Loving.* New York: Harper and Row.

———. 1992. *The Art of Being.* New York: Continuum.

———. 1994. *On Being Human.* New York: Continuum.

———, ed. 1965. *Socialist Humanism.* Garden City, N.Y.: Doubleday.

Funk, Rainer. 1982. *Erich Fromm: The Courage to Be Human.* Trans. Michael Shaw. New York: Continuum.

Gandhi, Mohandas K. 1957. *An Autobiography: The Story of My Experiments with Truth.* Trans. Mahedeu Desai. Boston: Beacon Press.

Hanh, Thich Nhat. 1988. *The Heart of Understanding.* Berkeley, Calif.: Parallax Press.

Kundera, Milan. 1984. *The Unbearable Lightness of Being.* Trans. Michael Henry Heim. New York: Harper and Row.

————. 1988. *The Art of the Novel.* Trans. Linda Asher. London: Faber and Faber.

Muste, A. J. 1942. *The World Task of Pacificism.* Wallingford, Pa.: Pendale Hill.

Quinney Richard. 1970. *The Social Reality of Crime.* Boston: Little, Brown.

Sartre, Jean-Paul. 1992 [1948]. *Truth and Existence.* Trans. Adrian Van de Hoven. Chicago: University of Chicago Press.

Sekida, Katsuki. 1975. *Zen Training: Methods and Philosophy.* New York: Weatherhill.

Seung, Sahn. 1982. *Only Don't Know.* San Francisco: Four Seasons Foundation.

3

Fromm, Sadomasochism, and Contemporary American Crime

Lynn S. Chancer

My doctoral dissertation about sadomasochism was so indebted to Erich Fromm that, in retrospect, I should have dedicated the finished manuscript to him (Chancer 1992). More than belatedly acknowledging an intellectual influence, however, my purpose in this essay is to tap Fromm's theoretical insights in order to illuminate a practical social problem—violent crime—through which sadomasochistic motivations regularly manifest themselves. Even if slowly decreasing through the 1980s and 1990s, rates of violent crime remain higher in the United States than in other advanced industrial societies, while offenders are being incarcerated at rates higher than any other country in the world.

If there is a relationship between crime, sadomasochism, and contemporary societies, how can the character of such a connection be better understood? Moreover, how does this connection between crime and sadomasochism relate to the psychological and social thought of Erich Fromm and to the Frankfurt School tradition with which he is associated? Generally, students of criminology in the United States turn to homegrown theories such as social ecology, differential association, and anomie to find causal explanations of crime. Fromm is rarely connected to broad explanatory insights into crime and its causation. This essay contends that, despite the relative unpopularity of Fromm's work in general and its lack of association with crime in particular, his ideas provide indispensable clues for developing a deeper theoretical and practical understanding of the persistence of crime in specific social and historical contexts, such as that of the United States in the 1980s and 1990s.

This claim makes little sense unless placed in the context of a more fully developed argument about Fromm's ideas overall. To this end, part I investigates Fromm's view of sadomasochism, using his interpretation to elaborate a theoretical case of my own about the widespread existence of sadomasochistic dynamics in contemporary capitalist societies. After linking Fromm's ideas with sadomasochism in general, part 2 suggests how sadomasochism and contemporary crime may themselves become interrelated in producing high levels of crime in our current American context. By way of conclusion, this essay proposes that factors at once conscious and unconscious, emotional and rational, must be incorporated into any approach to violent crime—in theory and practice—that genuinely aims at uprooting this social problem, rather than merely alleging to be concerned about its seriousness. Thus, I end by insisting that Fromm's work is extremely useful to criminology, whether or not his ideas have been specifically applied in this context.

As the sociologist Neil McLaughlin has argued, Fromm might be characterized as a "forgotten intellectual."[1] By conventional academic criteria, at least in the United States, Fromm has received little attention. Compared to other well-known contemporary European social theorists—for example, Foucault or Bourdieu—Fromm is rarely taught in social theory courses in the sociology and political science departments of major American universities. After writing *Sadomasochism in Everyday Life* (Chancer 1992), I was told by several reviewers that, while the book's perspective was interesting, both Fromm's writings and the broader set of ideas associated with the Frankfurt School critical theorists had become passé. While Critical Theory is often referenced respectfully in the 1990s (see, for example, Calhoun 1996), by no means is it fashionable to resuscitate the Frankfurt School's motivating project of combining Freudian and Marxist perspectives to understand concrete social problems and issues of collective behavior. Rather, as McLaughlin notes, Fromm's approach toward understanding social phenomena often strikes scholars as increasingly irrelevant. In a sociological field from which vestiges of positivism have by no means been eliminated, psychoanalytic perspectives that are not "provable" are placed at a disadvantage.

Yet if one does not conceive Fromm's intellectual significance merely in terms of academic acceptability or numbers of citations, but in terms of sheer ongoing relevance, I contend that his ideas are increasingly germane. Incarceration rates continue to skyrocket in the contemporary United States, even as violent crime has actually diminished. The 1994 Omnibus Crime Bill signed into law under the Clinton administration devoted no funding to preventive measures, nor to alternatives to incarceration. Getting "tough on crime" continues to be the leitmotif of the 1980s and 1990s, in both the statements of politicians and in media depictions, even as economic disparities between rich and poor are wider than in any decade since the 1940s. A number of writings have asked whether these trends cannot be explained simply in terms of rational and conscious motivations. Rather, there may be unconscious collective processes (such as displaced anger) that help to explain current trends in popular policy reactions. Thus, returning to Fromm's writings, both about sadomasochism in general and more specifically about crime, may be useful indeed. I start with Fromm's writings on sadomasochism because they offer perspectives that can be applied to criminologists' interests both in the causes of crime and in the reasons for mass collective reactions that channel responses to crime in particular directions.

Part 1: Expanding the Scope of Fromm and Sadomasochism

In a forward to *Escape from Freedom* written twenty-five years after the book's original publication, Fromm wrote soberly about the ongoing applicability of the book's thesis in a world where "the development of man's intellectual capacities has far out-stripped the development of his emotions. Man's brain lives in the twentieth century; the heart of most men lives still in the Stone Age. . . . How can mankind save itself from destroying itself by this discrepancy between intellectual-technical over-maturity and emotional backwardness?" (Fromm 1994 [1941]: xvi).

The thesis, and the heart of the discrepancy between technical and emotional maturity, is reminiscent of Durkheim's sociological understanding about the emergence of individualism and anomie in the transition from premodern to modern societies. The birth of the modern "individual," as Fromm contended, was accompanied by a painful loss of equally critical human needs for connections, security, and community. Freedom became negatively defined as that which we become liberated "from." Yet, without a positive alternative vision of what we become freed "to," insecurity and a sense of insignificance abound. Fromm cites the United States as a place where an individualistic ideology reigns poignantly and characteristically. Across different social strata, the average person is filled with fear and an overwhelming feeling of personal insignificance; consumer culture and intense economic competition only compound collective feelings of unbearable aloneness in a land that traditionally glorifies the loner and the frontier mentality. *Escape from Freedom,* originally written in 1941, anticipates precisely the kind of worsening economic insecurities described by contemporary Left theorists concerned about the loss of jobs (Aronowitz and DiFazio 1994). Fromm anticipated the worsening of unmet human needs and misery amid uncontrolled structural tendencies. "Although the support of the unemployed by public means has done much to counteract the results of unemployment," Fromm noted decades ago, "not only economically but also psychologically, the fact remains that for the vast majority of people the burden of being unemployed is very hard to bear psychologically, and the dread of it overshadows their whole life. To have a job—regardless of what kind of a job it is—seems to many all they could want of life and something they should be grateful for" (Fromm 1994 [1941]: 130).

This is where the concept of sadomasochism figures within Fromm's overall framework. If indeed a given culture "frees" the individual without providing feelings of security and belonging, people will seek to escape that painful and practically deathlike aloneness through the forging of symbiotic bonds with others. This apparently "free" individual is likely either to seek connection through submerging his or her identity within another's (the strategy classically enacted by the masochist), or by keeping someone else symbiotically connected through psychic and/or physical domination (the strategy classically enacted by a sadist). For Fromm, both options are defense mechanisms likely to flourish wherever, as in the United States, cultural values do not embrace both sides of human needs for autonomy and connectedness, dependence and independence.

Switch now from Fromm's words in *Escape from Freedom* to his prescient elaboration of such strategies in *The Sane Society* (1955). In this later text, sadism and masochism are no longer depicted separately. Rather, they are tied together by "common elements" that unite them at least in underlying motivation:

> man can try to unite himself with the world by having power over it, by making others a part of himself, and thus transcending his individual existence by domination. The common element in both submission and domination is the symbiotic nature of relatedness. Both persons have lost their integrity and freedom; they live on each other and for each other, satisfying their craving for closeness. . . . The realization of the submissive (masochistic) or the domineering (sadistic) passion never leads to satisfaction. They have a self-propelling dynamism, and because no amount of submission, or domination (or possession, or fame) is enough to give a sense of identity and union, more and more of it is sought. The ultimate result of these passions is defeat. It cannot be otherwise; while these passions aim at the establishment of a sense of union, they destroy the sense of integrity. The person driven by any one of these passions actually becomes dependent on others; instead of developing his own individual being, he becomes dependent on those to whom he submits, or whom he dominates. (Fromm 1955:36)

Here is a concise summation of Fromm's basic argument about sadomasochism: If an individualistic culture like that of the United States only appears to "free" the individual, but actually fails to provide him or her simultaneously with feelings of connection and belonging, people will nevertheless seek to escape this ironically deathlike "freedom." They will rebel unless both the needs and longings for freedom and autonomy, as well as connection and belonging, are simultaneously fulfilled. For Fromm, symbiotic sadomasochistic interactions with others, whether manifested through sadism or masochism, are likely to predominate in societies where human needs for acknowledged independence and dependence, autonomy and connections, are not both fulfilled. I argue in *Sadomasochism in Everyday Life* (Chancer 1992) that the structural characteristics shared by both capitalism and patriarchy, as modes of social organization, impede human beings' realization of simultaneous independence and dependence, autonomy and connections. Under capitalism, the individual is left to his or her own devices; the reality of dependency and vulnerability (which, as Aronowitz and DiFazio note in *The Jobless Future,* is more acute than ever in contemporary contexts) is demeaned or altogether denied. In the case of patriarchy, socialized masculinity reifies the alleged value of independence, while devaluing feelings of dependency that are differentially associated with socialized femininity. Consequently, it ought not be surprising if sadism and masochism become common defense mechanisms in contemporary life.

Extending some of Fromm's ideas, societies still structured around capitalistic and patriarchal assumptions are likely to produce high rates of what I have called "social symbiosis" (Chancer 1992). By coining the term "social symbiosis," I suggest that the structure of social institutions themselves make many people excessively dependent and insecure. Within socially symbiotic relationships, the differential power of others strongly affects our self-evaluations and feelings of self-worth; comparatively, it is hard to accord equal weight to our own internal judgments. For example, extreme dependence on intimate partners and family members is common in societies where these persons are the main (and often the only) source of community and connection to others. Similarly, if extremely concerned about job security, we may experience socially symbiotic dependency at the workplace as normal: we may be loath to question or challenge conditions at that workplace, literally as well as figuratively scared for our lives as well as our livelihoods. These specifically social experiences may have an effect as insidious as childhood factors, predisposing us to sadomasochistic tendencies within an excessively and socially symbiotic culture, across a wide range of social relationships from work through schools through familial relations.

Based on this analysis, one could conclude that sadomasochistic forms of interaction, both on individual and collective levels, may predictably become more common than rare in cultures like our own. Sadomasochism becomes the social psychology one would most expect to correspond with the life of "individuals" who have been left altogether too vulnerable and alone. And society is culpable, failing to provide the social security that Fromm in both *Escape from Freedom* and *The Sane Society* asserts that human beings desperately need in addition to individual freedoms.

It is at this point in Fromm's argument, however, that an additional theoretical dilemma arises, one not quite as developed in his own work as the description of sadistic and masochistic strategies themselves. Once tendencies toward sadism and masochism are generated in "everyday" modes of interaction under particular social conditions, how does this form of interaction unfold over time and in concrete social situations? In other words, how does it come to pass that social structures are not only produced but reproduced by agents engaged in defending themselves against the terrors of aloneness that contemporary U.S. culture ought to mitigate, although it has not yet learned how?

At this point, one can use Fromm's theoretical ideas to develop a related idea— that of "internal transformability" (Chancer 1992). Like Freud, Fromm believed that sadism and masochism are two sides of a coin. Even more importantly, they can coexist in the same person. But while Fromm recognized that the same person can regularly be sadistic in one social sphere while masochistic in another, he tended to describe each trait separately from the other. Moreover, Fromm did not explore in depth the patterned ways in which a given party's ability to be *both* sadistic and masochistic in different social spheres may serve to aid in the reproduction of relations of domination and subordination writ large. In this particular sense, though not in others, Fromm's work remained more psychologically general than historically specific.

Yet perhaps this aspect of Fromm's insightful analysis can be even further elaborated through the concept of internal transformability, placing this two-sided structure of sadomasochism in a specifically U.S. context. One could argue that within a given historical setting, sadists and masochists tend to act out relationships with one another in patterned ways. This can be referred to through the concepts of *dominant* and *subordinate* sadism and masochism to encompass this complex character of internal transformations from sadist to masochist (and from masochist to sadist) that take place when sadomasochistic social psychology is viewed within a specific hierarchical social structure. Dominant sadism and dominant masochism refer to the primary mode of interaction through which a person has come to relate to the world. This is the posture of which one is more or less conscious; it is the mode of behavior most perceived by others in describing another person in terms of sadism and masochism. But if one acts in a mode of dominant masochism in one sphere, subordinate sadism may be acted out in another. Conversely, if someone shows dominant sadism in one aspect of life, subordinate masochism may appear elsewhere.

In promulgating a concept that encompasses the coexistence of sadism and masochism in the same person, my intention is to facilitate a transition from "psyche" to "society." If it is true, as Fromm argued, that people regularly experience themselves as powerless to control how the social world is structured around them (that is, one experiences oneself as a dominant masochist), then sadomasochism's capacity for internal transformation may make us (collectively) eager to displace forms of anger that cannot be directly expressed at authorities onto those less powerful. For example, the white worker powerless on the job may vent racist, homophobic, or anti-Semitic feelings on a steady basis, perhaps displacing dissatisfactions subordinately onto others he or she sees as possible scapegoats, and who are even more powerless. To take another example: given the coercive mandates of the traditionally patriarchal family, a particular woman cast masochistically in relation to her husband might find herself exerting too much control over the lives of her children. Thus, power exercised in a subordinate mode can be viewed as an effort to compensate for anger at powerlessness experienced in the dominant position. While the dominant masochist or sadist embroiled in the vicissitudes of this form of sadomasochistic interaction may be totally unaware of the subordinate dimension, the reality of "acting out" the latter is an inescapable potential in a world where structures of power make it difficult or impossible to express dissatisfactions at the party who is actually generating such responses.

But this extension of Fromm's theories about sadistic and masochistic strategies to the concept of dominant and subordinate sadomasochisms carries even more important ramifications. Large-scale desires toward the expression of subordinate and compensatory sadism may also keep social hierarchies firmly in place by encouraging collective angers to be rechanneled. We may be powerless with regard to those in authority above us. But, on the other hand, the easy availability of others onto whom we can target subordinate resentments—those on welfare or criminals, both likely to be disproportionately poor in their social class and racial backgrounds—aids in reproducing an inequitably structured capitalist society through emotionally pleasurable feelings about which we may or may not be aware, and that we may or may not be willing to bring to conscious recognition.

At this juncture, perhaps we can move back from the general to the specific. What does any of this have to do with the specific focus of this essay, namely, the relationship of Fromm's ideas to crime in the context of the contemporary United States?

Part 2: Fromm, Sadomasochism, and Crime

Using Fromm's ideas about sadomasochism as a defense mechanism, and extending them further to develop the idea of sadism's and masochism's internal transformability, these ideas can now be applied to contemporary reactions to crime, which involve collective dynamics that are deeply emotional and often unconsciously motivated.

Let us apply this notion of internal transformability to a simple hypothetical case of crime. Sadism and masochism become linked insofar as a dominant sadist in one context (for example, the person who commits a violent act) may take the reverse position in another (for example, the person who at a workplace or in a home setting is situated as a quite powerless party). On the other hand, the dominant masochist in one setting (for example, the person who feels vulnerable to, or actually has been victimized by, a criminal act) may react by becoming subordinately sadistic elsewhere, such as in his or her eagerness for contemporary incarcerative and "get tough" attitudes toward crime. Indeed, as already noted, in the 1980s and 1990s harsh attitudes toward crime—a move toward punitive rather than rehabilitative philosophies of punishment—have become predominant, and public interest in social causes of crime has markedly diminished.

Nevertheless, the thesis of transformability expanded on the basis of Fromm's ideas provides an explanation not only for many criminal acts themselves but for a connection to be made between individual and social reactions to crime. Through this connection, individual acts of crime and their social context cannot be separated. Take an example from contemporary newspaper accounts. On October 17, 1994, the *New York Times* detailed "state of the art" prison designs that have already been adopted in twenty-five states and at a "model" federal facility in Florence, Colorado. The accompanying illustration proposed a postmodern-looking jail cell resembling a Foucaultian panopticon. The article went on to read:

This approach, resorted to after the murders of Federal corrections officers by hardcore inmates sentenced to prison for life, is as much a state of individualized captivity as imprisonment. . . . All involve techniques that limit the movement of dangerous prisoners beyond their cells to an hour or less a day, and then only with leg-irons, handcuffs, and an escort of two or three guards per inmate. . . . The maxi design, with cordons of cold steel painted in soft green and maroon, staggers the cell so that one inmate cannot make eye contact with his neighbors. Each cell has a double-entry door, with the classic barred cage door backed up by a windowed steel door that minimizes contact among prisoners. "An inmate first has to get over the first hurdle—

violent and predatory behavior," Mr. Vanyur [the associate warden] said, stressing basics in looking forward to throwing open Florence's cells to the inaugural incorrigible, and then firmly locking them up.

This article, which is not unusual among detailed journalistic depictions of increasingly severe criminal justice sanctions, aligns the reader with "roused" taxpayers and with Mr. Vanyur, the associate warden. In other words, there is an implicit agreement between writer and readers as to the "badness" of the dangerous criminals in the jail and the "goodness" of us—the writer, the reader, the viewer, the spectator—out here, knowing we only look in.

Yet we are also set up by the article to imagine ourselves in the place of the other, with whom we also identify. We view the prison cell on the front page of the *New York Times* both from outside and inside. The reader of this article about proposed punitive criminal justice policies, then, can be seen to occupy an intrinsically dual position: at once outside and inside; at once distanced and close; at once fearful and powerless as well as judgmental and powerful.

The example is meant to concretize connections between the societal level at which attitudes to policy are enacted and the supposedly individual level at which crime takes place. This relationship is shown here not by referring to abstract sociological explanations of crime (such as one finds in explanations like anomie theory or social ecology theory), nor to individualistic explanations (such as biological or psychic explanations that abstract from societal contexts) but through social psychological mechanisms that create often unconscious emotional connections between the individual and the social, the psychic and the collective.

More concretely, the internal transformability of sadism and masochism suggests the existence of a "psychopolitics" of crime. As in the above example, the tendency for one side to take precedence in a dominant mode leaves its subordinate side unconsciously dissociated and disowned. Consequently, the violent party who projects a dominant persona of power through sadistic acts (such as a batterer) may be loath to acknowledge a painful and generalized sense of powerlessness that he or she has felt compelled to bear in masochistically structured circumstances of everyday life. Or the "noncriminal" who has experienced predominant powerlessness (and an ongoing feeling of fear and victimization characteristic of a masochistic situation) is not likely to acknowledge retributive desires peculiarly reminiscent of their sadistic nemesis. Such analyses, though needing to be developed at far greater depth than in this cursory overview, have the advantage of connecting social structural and internal psychic experiences within the same explanatory framework. This is precisely where recourse to Fromm's conceptual vocabulary, at once insistent on criticizing capitalism as well as the social psychological defenses and problems it creates, has definite advantages over other well-known frameworks of analysis in criminology, whether or not Fromm's work has yet been adequately tapped by criminologists.

Part 3: The Relevance of Fromm to Current Thinking about Crime

In conclusion, I would like to return to the question of Fromm's relevance to criminology. Three points can be summarized by way of pointing to future applications of Fromm's work to the theoretical concerns of criminologists.

First, Fromm's ideas can help us better understand the causes of crime. Criminologists have frequently separated "individual" from "social" causes of crime. The former category generally entails biological as well as psychological interpretations of crime and its genesis within individuals. Social explanations of crime have traditionally included, among other theoretical perspectives, anomie and Marxist theory. Fromm's views, though, need to be placed in a third category—with interactive theories of crime such as labelling theory, phenomenological accounts, or differential association—that seek to understand how social and psychic factors combine in the backdrop of crime.

Fromm's explanatory framework differs from, and adds to, these other theories through its willingness to explore distinctly psychoanalytic factors. Fromm is concerned not only with taking emotional and rationalistic factors into account within a theory of crime: in addition, unconscious as well as conscious dimensions of individual and social life are seen to require serious investigation. Thus, as argued in part 2, capitalism can be seen as an economic system that produces a certain kind of social psychology. Expanding on Fromm's ideas, this social psychology could be defined as sadomasochistic, and frequently produces unconsciously sadistic and masochistic responses as defense mechanisms against society's failure to meet individuals' simultaneous needs for dependence and independence, connection as well as autonomy. Among these sadistic responses may be acts of crime. Moreover, a specific connection between the social and psychic levels can be shown to take place through the idea of internal transformability (Chancer 1992). Someone who is powerless in one sphere (say, at work) may exert power in other aspects of his or her life by way of seeking compensatory satisfaction. Such "subordinate sadism" may express itself from time to time in criminal acts, such as domestic violence or hate crimes. Other examples, too, could be cited to illustrate how sadomasochistic dynamics (sometimes criminal sadomasochistic dynamics) originate not only in capitalistic and hierarchically organized social structures, nor only in individual psychic defense mechanisms, but in concrete interactions between both these levels, as such connections were developed in the work of Fromm.

Second, Fromm's ideas are potentially applicable to better understanding solutions to crime. An integrated sociological/psychoanalytic understanding of
crime's origins—implicit in Fromm's work—would require two-sided strategies
to deal pragmatically with crime at the level of social and public policy. One prong
of this strategy would have to be overtly political, and would have to involve social
and economic changes. On the one hand, Fromm's critiques of capitalism in
Escape from Freedom and *The Sane Society,* among other works, intimate that some
degree of crime is likely to continue in societies characterized by huge income
disparities and structural economic inequities. Indeed, as noted in this essay's
introduction, income gaps between rich and poor are greater in the 1980s and
1990s than in any decade since the 1930s and 1940s. But on the other hand,
Fromm's perspective simultaneously suggests the importance of policy measures
specifically oriented toward helping individuals cope with problems of loneliness
and alienation, as well as with defenses that come into being precisely when individuals' needs are denied within the society they occupy. Thus, Fromm would
likely have believed that the provision of psychotherapy to large numbers of people
was not simply an "individual" matter but a social right. Without such psychological assistance providing support en masse, outlets may not be available for
individuals to talk about (rather than to "act out") intense feelings of rage, frustration, and resentment that stem both from personal psychic situations and from
"political" collective realities. Consequently, from Fromm's ideas emerges the
notion that treating crime has to be a multifaceted endeavor oriented at once
toward external societial transformation and providing internal individual assistance aimed at rehabilitation. This level of complexity is exactly analogous to the
interactive social/psychic character implicit in Fromm's views of the origins of
crime itself.

Third, Fromm's ideas are potentially applicable to better understanding the
mass psychology of crime. Just as Wilhelm Reich wrote about the mass psychology of fascism, so there may indeed be a mass psychology of crime. By this, I mean
that Fromm's ideas can be used to suggest that public attitudes toward questions
of crime—for instance, whether notions of rehabilitation have been eschewed in
a given time and place in favor of punitive measures—are likely to be intertwined
with crime itself. This mirroring relationship between attitudes toward crime and
crime itself has a long history in the sociological subfields of deviance and criminology. Durkheim discussed society's need for crime in order to define its own
sense of right in opposition to the criminal's wrongdoing. From Hall et al.'s *Policing the Crisis* to Erikson's *Wayward Puritans,* this idea has been applied to various "moral panics" in British and early American contexts, panics that have much
more to do with societal needs for definition than with what is being defined per

se. Fromm's work can add to this history through its explicit stress on unconscious as well as conscious mass dynamics. Drawing on Fromm's ideas allows one to explore more deeply whether trends toward increased incarceration in the United States in the 1980s and 1990s are really what they appear. Does the insistent buildup of jails in the United States have as much to do with crime, especially since crime rates have been diminishing, as it does with economic trends that have been displacing jobs and increasing economic insecurities? Do underground economies become increasingly interrelated with the "prison economy," in ways that demonstrate denied and unconscious connections between actual social realities and conscious pretensions as to such a prison economy's underlying motivations? While it is beyond the purview of this essay to explore this question in detail, the Frankfurt School tradition with which Fromm was associated allows—indeed, it encourages—these connections to be analyzed in ways that incorporate, rather than shirk from, admitting the existence of mass unconscious dynamics and social processes.

It remains for others to continue the process of applying the work of Erich Fromm to contemporary issues in the theory and practice of criminology. For now, though, suffice it to surmise that the time is more than ripe for Fromm to emerge from relative obscurity. Even if a forgotten intellectual in the past, the "psychopolitics" of crime call for Fromm's reintroduction into the context of an increasingly punitive, yet socially and economically anxious, present.

Note

1. I take the term "forgotten intellectual" from McLaughlin's fascinating and as yet unpublished dissertation (CUNY Graduate Center, 1995).

References Cited

Aronowitz, Stanley, and William DiFazio. 1994. *The Jobless Future*. Minneapolis: University of Minnesota Press.

Calhoun, Craig. 1996. *Critical Social Theory*. London: Basil Blackwell.

Chancer, Lynn. 1992. *Sadomasochism in Everyday Life*. New Brunswick, N.J.: Rutgers University Press.

Erikson, Kai T. 1966. *Wayward Puritans: A Study in the Sociology of Deviance*. New York: Macmillan.

Fromm, Erich H. 1955. *The Sane Society*. Greenwich, Conn.: Fawcett Books.

———. 1994 [1941]. *Escape from Freedom*. New York: Henry Holt and Co.

Hall, Stuart, et al. 1978. *Policing the Crisis: Mugging, the State, and Law and Order*. New York: Holmes and Meier.

4

Alienation and Crime: Lessons from Erich Fromm

John F. Wozniak

Throughout a scientific career that spanned over six decades (from the early 1920s to 1980), Erich Fromm produced twenty books and numerous articles and reviews (Knapp 1993:1; Funk 1982:374–83). His writings focus heavily upon the psyche and behavior of the individual. Hence, many authors of psychology textbooks treat Fromm as a psychologist or as a psychoanalyst. In fact, Fromm has been identified even more specifically as a theorist who endeavored to blend together "lines of thought from both psychoanalysis and Marxism" (Israel 1971:153).

Rainer Funk (1982) and Gerhard Knapp (1993) have undertaken extensive overviews of Fromm's life and research. Although they make the argument in different ways, both contend that along with his psychological interests, sociological leanings have been demonstrated in many of Fromm's writings. Funk (1982) and Knapp (1993) also maintain that it is beneficial to conceive of Fromm's work as highly interrelated.

Notably, the richness and depth of Fromm's sociological thinking can be ascertained through an examination of his classic book, *The Sane Society* (1955), which analyzes the problem of "alienation" in industrialized society. In this book, Fromm developed a sociological theory of alienation that is pertinent for contemporary studies of crime. Therefore, it is the purpose of this essay to illustrate ways in which Fromm's theoretical perspectives on alienation can be usefully applied within criminological research.

Essentially, this essay is divided into three parts. The first shows how Fromm's analyses of alienation have the potential to advance the development and growth of critical/humanist/peacemaking criminology. Second, the essay indicates how Fromm's theory of alienation can heighten understanding of crimes that have received national attention. The third segment explores various criminal justice policy implications stemming from Fromm's work on alienation.

Links between Fromm's Theory of Alienation and Critical/Humanist/Peacemaking Criminology

In the foreword to *The Sane Society*, first published in 1955, Erich Fromm indicates that he tried to develop basic concepts for a "humanistic" analysis of life in the twentieth century. One set of concepts, formulated by Fromm, pertains to needs that stem from the conditions of human existence. More specifically, Fromm implored his readers to consider how five needs—relatedness, transcendence, rootedness, sense of identity, frame of orientation—are common in the human situation. Fromm then proceeds to describe how another set of concepts—the phenomenon of alienation and its various manifestations—elucidates ways that these common human needs are generally experienced over time. Thereby, both of these sets of concepts constitute the core elements in what can be termed "Fromm's theory of alienation."

In this context, it is proposed that Fromm's theory of alienation continues to have fruitful applicability for sociological research into present-day society, particularly in scientific studies of crime and its control. As such, this section will demonstrate how Fromm's theory of alienation has the potential to enhance the development of critical/humanist/peacemaking criminology.

Each of these latter criminological orientations has received growing attention among crime scholars in recent years.[1] For the most part, criminologists adopting insights from critical/humanist/peacemaking criminology strive to conduct analyses about transforming society "progressively" toward the lessening of harms arising from social injustice, law-breaking behavior, and their interrelationship (cf. Bohm 1982; Maguire 1988; Michalowski 1983; Platt 1984). For example, Werner Einstadter and Stuart Henry write that critical criminologies "prefer to define crime as social harm and/or as violations of human rights . . . oppose the existing social order of power based on inequality . . . usually demand a radical transformation, not just of criminal justice, but of the total social and political organization of society" (1995:227). Similarly, "the task of a humanistic criminology," in Ronald Kramer's view, "is to combine a theoretical concern with the historically generated structural context within which crime and social control are produced and constructed with a practical concern for human liberation and the realization of social justice. . . . Humanistic criminologists must describe and explain those actions which cause willful social harm whether those harmful acts are engaged in by lower class youths, middle class businessmen, corporate organizations, or ruling elites" (1985:469, 476).

Along the same lines, Richard Quinney suggests that peacemaking criminology "seeks to end suffering and thereby eliminate crime. It is a criminology that is based on human transformation in the achievement of peace and justice. Human transformation takes place as we change our social, economic, and political structure" (1991:11–12).

At present, criminologists working within the broad scope of critical/humanist/peacemaking criminology have not often seen themselves as falling within a common paradigm of analysis.[2] Nonetheless, it is possible to capture the essence of critical/humanist/peacemaking criminology, particularly as it can be applied in relation to Erich Fromm's "humanistic" analysis of life in the twentieth century. Hence, key passages furnished by authors about the nature of critical/humanist/peacemaking criminology will next be identified and then will be elaborated upon with direct linkage to Fromm's theory of alienation.[3]

For the purposes of this essay, useful remarks concerning "critical criminology" have been put forth by Richard Quinney and John Wildeman, who assert that this approach involves "a radical questioning of the justness and effectiveness of all our social institutions" (1991:72). They observe:

> The critical criminology that began to flourish in the 1970's essentially tried to realize two goals: first, to analyze crime in American life through a critical inspection of the contradictions of our master institutions and, second, to define crime as more than just behavior in violation of the law of the state but also as behavior that causes social harm and social injury to great numbers of people. Crime was now conceptualized as institutionalized behavior in violation of basic human rights. (1991:73; cf. Michalowski 1985:14)

Similarly, David Friedrichs posits that "a humanist criminology must concern itself with the larger traumas endured by our society" (1982:210). "A humanist criminology," according to Friedrichs "gives priority to those problems which are restrictive to the exercise of human freedom and dignity, and to the quality of life for all members of society" (1982:210; cf. Hartjen 1985:443).

Likewise, Richard Quinney contends that peacemaking criminology must "search for the reasons that make us suffer" (1991:9). In this light, peacemaking criminology also "seeks to end suffering and thereby eliminate crime," which can help to form "the basis of a nonviolent criminology" (Quinney 1991:11, 12).

Harold Pepinsky, in his article titled "Peacemaking in Criminology," tells us that an aim of this perspective is to "figure out how we can get along without criminalizing and victimizing one another" (1989:6). Michael C. Braswell stipulates further that one of the principal themes of peacemaking criminology is "connectedness" (1990:3). He goes on to say that: "In truth, we are all connected; most of us just can't see the glue" (cf. Lozoff and Braswell 1989).

With these latter passages in mind, let us now turn to a consideration of how

Erich Fromm's work on alienation in *The Sane Society* may have application for future research within critical/humanist/peacemaking criminology. First, peacemaking criminology themes are apparent in Fromm's view of human nature. Like other analysts, Fromm recognizes that every human has essential biological needs. As such, any person can feel a sense of satisfaction when one or more biological needs, such as adequate nourishment or protection from the environment, are met.

However, clearly demonstrating sociological insights, Fromm specifies that every human has five other social needs (Israel 1971:159). These social needs are: (1) the need to establish social relations with others; (2) the need to be actively creative; (3) the need for fixed roots; (4) the need for one's own identity; and (5) the need to orient oneself in the world intellectually. Notably, these five social needs can, with some imagination, be conceived to be close to the issue of "connectedness" that peacemaking criminologists such as Michael C. Braswell desire us to see. In other words, are these five social needs part of the "glue" that peacemaking criminologists want us to recognize and possibly promote as a way to "end suffering and thereby eliminate crime," as Richard Quinney has suggested? In any event, it is hard to realize how any of these five needs could become fully satisfied in isolation from others in society.

Second, Erich Fromm's theory of alienation proposes that the conditions of human existence arising from the nineteenth and twentieth centuries often make it difficult for the individual to satisfy these five social needs. It is at this point in his analysis that Fromm evokes themes of critical criminology and peacemaking criminology.

For instance, as noted earlier, critical criminology claims that it is important not only to inspect the contradictions of our social institutions, but also to radically question their justness and effectiveness (e.g., Quinney and Wildeman 1991). Correspondingly, it is a central tenet of *The Sane Society* that it has become increasingly problematic for the individual to satisfy all of the five social needs as the social institutions arising out of capitalism become more fully developed in the nineteenth and twentieth centuries. Thereby, Fromm's investigation of the societal conditions of the seventeenth and eighteenth centuries led him to write that, at this time, "The practices and ideas of medieval culture still had a considerable influence on the economic practices of this period. Thus it was supposed to be un-Christian and unethical for one merchant to try to lure customers from another by force of lower prices or any other inducements" (1955:81). Fromm also said that, during this period, "no economic progress was supposed to be healthy if it hurt any group within the society" (1955:82).

Societies began to slowly change with the coming of the nineteenth century. As Fromm reports: "The most characteristic element of nineteenth-century capitalism was first of all, ruthless exploitation of the worker; it was believed to be a natural or a social law that hundreds of thousands of workers were living at the point of starvation. The owner of capital was supposed to be morally right if, in the pursuit of profit, he exploited to the maximum the labor he hired. There was hardly any sense of human solidarity between the owner of capital and his workers. The law of the economic jungle was supreme. All the restrictive ideas of previous centuries were left behind" (1955:82). It is here that Fromm seems to address a humanist criminology theme noted earlier by Friedrichs, that this perspective "must concern itself with the larger traumas endured by our society" (1982:210).

Fromm further emphasizes that the world of the nineteenth century was "competitive, hoarding, exploitative, authoritarian, aggressive, individualistic" (1955:93). He then states that there is a major difference between the nineteenth and twentieth centuries—"instead of the exploitative and hoarding orientation we find the receptive and marketing orientation" (1955:93). In other words, the social structure of the nineteenth century necessitated persons who liked to save; the social structure of this current century requires persons who are interested in spending and consuming (Israel 1971:154–55).

According to Fromm, the work world of the twentieth century exhibited other classic features, such as: "the disappearance of feudal traits, the revolutionary increase in industrial production, the increasing concentration of capital and bigness of business and government, the increasing number of people who manipulate figures and people, the separation of ownership from management" (1955:101). It is Fromm's main contention that these social conditions arising during the last two centuries produced "the central issue of the effects of capitalism on personality: the phenomenon of alienation" (1955:111). He defines alienation as: "A mode of experience in which the person experiences himself as an alien. He has become, one might say, estranged from himself. He does not experience himself as the center of his world, as the creator of his own acts—but his acts and their consequences have become his masters, whom he obeys, or whom he may even worship. The alienated person is out of touch with himself as he is out of touch with any other person" (1955:111).[4] Here, one may consider how Michael C. Braswell's peacemaking criminology themes of "connectedness" clash and contrast with Fromm's themes underlying the experiences of alienation. All this also seems to recall Ronald C. Kramer's concerns for humanist criminologists that they must strive to "describe those actions which cause willful social harm" (1985:476; cf. Quinney and Wildeman 1991). In addition, it seems that

Fromm's theory of alienation potentially furnishes a "historically generated structural context" from which humanist criminologists could explore how, as Kramer
puts it, "crime and social control are produced and constructed" (1985:469).

Finally, let us note that, for Erich Fromm, alienation during the twentieth
century is almost total—it pervades the lives of workers, managers, stockholders, owners, man-to-fellow-man, and it even affects our leisure activities. In fact,
Fromm has argued that the social character of industrial society today is characterized by alienation (Israel 1971:156). In this regard, Fromm stresses that the
alienated person cannot be thought of as truly healthy because the more he/
she is manipulated by others, the more he/she tends to lack a sense of self. As
Fromm further adds, such a lack of self can create deep anxiety (1955:181), which
again recalls peacemaking criminology themes, that is, to "seek to end suffering" by "trying to figure ways to get along without victimizing one another"
(Quinney 1991:11; Pepinsky 1989). Fromm's notion of deep anxiety seems to
parallel Friedrichs's humanist criminology construct of "larger traumas" and
giving "priority to problems which are restrictive to the exercise of human freedom and dignity" (1982:210). In sum, various insights from Fromm's theory of
alienation have been linked to themes underlying critical/humanist/peacemak-
ing criminology. In the next section of this essay, attention will be directed
toward a second application of Fromm's theory of alienation—i.e., how this
theory can offer insight into highly publicized crimes.

The Applicability of Fromm's Theory of Alienation to Criminal Behavior

Before addressing the main concern of this part of the essay, it seems instructive
to note that recent developments in criminology have neglected the concept of
alienation. I examined twenty-nine criminology textbooks published since 1980.
Of these texts, only five (Balkan et al. 1980; Fox 1985; Quinney and Wildeman
1991; Sykes and Cullen 1992; Yablonsky 1990) include the topic of alienation in
the subject index. During this same period of time, the concept of alienation has
not received much focus in journals such as *Criminology* and *Justice Quarterly.*

Even though the concept of alienation has played a less vital role in most recent criminology research, it continues to have relevance in understanding contemporary life. David Simon and Stanley Eitzen reveal this relevance as they state:
"Since 1986, American society has witnessed scandal after scandal in its political
and economic institutions. What's more, there is no end in sight to either the
revelations of wrongdoing or their harmful effects on the public's health, pock-
etbooks, and/or trust" (1993:1).

It seems like every day a crime takes place that receives massive national attention. It is interesting to observe how U.S. citizens react once such illegality is illuminated: some may feel outrage, others may become more cynical, and still others may tend to be bewildered by the seemingly strange and bizarre behaviors that come to light. As citizens of our country, criminologists may initially react with similar outrage, cynicism, and bewilderment. However, as criminologists we might do well to contemplate the value of examining these highly publicized crimes—as well as less publicized offenses—through the concept of alienation.

In this light, Erich Fromm's theory of alienation offers a promising framework through which to analyze unlawful conduct as examples of alienated behavior. Of course, it must be acknowledged that Fromm's research on alienation did not focus directly upon the study of crime nor highly publicized offenses in the strictest sense. Still, as shown in the previous section, Fromm's theory of alienation can be quite suitably utilized by progressive (i.e., critical/humanist/peacemaking) criminologists and others who desire to investigate how the development of social structure relates to various forms of crime and victimization. In other words, *macro-level* studies of alienation and crime can be devised by adopting themes from Fromm's theory of alienation—particularly his envisioning of the social structural conditions arising out of capitalist societies.

Likewise, *micro-level* insights about the relationship between alienation and crime can also be gained by employing Fromm's theory of alienation as a guidepost for further study. Erich Fromm devoted over eighty pages in *The Sane Society* to various macro- and micro-level dimensions in which alienation can be experienced under the conditions of capitalist societies. It is not the intention here to delineate all these various micro-level dimensions of alienation.[5] Rather, in the discussion below, five examples of highly publicized crimes will be identified and then linked to micro-level dimensions in Fromm's theory of alienation. In addition, an attempt was made here to connect micro-level aspects of this theory to major forms of crime often specified in the criminology textbooks mentioned earlier. Readers may note that each of these events can be thought of as examples of street crime, white collar crime, victimless crime, organized crime, and corporate crime.[6] Again, the purpose is not to furnish a complete theoretical explanation of each criminal event but to show, in a preliminary way, how elements of Fromm's work on alienation might cast a different light on the event.

As the first example of a highly publicized crime, let us consider the following scenario: Why did a graduate student at the University of Iowa shoot to death his advisor and others employed at this university on the day after he was not given a top academic achievement award?

Commentators may attribute this mass murder to the frustrations of academic life, to the student's difficulty adjusting to another culture, or to individual pathology. Using Erich Fromm's framework, however, it is possible to see how this violence may have been fostered by alienation. Thus, in *The Sane Society*, Fromm argues that a core aspect of "the alienated person" is that his/her "sense of worth is based on approval as the reward for conformity" (1955:181). In Fromm's words, the person "feels naturally threatened in his sense of self and in his self-esteem by any feeling, thought or action which could be suspected of being a deviation" (1955:181). But, of course, as a "human . . . he cannot help deviating, hence he must feel afraid of disapproval all the time" (Fromm 1955:181). The alienated person's only respite is "the feeling of not having lost close touch with the herd" (Fromm 1955:181).

In this context, the student, if alienated, would have experienced a continual threat to his self-worth, living under the burden that authority figures would disapprove. The failure to receive an award, a seemingly trivial slight, would signify a profound and public manifestation of the student's "deviation" from and perhaps devalued status within the "herd." If so, striking out with violence at the "herd" might seem understandable.[7]

A second example of a highly publicized crime: Why did Jim Bakker, the famous television evangelist, ask his viewers to donate funds to his ministry and then misappropriate these funds, while committing other crimes such as mail fraud in relation to these donations?

Again, employing Fromm's analysis, one might assert that some individuals, like Jim Bakker, become alienated by spending much energy on building an idol that they worship and submit to. In Fromm's words, the alienated person has a mode of experience in which: "His life forces have flown into a 'thing,' and this thing, having become an idol, is not experienced as a result of his own productive effort, but as something apart from himself, over and against him, which he worships and to which he submits. . . . In idolatry man bows down and submits to the projection of one partial quality in himself. He does not experience himself as the center from which living acts of love and reason radiate" (1955:112). For Jim Bakker, his idol became his television ministry work and the fame and lifestyle it permitted. This work tended to dominate him so much that the idol prompted him into an alienated form of behavior, abusing donations from his television viewers.

Based on Fromm, moreover, the *audience's* alienation would have furnished the context for the scandal. Bakker's idolatry may have been in transforming his ministry from a means to do good into an end, but he also became an idol for those far away, if not close by. In this case, the alienated "individual projects all his powers into" the idol, "hoping to regain some of his powers by submission and worship" (Fromm 1955:113). The result is a corrupt relationship in which true spirituality and love move beyond reach. The idol, says Fromm, "becomes a thing, his neighbor becomes a thing, just as his gods are things" (1955:112).

A third example of a highly publicized crime: A prostitute, known as the "Rolodex Madam," was hired by a head of a savings and loan bank in San Diego to supply prostitutes to close deals among the bank's depositors. Why did the Rolodex Madam, her prostitutes, and the others in this arrangement engage in such behavior?

This web of illegal relationships would remind us of Fromm's observation, noted earlier, that "alienation . . . in modern society is almost total; it pervades the relationship of man to his work, to the things he consumes, to the state, to his fellow man, and to himself" (1955:114–15). In this particular case, it seems that the participants—the Madam, the prostitutes, the savings and loan owner, and the bank customers—were fundamentally alienated. Their relationships were made so instrumental and impersonal that they could, in Fromm's terms, experience themselves "as a thing, an investment to be manipulated" (1955:181).

A fourth example of a highly publicized crime: Why did various businesses in the 1940s hire gangsters to terrorize and infiltrate the labor unions and to act as strike breakers?[8]

Based on Fromm's perspective, this use of illegal means to obtain corporate ends reflects the fundamental alienation between manager and worker (1955:111–37). As Fromm points out, the relationship of the "manager-bureaucrat" to workers is "one of complete alienation" (1955:116). In fact, the manager-bureaucrat considers "the people to be administered" as "objects" to be regarded "neither with love nor with hate, but completely impersonally. . . . he must manipulate people as though they were figures, or things" (Fromm 1955:116). Accordingly, when corporate interests are threatened, businesses will "unleash powerful forces," even illegal forces, to try to gain back control of the organization from the workers. The more general context for the insensitivity to the welfare of workers—or, for that matter, to the welfare of consumers or the public—is the alienation inherent in the larger economic and institutional system. As Fromm states: "Capitalism is based on the principle that is to be found in all class societies: the use of man by man. . . . The owner of capital uses other men for the purpose of his own profit. . . . One man serves another for purposes which are not his own but those of the employer" (1955:88).

The final example of a highly publicized crime: Why did Ford sell Pinto cars that were found to have defective fuel tanks, even though test results showed that rear-end collisions would lead to massive fiery explosions? Moreover, why did the company choose to market defective cars even though repair would cost only about eleven dollars per vehicle?

Similar to the previous example, Fromm's perspective would immediately focus on the effects of capitalism in alienating corporate managers from consumers, causing them to see consumers not as humans whose lives are tragically affected by a Pinto fire but as objects, or sources of potential profits. More specifically, Fromm may well link such corporate insensitivity and the physical harm it wreaks to the alienation that comes from the "exclusive pursuit of passion for money" (1955:114).

In *The Sane Society,* however, Fromm also notes a unique and alienating feature of the modern "big business": managers do not own the company they run, while stockholders do not run the company they own. Concern and *responsibility* for the well-being of consumers are often lost in the cleavage between managers and stockholders. According to Fromm, the manager thus "is alienated from his product as something concrete and useful"; his goals are reduced to "the efficient operation and expansion of the enterprise" (1955:15). The stockholder may own the modern corporation, but he or she "has little control" over and thus "bears no responsibility with respect to the enterprise and its physical property" (Fromm 1955:118). "It has often been said," writes Fromm, "that the owner of a horse is responsible. If the horse lives he must feed it. If the horse dies he must bury it. No such responsibility attaches to a share of stock" (1955:118). In the Pinto case, managerial efficiency and stockholder neglect may be seen as key factors in allowing dangerous automobiles to be marketed with few moral qualms and little concern for the potential risks unknowingly incurred by consumers.

In sum, Erich Fromm's perspective, while undoubtedly not a complete explanation of illegal activities, has the advantage of sensitizing criminologists to the ways that alienation penetrates the fabric of macro-level social institutions and, on the micro-level, the lives and minds of individual actors. Furthermore, this section hopefully has illuminated how alienation and the aspects of the phenomenon discerned by Erich Fromm are implicated in a range of crimes—from individual acts of violence, to the so-called victimless crime of prostitution, to offenses by elite individuals and corporate malfeasance.

Criminal Justice Policy Implications Underlying Fromm's Theory of Alienation

As a way to conclude this essay, focus will be directed toward how Erich Fromm suggested we might attempt to overcome alienation in the future. In essence, this final part will delineate some of the larger policy implications, especially in regard to criminal justice on the whole. Four key criminal justice policy implications will be examined in detail.

First, Erich Fromm ends *The Sane Society* by considering what he termed "various answers" to deal with the problems of life in the twentieth century. It is significant to note that Fromm identifies authoritarian idolatry, supercapitalism, and socialism as possible ways to end alienation of individuals within society. Each of these alone does not constitute his vision of the roads we need to take toward bringing about a sane society. In his "Roads to Sanity" chapter, Fromm's suggestion for the solution of the problem of alienation is not to totally destroy or eliminate capitalistic social structure. Fromm also does not recommend a societal revolution to change the present conditions.

Gerhard Knapp has pointed out that Erich Fromm basically "envisions a compromise solution which would on the one hand incorporate some remnants of the present system and, on the other, establish a new state which might be called predominantly socialistic" (1993:153; cf. Scimecca 1995:171–86; Simon 1996:317–41). Unlike many orthodox Marxists, Fromm does not visualize effective social change if we restrict such change to the institution of the economy. Instead, Fromm believes a sane society is more likely to result if humans can all work toward restructuring the economic, political, and cultural levels of society.

Fromm's "Roads to Sanity" chapter is relevant for those interested in furthering the development of critical/humanist/peacemaking criminology. That is, efforts must be made "to radically question and critically inspect the workings of our social institutions." Space limitations do not permit a concrete discussion of more specific suggestions made by Fromm in "Roads to Sanity." Suffice it to say that Erich Fromm was extremely optimistic about the potential of humanity to work a way out of social conditions that engender alienation and other social problems characteristic of the twentieth century.

A second important criminal justice policy implication emanating from Fromm's work on alienation pertains to his analysis of social needs. Peacemaking criminologists who strive to provide treatment for prisoners might adopt Fromm's social needs framework into their counseling programs (cf. Lozoff and Braswell 1989; Bartollas and Braswell 1993). Perhaps such correctional clients can be influenced into recognizing that their shortcomings and unlawful behavior might link to one of the unmet social needs outlined by Fromm. One possible benefit in using Fromm's social needs construct with prisoners is that it could potentially work for both their individual treatment and group treatment sessions (cf. Gibbons 1965).[9]

A third implication is that greater promotion of Erich Fromm's approach toward examining a problematic issue in our society—at both structural and individual levels—may potentially inspire other criminologists to undertake more elaborate and broader-based research on crime. Consider how greater inclusion of the social construct of alienation into crime-related studies might lead criminology and criminal justice into novel directions in the twenty-first century. In other words, the disciplines of criminology and criminal justice could certainly use more studies in Fromm's vein so that complex issues pertaining to crime can be scientifically investigated in more multifarious fashion.

The final implication is that a study like Erich Fromm's on alienation offers a point of view from which to assess some of the ongoing crime solutions that have been emerging from our government. Current attempts to solve crime include: "three strikes and you're out" legislation, boot camps for criminal offenders, electronic monitoring of correctional clients, and midnight basketball programs for inner city youths (see Turner et al. 1995; Burton et al. 1993; MacKenzie 1990; Ball et al. 1988; Baumer et al. 1993; Cullen et al. 1996; Feeley and Simon 1992).

Again, when viewed through Fromm's framework on alienation, none of these solutions addresses the macro-level societal conditions that Fromm had emphasized as pivotal factors producing the consequence of alienation and its various dimensions. To be fair, these proposals were not conceived specifically to analyze or solve the problems stemming from alienation. Nor were these crime solutions intended to be macro-level societal solutions as focused upon by Fromm in his "Roads to Sanity" chapter. Be that as it may, it would be far-fetched to argue that all of these newer crime solutions are along the same lines of thought embraced by Fromm in *The Sane Society*.

It seems likely that Fromm might have treated such crime solutions as further evidence of how alienation can be experienced under the structural conditions of capitalist society. In fact, there is very little about these crime solutions that easily fits into Fromm's considerations about how to overcome alienation. That is, through the lens of Fromm's theory of alienation on the whole, can we expect to overcome alienation produced by social structural conditions by adopting "three strikes and you're out" legislation for criminals, or by closely monitoring criminals through electronics and boot camps, or by setting up programs for inner city youth to play basketball at night?

Erich Fromm's "Roads to Sanity" chapter sets much more socially extensive goals than such unidimensional crime solutions (cf. Cullen and Wozniak 1982). Again, Fromm's analysis tends to be more in keeping with the perspectives of critical/humanist/peacemaking criminologists. Hence, can we adequately maintain that any of these crime solutions can exemplify parts of the "social glue" that holds us all together in society? Or, to put it into the terms of Quinney and Wildeman, are such crime solutions "the best of all possible ways to achieve the fullest development and realization of the human potential of all the people?" (1991:72).

Regardless of whether or not any of these newly proposed crime solutions can render favorable findings upon evaluation research, such remedies are limited given that they do not deal with the macro-level conditions of society that commonly propel offenders into jails and prisons in the first place. It is equally plausible that these crime solutions, since they are mostly designed to restrict offenders from full participation in the rest of society, may further "alienate" offenders who encounter difficulties adjusting to these crime control programs (cf. Cullen et al. 1996).

In this light, Erich Fromm's theoretical perspective enables us to "see through" alienating solutions to societal ills. Hopefully, this essay will play a part in motivating others to reexamine Erich Fromm's writings as a potentially useful vantage point from which to work toward achieving goals of a critical/humanist/peacemaking criminology.

Notes

1. Regarding "critical criminology," see, for example: Groves and Sampson 1986; Henry and Milovanovic 1991; MacLean and Milovanovic 1991; Thomas and O'Maolchatha 1989. Examples of "humanist criminology" include: Friedrichs 1982; Hartjen 1985; Kramer 1985; Pfuhl 1985. Concerning "peacemaking criminology," see for example: Braswell 1990; Friedrichs 1991; Lozoff and Braswell 1989; Pepinsky 1988, 1989; Pepinsky and Quinney 1991; Quinney 1988a, 1988b, 1993; Quinney and Wildeman 1991.

2. Authors who have written books on various types of past and present criminological theories also have not drawn a clear linkage between critical, humanist, and peacemaking criminology (e.g., Akers 1994; Curran and Renzetti 1994; Einstadter and Henry 1995; Gibbons 1979; Lilly et al. 1989; Pelfrey 1980; Vold and Bernard 1986; Williams and McShane 1994).

3. For a more detailed discussion of the central dimensions of each of these orientations, see, for example: Einstadter and Henry 1995 and Thomas and O'Maolchatha 1989—on critical criminology; Friedrichs 1982 and Hartjen 1985—on humanist criminology; Pepinsky and Quinney 1991—on peacemaking criminology.

4. Following the example of the humanist sociologist Joseph Scimecca (1995), I have tried to use nonsexist pronouns in this essay and also have chosen to not alter Fromm's original wording. Presumably, Fromm's concept of alienation would apply to woman and man alike.

5. See Israel 1971:151–62 for an example of such a synopsis.

6. Some of these criminal scenarios would fall into one or more of these offenses.

7. Of course, any behavior may have multiple motives, but Fromm's depiction of this

side of alienation seems relevant. Parenthetically, the victimization resulting from this type of alienated behavior could be further examined by criminologists as a way to move beyond Fromm's original formulation.

8. For more detailed discussion of such criminal activities, see Simon 1996:79–81.

9. See, in particular, Gibbons's chapter titled "On The Nature And Forms Of Treatment."

References Cited

Akers, Ronald L. 1994. *Criminological Theories: Introduction and Evaluation.* Los Angeles: Roxbury.

Balkan, Sheila, Ronald J. Berger, and Janet Schmidt. 1980. *Crime and Deviance in America: A Critical Approach.* Belmont, Calif.: Wadsworth.

Ball, Richard A., C. Ronald Huff, and J. Robert Lilly. 1988. *House Arrest and Correctional Policy: Doing Time at Home.* Newbury Park, Calif.: Sage.

Bartollas, Clemens, and Michael Braswell. 1993. "Correctional Treatment, Peacemaking, and the New Age Movement." *Journal of Crime and Justice* 26 (2): 43–48.

Baumer, Terry L., Michael G. Maxfield, and Robert I. Mendelsohn. 1993. "A Comparative Analysis of Three Electronically Monitored Home Detention Programs." *Justice Quarterly* 10 (March): 121–42.

Bohm, Robert M. 1982. "Radical Criminology: An Explication." *Criminology* 4 (February): 564–89.

Braswell, Michael C. 1990. "Peacemaking: A Missing Link in Criminology." *The Criminologist* 15 (May–June): 1, 3–5.

Burton, Velmer S., James W. Marquart, Steven J. Cuvelier, Leanne Fiftal Alarid, and Robert J. Hunter. 1993. "A Study of Attitudinal Change among Boot Camp Participants." *Federal Probation* 57 (September): 46–52.

Cullen, Francis T., and John F. Wozniak. 1982. "Fighting the Appeal of Repression." *Crime and Social Justice* 18 (Winter): 23–33.

Cullen, Francis T., John Paul Wright, and Brandon K. Applegate. 1996. "Control in the Community: The Limits of Reform?" In *Choosing Correctional Options That Work: Defining the Demand and Evaluating the Supply.* Ed. Alan T. Harland. 69–116. Thousand Oaks, Calif.: Sage.

Curran, Daniel J., and Claire M. Renzetti. 1994. *Theories of Crime.* Boston: Allyn and Bacon.

Einstadter, Werner, and Stuart Henry. 1995. *Criminological Theory: An Analysis of Its Underlying Assumptions.* Fort Worth, Tex.: Harcourt Brace.

Feeley, Malcolm M., and Jonathan Simon. 1992. "The New Penology: Notes on the Emerging Strategy of Corrections and its Implications." *Criminology* 30 (November): 449–74.

Fox, Vernon. 1985. *Introduction to Criminology.* 2d ed. Englewood Cliffs, N.J.: Prentice-Hall.

Friedrichs, David O. 1982. "Crime, Deviance and Criminal Justice: In Search of a Radical Humanistic Perspective." *Humanity and Society* 6 (August): 200–226.

———. 1991. "Introduction: Peacemaking Criminology." In *New Directions in Critical Criminology.* Ed. Brian D. MacLean and Dragan Milovanovic. 101–6. Vancouver: Collective Press.

Fromm, Erich. 1955. *The Sane Society.* New York: Holt, Rinehart and Winston.

Funk, Rainer. 1982. *Erich Fromm: The Courage to be Human.* New York: Continuum.

Gibbons, Don C. 1965. *Changing the Lawbreaker: The Treatment of Delinquents and Criminals.* Englewood Cliffs, N.J.: Prentice-Hall.

———. 1979. *The Criminological Enterprise: Theories and Perspectives.* Englewood Cliffs, N.J.: Prentice-Hall.

Groves, W. Byron, and Robert J. Sampson. 1986. "Critical Theory and Criminology." *Social Problems* 33 (December): S58–80.

Hartjen, Clayton A. 1985. "Humanistic Criminology: Is it Possible?" *Journal of Sociology and Social Welfare* 12 (September): 444–68.

Henry, Stuart, and Dragan Milovanovic. 1991. "Constitutive Criminology: The Maturation of Critical Theory." *Criminology* 29 (May): 293–316.

Israel, Joachim. 1971. *Alienation: From Marx to Modern Sociology.* Boston: Allyn and Bacon.

Knapp, Gerhard P. 1993. *The Art of Living: Erich Fromm's Life and Works.* New York: Peter Lang.

Kramer, Ronald C. 1985. "Defining the Concept of Crime: A Humanistic Perspective." *Journal of Sociology and Social Welfare* 12 (September): 469–87.

Lilly, J. Robert, Francis T. Cullen, and Richard A. Ball. 1989. *Criminological Theory: Context and Consequences.* Newbury Park, Calif.: Sage.

Lozoff, Bo, and Michael Braswell. 1989. *Inner Corrections: Finding Peace and Peacemaking.* Cincinnati: Anderson.

MacKenzie, Doris Layton. 1990. "Boot Camp Prisons: Components, Evaluations, and Empirical Issues." *Federal Probation* 54 (September): 44–52.

MacLean, Brian D., and Dragan Milovanovic, eds. 1991. *New Directions in Critical Criminology.* Vancouver: Collective Press.

Maguire, Brendan. 1988. "The Applied Dimension of Radical Criminology: A Survey of Prominent Radical Criminologists." *Sociological Spectrum* 8:133–51.

Michalowski, Raymond J. 1983. "Crime and Control in the 1980's: A Progressive Agenda." *Crime and Social Justice* 19:13–23.

———. 1985. *Order, Law, and Crime: An Introduction to Criminology.* New York: Random House.

Pelfrey, William V. 1980. *The Evolution of Criminology.* Cincinnati: Anderson.

Pepinsky, Harold E. 1988. "Violence as Unresponsiveness: Toward a New Conception of Crime." *Justice Quarterly* 5 (December): 539–87.

———. 1989. "Peacemaking in Criminology." *Critical Criminologist* 1 (Summer): 6–10.

Pepinsky, Harold E., and Richard Quinney, eds. 1991. *Criminology as Peacemaking.* Bloomington: Indiana University Press.

Pfuhl, Erdwin. 1985. "Humanistic Criminology: Future Prospects." *Journal of Sociology and Social Welfare* 12 (September): 604–38.

Platt, Anthony M. 1984. "Criminology in the 1980's: Progressive Alternatives to 'Law and Order.'" *Crime and Social Justice* 21–22:191–99.

Quinney, Richard. 1988a. "Crime, Suffering, Service: Toward a Criminology of Peacemaking." *The Quest* (Winter): 66–75.

———. 1988b. "The Theory and Practice of Peacemaking in the Development of Radical Criminology." Paper presented at the annual meeting of the American Society of Criminology, November, Chicago.

———. 1991. "The Way of Peace: On Crime, Suffering, and Service." In *Criminology as Peacemaking*. Ed. Richard Quinney and Harold E. Pepinsky. 3–13. Bloomington: Indiana University Press.

———. 1993. "A Life of Crime: Criminology and Public Policy as Peacemaking." *Journal of Crime and Justice* 16 (2): 3–9.

Quinney, Richard, and John Wildeman. 1991. *The Problem of Crime: A Peace and Social Justice Perspective.* Mountain View, Calif.: Mayfield.

Scimecca, Joseph A. 1995. *Society and Freedom: An Introduction to Humanist Sociology.* 2d ed. Chicago: Nelson Hall.

Simon, David R. 1996. *Elite Deviance.* 5th ed. Boston: Allyn and Bacon.

Simon, David R., and D. Stanley Eitzen. 1993. *Elite Deviance.* 4th ed. Boston: Allyn and Bacon.

Sykes, Gresham M., and Francis T. Cullen. 1992. *Criminology.* 2d ed. Fort Worth: Harcourt Brace Jovanovich.

Thomas, Jim, and Aogan O'Maolchatha. 1989. "Reassessing the Critical Metaphor: An Optimistic Revionist View." *Justice Quarterly* 6 (June): 143–72.

Turner, Michael G., Jody L. Sundt, Brandon K. Applegate, and Francis T. Cullen. 1995. "'Three Strikes and You're Out' Legislation: A Treatment and Supervision Approach." *Federal Probation* 59 (September): 16–35.

Vold, George B., and Thomas J. Bernard. 1986. *Theoretical Criminology.* 3d ed. New York: Oxford University Press.

Williams, Frank P. III, and Marilyn D. McShane. 1994. *Criminological Theory.* 2d ed. Englewood Cliffs, N.J.: Prentice-Hall.

Yablonsky, Lewis. 1990. *Criminology, Crime, and Criminality.* New York: Harper and Row.

5

Gender, Social Character, Cultural Forces, and the Importance of Love: Erich Fromm's Theories Applied to Patterns of Crime

Polly F. Radosh

Mental health, in the humanistic sense, is characterized by the ability to love and to create, . . . by a sense of identity based on one's experience of self as the subject and agent of one's powers, by the grasp of reality inside and outside of ourselves, this is by the development of objectivity and reason. The aim of life is to live intensely, to be fully born, to be fully awake. (Fromm 1955:180)

Social character . . . [is] the nucleus of the character structure which is shared by most members of the same culture. (Fromm 1962:78)

I am what I have and if what I have is lost, who then am I? (Fromm 1976:109)

In American society, men have a virtual monopoly over crime. Over 90 percent of those accused, convicted, and incarcerated for crimes in the United States are men. The most recent Department of Justice data indicate that the rate of incarceration for men with sentences of more than one year is 819 per 100,000 population, compared to 51 women incarcerated for more than one year per 100,000 population (Mumola and Beck 1997:5). Given the high rates of nonreporting for several crimes committed almost exclusively by men, such as sexual assault, rape, and domestic battery, the very low conviction rates among reports of these crimes, and the exceptionally low likelihood of punishment for such crimes, the official rates estimate only a small portion of men's crime. In 1993, for example, the Federal Bureau of Investigation (FBI) recorded 106,010 reports of rape, which is believed to be about half of all rapes committed in that year. Fewer than 22,000 people were convicted of rape and under 8,000 were actually sentenced to prison for the crime of rape in 1993 (FBI 1995:225; Maguire and Pastore 1995:230, 445, 485). In other words, less than four percent of rapes resulted in incarceration of an offender in 1993.[1]

In addition, men are the primary perpetrators of the seldom-prosecuted crimes associated with occupations, or white collar crime (Simon and Eitzen 1993). Crimes against human societies, such as those involving the environment, armaments, global endangerment, governmental crime, and other nearly-never prosecuted offenses also fall within the male monopoly over crime (Simon and Eitzen 1993).

More than 1.1 million men were incarcerated in state or federal prisons and jails in 1996, compared to 74,730 women (Mumola and Beck 1997:5). Most offenders incarcerated in the United States have committed an "index offense," or one of eight crimes statistically tracked by the FBI. Unmeasured crimes against human society and white collar crime are not included in usual crime statistics and offenders are rarely incarcerated. From the limited information available about these crimes, men maintain their preeminence in these fields as well. Women, by comparison to men, are infrequent perpetrators of crime in all cultures. That is, women's crime is rare by comparison to men's crime.

In spite of the predominance of men as the perpetrators of virtually all categories of crime, in recent years there have been many sources in both academic and popular literature citing rising crime rates among women.[2] Academics and statisticians have cited the fact that crime and incarceration rates among women have increased, and women's rates are increasing faster than men's (Gilliard and Beck 1994). The rate of incarceration for men grew 53 percent between 1986 and 1991; the rate of incarceration for women rose 75 percent in the same period (Snell 1994). While the percentage increases may be alarming at first glance, the absolute numerical increases indicate that officially calculated crime statistics still reflect predominantly male activity in the crime arena. Percentage increases are deceptive because they do not indicate the original wide disparity in male and female offending patterns. Table 5.1 shows gender and race differences in incarceration rates in the United States since 1980.

As illustrated by the table, increases in women's incarceration are much less significant than the predominant presence of men in American prisons. Changes in incarceration rates for ethnic minorities, especially for African-American men, reflect more alarming shifts since 1980 than increased incarceration of women. Social or economic factors that have triggered increased incarceration of African Americans should probably receive greater attention than increases in the number of women in prison. Yet, theorists and the public are alarmed by rising incarceration rates among women because female criminality challenges common perceptions of culturally prescribed roles for women. Increased incarceration of African Americans confirms many underlying racial prejudices that linger in American society. That is, more imprisonment of African Americans provides an

Table 5.1. Rates of Incarceration per 100,000 Population by Gender and Race, 1980–96

| Year | Total | Men | | | Women | | |
		All	Black	White	All	Black	White
1980	139	275	1,111	168	11	45	6
1985	202	397	1,559	246	17	68	10
1990	297	575	2,376	339	32	125	19
1993	359	698	2,920	398	41	165	23
1996	427	819	3,250	461	51	178	29

Sources: Tracy L. Snell, "Correctional Populations in the United States, 1993," *Bureau of Justice Statistics Report* (Washington, D.C.: U.S. Government Printing Office, 1995), 9; Thomas P. Bonczar and Allen J. Beck, "Lifetime Likelihood of Going to State or Federal Prison," *Bureau of Justice Statistics Special Report* (Washington, D.C.: U.S. Government Printing Office, 1997), 1; Christopher J. Mumola and Allen J. Beck, "Prisoners in 1996," *Bureau of Justice Statistics Bulletin* (1997): 5, 9.

intellectual justification for racial prejudice for many people. The rising rate of incarceration among African Americans does not create the same alarm as increased imprisonment of women because denigration of the character of African Americans is culturally implied.[3] Women, however, are stereotyped as law-abiding.

Figure 5.1 illustrates incarceration trends for both men and women since 1925. As indicated here, incarceration has increased rather drastically since 1980, but the proportionate differences between men and women have not changed significantly.

Women's crime is often seen as an especially troubling side-effect of increased opportunity for women (Adler 1975), or as a symptom of the failures of feminism.[4] The increase in women's crime rates is indeed a troubling concern. However, the same question in reverse is just as intriguing: why are women's rates of offense and incarceration so low when compared to men? Both questions will be addressed here.

Erich Fromm on Social Character

Much has been written about women's socialization into law-abiding behavioral patterns, the strength of women's family responsibility as a force that restrains women from crime, the cultural forces that restrict women's expression of aggression and foster dependence, and the criminal opportunities that have been held predominantly by men.[5] All of these ideas hold some importance for explaining the differences between men and women in the criminal arena. Each of these observations points to cultural patterns that have in some way restricted women

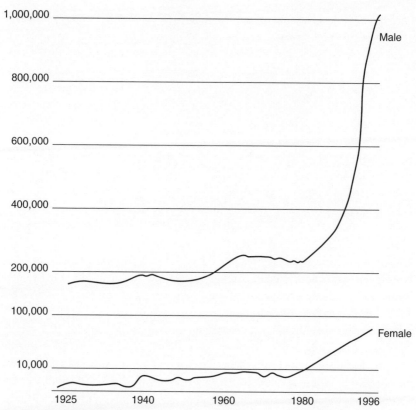

Sources: Kathleen Maguire and Ann L. Pastore, Sourcebook of Criminal Justice Statistics (Washington, D.C.: U.S. Government Printing Office, 1995), 538–39; Christopher J. Mumola and Allen J. Beck, "Prisoners in 1996," Bureau of Justice Statistics Bulletin, 5, 9.

Figure 5.1. Sentenced Male and Female Prisoners in State and Federal Prisons, 1925–98

to culturally approved roles, while releasing men to behave in ways that are illegal, socially reprehensible, or dangerous to the whole of humanity. Why, then, does culture restrain women, but not men? And are restraints of women lessening if women's crime rates are rising?

Motivations for behavior and restraint from unacceptable behavior are rooted in both individual character traits and cultural requirements. The fact that some people are restrained from criminal behavior while others are not has fostered perennial concerns regarding moral development, psychological differences, internal and external forces of social control, frustration and anomie resulting from social structural pressures, the impact of in-group enticements, and a wide variety of other possible reasons for the development of criminal patterns in some and the absence of crime in others.[6] While it is not within the scope of this essay to reiterate the theories and research developed over the last half-century to explain this phenomena, it is sufficient to state that this concern is central to the study of crime. What has not been fully developed in the literature is an explanation of the cultural forces that differentially motivate men and women to criminal or noncriminal behavior (Messerschmidt 1993). Among the most useful sources for illuminating these differences is Fromm's discussion of social character.

Fromm (1962) has distinguished two types of character, both affected by culture, but that influence human behavior through different spheres of motivation. Individual character is shaped by personal characteristics that develop, in part, through a person's interaction with the culture within which he or she lives. Social character represents the shared values, ideals, and prevailing sentiments that result from particular cultural patterns in any given society (Fromm 1962:78). Social character is influenced by social structure, economic conditions, and social trends. As with individual character, social character is shaped through interaction with the society within which a person lives. The family is the institution most commonly identified with imparting the requirements of society. Fromm saw the family fulfilling this function in two ways: "(1) by the influence the character of the parents has on the character formation of the growing child; since the character of most parents is an expression of the social character, they transmit in this way the essential features of the socially desirable character structure to the child. (2) In addition to the character of the parents, the methods of childhood training which are customary in a culture also have the function of molding the character of the child in a socially desirable direction" (Fromm 1962:83).

For Fromm, character is subject to both the micro-environment of the family and the macro social, economic, and cultural influences of the wider society (Burston 1991:88). Individual character changes throughout life, and the prevailing social character requirements have a profound impact on the individual, despite family idiosyncrasies. The means by which individuals personally adapt to the society in which they live is influenced by the imprint of social character on their ideals, values, and aspirations.

Male and Female Social Character Development

In all societies the cultural requirements for behavior apply different standards to males and females; the socialization process imparts the particular rules for behavior to each new individual in the society. In America, as in virtually all other societies, boys are trained through socialization for adult male roles that reinforce the traditional male values of independence, achievement, focus upon future occupational roles, and personal characteristics that require perseverance, endurance, and rationality. Emotionality, lack of achievement orientation, or too much concern for family have been traditionally viewed as signs of weakness in American men. Male children are conditioned to these traits through the supply of occupational toys (trucks, building materials, war toys, and a dearth of familial toys), competitive sports, and occupational roles that require danger, competition, or subordination of familial involvement (see French 1992).

Female children in American society are trained toward familial responsibility from a very early age. Toys for girls reaffirm age-old emphases on family, domestic responsibility, beauty, and love. While there have been consistent efforts to bring achievement imagery for girls into educational materials and to increase female participation in a wide array of athletic, academic, and occupational opportunities, only limited avenues of achievement have opened for girls in recent years (Sapiro 1994). Primary achievement imagery and opportunities remain decidedly male phenomena. In spite of three decades of discussion of the impact of socialization models on adult aspirations, little has been added to either boy or girl toys to impart other than traditional imagery of male and female roles (Faludi 1991).[7] Likewise, socialization of boys toward achievement and girls toward familial responsibility remains consistent. Ideal standards have softened considerably, but patterns of differential treatment and fewer opportunities for girls remain intact (Sadker and Sadker 1994). Cultural norms reflect this pattern throughout childhood in American society, resulting in differential treatment of male and female children and identification with gendered roles for adult men and women.

Differential character requirements for males and females are expected by parents and society. Early childhood socialization, school experiences, occupational models, and stereotypical distinctions between male and female character traits all illustrate predominant cultural expectations. Academic literature consistently reaffirms the predominance of males in virtually all walks of life, from childhood through adulthood.[8] Early childhood socialization, education, and occupational opportunities reinforce the cultural stereotypes that males are to be competitive, achievement-oriented, aggressive in pursuit of both occupational goals and interpersonal competition, and that male leadership in all areas is a predominant concern. Likewise, girls are expected to be family-oriented, concerned with beauty and all aspects of love, and they are tacitly expected to be dependent upon men for economic support, protection, and political leadership. While many values emphasizing opportunity, achievement and independence for girls may be emerging, the cultural reality is that men continue to dominate all aspects of political, economic, and occupational hierarchies.[9] With nearly immovable wage disparities (Reskin and Padavic 1994:108–13), cultural devaluation of work done by women (see French 1992), and the recent upsurge in political rhetoric calling for a return to traditional family values which, of course, have by longstanding tradition emphasized female dependence upon male economic support (see Faludi 1991), the likelihood that cultural expectations for male independence and female dependence will change in the near future is slim at best.

Stereotypic gender traits are both the result of social structural differences in opportunities for males and females and the provocation of continued differences in social participation for men and women. In Fromm's (1962) scheme, males in American society behave in competitive, aggressive, and protective ways because they have developed personal characteristics that reflect the cultural expectations for males that are grounded in ideals of male leadership, male prerogative, and male authority. Likewise, females in American society have personal characteristics that result from their interaction with a culture that prefers to have men in positions of economic, political, and occupational leadership. Women develop personal character traits that allow them to accommodate, in one way or another, to patriarchal culture. Women are idealized as nurturers, cleaners, caretakers, and supporters.

Social Character and Male Crime

The existence of crime in any society is a reflection of a variety of social structural factors. Poverty, alienation from economic opportunity, lack of moral restraint, anomie resulting from structural strain, and sheer frustration are all among the myriad causes of male crime.[10] Each of these explanations also reflects underlying connections with the social character of males in American society. Aggression, competition, economic success, power, control, and authority are all components of normal male social character, and all are components of male crime. That is, men who commit crimes behave in ways that are consistent with male social character, as well as in ways that reflect character traits derived through interaction with the cultural expectations for men in American society. Men are socialized to be aggressive, to win at all costs, to denigrate and destroy opponents (as illustrated by sports imagery), and to dominate those who are weaker. Images of failed masculinity imply weakness, femininity, homosexuality, and attendant stereotypes of effeminacy, retreat, and *wimpishness,* or failure to act aggressively.

Whether men commit index offenses such as robbery, illegal business transactions for profit or greed, violations of environmental laws to increase industrial production, or territorial aggression related to gang activities, underlying values reflecting male social character are emphasized. In each type of crime, competition, aggressive usurpation of economic rewards, and pursuit of power, authority, and control prevail among the individual motivations for the illegal behavior. As Messerschmidt points out, "*boys will be boys* differently, depending upon their positions in social structure, and therefore upon their access to power and resources" (1993:87). In other words, male criminal activity is consistent with culturally defined male social character. As Messerschmidt points out, the *types* of male crime are influenced primarily by social class.

There is a subtle yet identifiable link between legitimate expression of male aggression and illegal expression of the same. Garland White and colleagues (1992), for example, found that the frequency of admissions of women victims of gun shots, stabbings, assaults, falls, lacerations, and injury from beatings with objects in Virginia hospitals increases when the Washington Redskins football team wins a game. While not all male Redskins fans beat their wives when the team wins, there is a statistically traceable relationship between legitimate male aggression and illicit violence. Beatings do not rise, statistically, when the team loses. Only the enthusiasm of winning, or of aggressive triumph over opponents, is associated with assaultive acts perpetrated against women. Similarly, a link between highly publicized boxing matches and an increase in homicide rates for several days after each match illustrates the thread of consistency that knits together patterns of male aggression and criminal violence (Phillips 1983).

Social Character and Female Crime

Fromm (1956, 1970) suggests that women's familial involvement has fostered a focus on relationships and nurturance that has never been accepted as meaningful, outside of the narrow parameters of family, by the male domain of business or government. Similarly, Carol Gilligan (1982) has suggested that women are motivated by different ideals, values, and moral requirements from those that motivate men. The values that call women to social action are antithetical to the values of men. Both Fromm (1970) and Gilligan (1982) have proposed that women are motivated to maintain peace, stop pain, heal iniquities, and foster loving relationships. Women's motivations to protect peace and to promote love are grounded in the culturally transmitted social character of women, which is nonviolent and maternal. Women are familiar with the components of love as illuminated by Fromm (1956), in that culture promotes kindness, compassion, nurturance, responsibility, and communication of feelings as feminine character traits.

As a result, women's crime is closely tied to the social character requirements of women. Women's crime is limited and highly circumscribed. It is generally associated with economic need, rarely predatory, often pressured by inadequate resources for child support, and when violent, it is increasingly associated with patterns of abuse and mistreatment by men (Browne 1987). Most women's crime is concentrated among low-level property offenses (shoplifting, check fraud, fraudulent theft of services), drug offenses, and defensive violence against male abusers (Snell 1994). This has been true of women's crime for two centuries (Kellor 1900; "What Should Be Done" 1916; Feinman 1986; Snell 1994).

Women's property crime reflects contemporary responsibilities among women that make provision of basic necessities for their children increasingly difficult. Women who do not have the culturally designated male provider, or who lack marketable skills for employed labor, often resort to theft or fraud as a means of support of their children (Milkman and Tinkler 1993). Women's violent crime is rare. When it occurs it is most commonly associated with defense of themselves or their children in the face of sexual or physical abuse by men. Forty-three percent of women incarcerated in state prisons in 1991, for example, reported that they had been victims of physical or sexual abuse prior to their incarceration, compared to five percent of men (Snell 1994). Violence by women is an affront to cultural expectations for women's behavior and often results in longer average sentences for women who commit violent crimes, compared with those awarded to men under similar circumstances (Illinois Clemency Project 1994).[11]

Recent Increases in Women's Crime

The very act of crime is itself a male activity. Women who commit crimes not only violate the law, they challenge culturally determined values about female social character. It is the violation of cultural expectations about appropriate female behavior that has attracted the greatest attention in recent years. The focus has been not only upon patterns of offense, but also upon the similarity of women's crime to typically male behaviors. One of the most consistent themes running through twentieth-century theorizing about women's crime is that women who commit crimes are viewed as traitors to natural female social character: "Few women are born with criminal tendencies; but when these are present the criminality is more intense and depraved in them than in male delinquents. They are found wanting in every attribute belonging to normal women. For example, there is a total lack of maternal affection, pity, and love; they are excessively revengeful—revenge among this class being one of the chief motives for crime. In the place of real and strong sentiment there is a mawkish sentimentality" (Harrell 1900:109). "The officials of the law are genuinely more shocked; they feel, from judge to policeman, their sense of what is right more outraged by the woman who is not normally well behaved than they do by the man guilty of the same misconduct" (Amos 1898:804).

Implicit in the supposition that women's crime represents a loss of social character distinctions between men and women is the belief that women's crime will continue to escalate if women achieve higher levels of social equity. In other words, increases in social opportunity forecast increased crime for those who believe that an erosion in cultural requirements for women will result in an increase in behavior that is typically associated with male social character. The implication of such reasoning is that male social character is primordial and female social character is held in check by cultural requirements that restrain women from criminal behavior. Theorists throughout the twentieth century have forecast explosions in female crime, if women's opportunities were to coincide with male social roles:

> It is probable that as women come more into line with men in their occupations, in their struggles for existence, in their independence and the like, . . . [they] exhibit similar signs of degeneracy and an equal tendency to criminality. (Harris 1907:783)

> It is possible, of course, that the comparative emancipation of women, her greater participation in commercial and political affairs and the tendency towards greater sexual freedom may be playing their part in bringing about [increases in the numbers of female prisoners]. (City of New York Department of Corrections 1929)

> The forces behind equal employment opportunity [and] women's liberation movements . . . have been causing and reflecting a steady erosion of the social and psychological differences which have traditionally separated men and women. It would be natural to expect parallel developments in female criminality. . . . But what is clear is that as the position of women approximates the position of men, so does the frequency and type of their criminal activities. (Adler 1975:251)

The fact that male crime is accepted as an understandable, yet regrettable, component of male social character attests to the conceptual linkage between legitimate male pursuits and illegal behavior by men. To engage in aggressive criminal activities is an extension of men's cultural license to participate in legal aggressive activities; women's pursuit of the same is an anomaly inconsistent with women's social character. Thus, fear of unleashed feminine aggression is a threat that affronts not only the arena of crime, but also more subtle societal structures such as patriarchy.

Those who believe that greater social equity will result in more antisocial behavior among women who take on traits of male social character fail to make a significant conceptual linkage. Greater labor-force participation, opportunities for occupational choice, and increased social mobility are generally middle- and upper-class phenomena. Women's crime is a decidedly lower-class phenomenon. Women who have achieved representation in politics, business, or professions are not committing the crimes most typically associated with female offense patterns, such as check fraud, shoplifting, or theft of welfare services. On the contrary, women who are outside of the ring of opportunity afforded to middle- and upper-class women are most likely to engage in crime. Desperation, lack of economic opportunity, and hopelessness are common motivations for women's crime, not upward mobility (see Daly 1994). Thus, women's crime is likely to increase along with poverty and lack of opportunity.

The downward mobility of many women since 1980 has been dubbed the *feminization of poverty.* This social trend accelerated with astonishing speed through the 1980s and is likely to continue into the twenty-first century (Rodgers 1987; U.S. Department of Labor 1993). Women's crime has increased most dramatically since the feminization of poverty became a measurable social trend in the early 1980s (Radosh 1990). While a causal relationship between the two phenomena has yet to be established, it appears to many observers that lack of economic opportunity may explain more of women's crime than the previously hypothesized increases in social equality (Milkman and Tinkler 1993).

In addition, the focus on women's increasing criminality obfuscates the reality of crime, which is that women commit a tiny portion of all crime. Rising rates among women are a concern, but a matter of more grave attention should be the question of why men engage in predatory crime, street crimes, endangerment of humanity, and myriad crimes of aggression as a matter of course. The question of why women's crime has increased to almost 10 percent of men's *recorded* crime is insignificant when compared to the volume of aggression and antisocial behavior, both legal and illegal, committed by men (Pollock-Byrne 1990:23). Women's crime does not include global endangerment, crimes against human societies or the environment, or lucrative occupational crimes associated with fraud and theft in the business world. Most women who commit crimes are mothers responsible for primary custodial care of their children (Baunach 1992). Motivations for their crimes commonly reflect economic needs, fears of economic insecurity for their children, or escape through drugs from the pains of economic insecurity or abuse (Pollock-Byrne 1990). The circumscribed nature of their crimes should signal to even casual observers that women's crime is concentrated in particular social structural factors, whereas men's crime crosscuts all parameters of social structure. Given the distinct downward mobility of large numbers of women since 1980, the marvel is not why women's crime is rising, but rather, why it hasn't gone up more dramatically than current trends indicate.

Fromm's Theories Applied to Gender Differentials in Crime

In *The Art of Loving* (1956), Fromm argues that society is the mirror of the family, which is patriarchal. The mother represents unconditional, mature love that grows from the interdependent attachment between the mother and her child. The father's love is conditional, authoritative, and motivated by a desire for the child to learn the consequences of wrongdoing. Mothers' love is exemplified by protection, care, and acceptance, while fathers' love is grounded in authority, power, and principles of law and order (Fromm 1956:43–45). The unconditional nature of mothers' love is characterized by an acceptance of the child and forgiveness for wrongful or inappropriate behavior. The voice of conscience grounded in mothers' love is an admonishment to duty, responsibility, and forgiveness (Fromm 1955:50). Fathers' love is hierarchical, includes penalties and rewards, and is likely to be withdrawn for wrongful behavior.

For Fromm the distinctions between mothers' love and fathers' love provide prototypical differences between matriarchal and patriarchal societies. In *The Crisis of Psychoanalysis* (1970) he articulates the importance of matricentric or patricentric principles in the formation of matriarchal or patriarchal societies. Matricentric values derive from mothers' love and are essentially supportive and nurturant. Matriarchal societies reflect the "nature" of women, which has developed through women's "practice" in life. Care of others and nurturance promote compassion and maternal love as dominant moral principles. The most serious offense in matriarchal societies is the injury of a human being. Gynocratic democracy, or democratic practices derived from matricentric values, prohibits tyranny, exploitation, or ownership of private property (Fromm 1970:92–93).[12]

Patricentric values derive from principles of fathers' love, which is based upon justice, punishment, and control through domination. Patriarchal societies are hierarchical, dependent upon authority, duty, guilt, and adherence to rules. Fromm says, "These guilt feelings are of great social importance. They account for the fact that suffering is experienced as just punishment for one's own guilt, rather than blamed on the defects of the social organization. They eventually cause emotional intimidation, limiting people's intellectual—and especially their critical—capacities, while developing an emotional attachment to the representatives of social morality" (Fromm 1970:99).

In patriarchal societies, the principles of fathers' love dictate, whereas in matriarchal societies mothers' love is dominant (Fromm 1973:159–161; 1970). Patriarchy focuses on ownership of private property and attendant restrictions to access of property by nonowners, control over nature and human hierarchies, struggle for power and control, and the exercise of authority through violence (Greisman

1981). While Fromm sees some positive qualities associated with fathers' love, such as discipline and conscience, the expression of oppression, inequality, and submission are clearly negative aspects of patriarchy (1955:50). Matriarchal societies are punctuated by peace, equality, cooperation, universality and acceptance, and communion with nature (Fromm 1973; Greisman 1981).

Both patriarchy and capitalism exist through the exercise of authority, or the expression of superiority in social relations (Fromm 1955:90). Both systems are based on principles of exploitation, with control and manipulation of others as the proof of success in either. As an economic force, capitalism breaks down the principles of solidarity in favor of exploitation and undermines gynocentric democracy and matricentric values (Fromm 1955; 1970:99). Patriarchy suppresses the humanistic connections among individuals by rendering "the ever-increasing importance of man-made laws and secular hierarchies" (Fromm 1955:58). Patricentric principles are inherently restrictive and imply limitations throughout life; matricentric principles are universal, know no barriers, and promote unity among all people (Fromm 1970:98). Fromm summarizes patricentric and matricentric principles:

> patricentric [society] . . . is characterized by a complex of traits in which the following are predominant: strict [adherence to rules], guilt feelings, docile love for paternal authority, desire and pleasure from dominating weaker people, acceptance of suffering as a punishment for one's own guilt, and a damaged capacity for happiness. The matricentric complex, by contrast, is characterized by a feeling of optimistic trust in mother's unconditional love, far fewer guilt feelings, a far weaker [adherence to strict rules] and a greater capacity for pleasure and happiness. Along with these traits there also develops the ideal of motherly compassion and love for the weak and others in need of help. (Fromm 1970:104)

Patriarchal capitalism, as the dominant social structural force in American society, merges personal exploitation endemic to patriarchy with economic hegemony under capitalism. Political and economic ideologies are unified by patriarchal values modeled after the exercise of fathers' love in the family and patricentric cultural patterns. That is, cultural components of male social character reiterate the exercise of authority, control, domination, punishment, and preservation of justice models as character-building qualities to be pursued either by individuals or by society as a whole (Fromm 1955:50). Punishment, either in the legal use of justice models or in the colloquial "just deserts" models, is consistent with the patriarchal emphasis on exercise of authority and control through domination. Violence, either exercised through state-sanctioned punishments or through illegal violence used as a proof of authority, control, or dominion, is also consistent with patriarchal exercise of authority. Patriarchal society is completely dedicated to the concept of "free will," according to Fromm, because the external hierarchical forces are internalized by personal requirements for adherence to authority. Fulfilling the dictates of law is supposed to provide internal satisfaction, which "contribute[s] greatly to the solidification of the patricentric structure. . . . This satisfaction, however, [is] quite limited, because fulfillment of duty and economic success [are] poor substitutes for traits now lost: the capacity to enjoy life, and the inner security derived from knowing that one is loved unconditionally" (Fromm 1970:107).

Under modern patriarchal capitalism the characteristics of mothers' love have not disappeared, but they have been transformed from their natural function of offering protection to those in need into figures in need of protection (Fromm 1970:104). Patricentric authority, with emphasis on domination of those who are weaker, rigid inflexibility, denigration of nurturance as sentimentality, and promotion of hierarchical distinctions, has permeated all social institutions, including criminal justice.

In many ways the legal expression of male social character is much the same as the criminal application of the same principles. Justice, authority, exercise of power, coercion through force, and an underlying "just deserts" orientation toward opponents permeate both legal political and economic activities and most illegal activities typical of male offending patterns. Dominant patriarchal social values are linked to male crime, as well as to legitimate activities within the larger culture. Male crime, in other words, is pervasive through all societal components because it is an extension of general values and principles of patriarchy, which dictates male social character. Crime is an understandably male phenomenon because it bears striking similarity to many legitimate activities predominant within male social roles. Warfare, economic competition, pursuit of capitalistic goals, and demolition of opponents in sports share the same cluster of values that foster murder, environmental degradation for corporate profit, gang activities, degradation and mistreatment of women and children, and a host of other crimes committed by men. While moral restrictions binding individual men to lawful activities may intercede to prevent crime for many, among those men who do engage in crime, the values expressed through legitimate male activities and crime are variations on a continuum of values coincidental to patriarchy and capitalism.

In spite of recent challenges to cultural proscriptions for women in American society (ca. 1960–present), underlying matriarchal values exemplified in female social character are still evident in the daily lives of women, as well as in differences between male and female crime. That is, women may aspire to equity of opportunity, but as both Fromm (1970) and Gilligan (1982) have proposed, underlying values orienting social behavior may be grounded in a different ideological framework for women. Gilligan (1982), like Fromm, sees the predominant moral attitude among men as resounding what she calls the *ethic of justice*. This concept is similar to Fromm's ideas of fathers' love, patricentric values, and patriarchy. Women's moral attitude, according to Gilligan (1982), is dominated by what she calls the *ethic of care*. This, like Fromm's concept of mothers' love, prods women to focus upon concrete relationships, concern for others, and responsibility. Virtues of sympathy, nurturance, patience, concern, and love are by no means only associated with women, but they are quintessentially associated with female social character.[13]

Women rarely engage in crime because the orientations toward love, peace, and care that are nurtured throughout women's lives conflict with the underlying values associated with most crime. That is, women do not commit crimes that are comparable to typical male crime because the underlying components of patriarchy represent foreign values. Whether by socialization, as a result of cultural restraints, or because of differential male and female moral schemes, women are less inclined to identify with the values, the motivations, or the behavioral characteristics associated with male crime. Occasional exceptions occur, but for the most part the offending patterns of women are consistently defined by social structural characteristics. Women are rare offenders outside of the particular social and economic parameters of women's limited involvement in crime. Women commit crimes as a result of economic need, or out of hopelessness resulting from abuse or economic marginality. Women's crime is concentrated primarily in the lower classes. Men's crime is not class-specific; it is common among all social classes or demographic distinctions.

Socialization of female children to *maternal thinking* may ultimately promote the values that underlie women's distinct social character and rare involvement in crime. Women's adult roles as mothers and caretakers allow them to activate values illustrated by their own mothers and instilled since childhood as desirable for all women. That is, caring, nurturance, support, preservation of peace and communication, and attention to growth and change constitute important aspects of maternal thinking (Ruddick 1989). Fromm refers to this as the "practice" of mothers' love (1970:92).

All women are attuned to the concept of mothers' love, either as recipients, observers, or practitioners of the art of mothering. Maternal life is typified by continual conflict and demand for accommodation of the needs, rights, and privileges of all household members. Mothers' attention to peacemaking, primarily through nonviolent means, is an active practice of unconditional, protective, and supportive love (Fromm 1956). Culture reinforces differential roles for men and women, but the underlying values, moral distinctions, and personal restraints from antisocial behavior are grounded in mothers' love. They are essential to

Fromm's concept of matriarchy (1970, 1973), and they foster the promotion of peace by women, who live by matricentric values. Even for women who are not mothers themselves, or who never knew their own mothers, these values predominate as essentially feminine in nature (Held 1993). The subtle infusion of ideals of responsibility, care, and promotion of peace and love constitute female social character distinctions that make crime improbable for most women.[14]

Discussion

One of the consistent shortcomings among theories of crime developed in the last century is that they have failed to explain all types of crime (Taylor, Walton, and Young 1973). Likewise, these dominant theories have not addressed the predominance of crime among men, and the relatively rare occurrence of crime among women (Price and Sokoloff 1982). The failure of the most widely accepted theories of crime to try to explain women's crime has been significantly criticized by feminist theorists (Daly and Chesney-Lind 1980). For the most part, theories have focused either upon certain types of crime, such as juvenile delinquency, street crime, or white collar crime, or they have focused upon men or women exclusively. The problem with these approaches is that the relationship between crime and culturally defined gender differences is insufficiently addressed.

All of the early attempts to theorize women's crime focused upon deficiencies in women criminals that set them apart from "normal" women (see Price and Sokoloff 1982 or Radosh 1990 for discussion). The early theories included an implied cultural expectation of lawfulness among women and an essentially masculine predisposition in all criminal offenders. An important implication, however, was left unaddressed. The question should not have been, why do relatively few women engage in crime? but rather, why is crime accepted as "normal" male behavior? While male criminal behavior is not "normal" in the sense that all men engage in crime, it falls within the realm of understandable male behavior (see Messerschmidt 1993 for discussion). It is intriguing to address the rare criminal behavior of some women, but it is a frightfully accurate commentary upon our society to accept the idea that crime is among the understandable patterns of normal male activity.

Traditional theories attempt to explain crime by focusing upon some aspect of social structure, fraternal group affiliations, deficiencies in socialization or moral development, or other possible triggers of criminal activity. But if social structural pressures or anomie cause crime (Merton 1968), why is crime typified as male behavior? Women also experience anomie and blocked goals to social structural achievement, but only a small proportion of women resort to criminal activity under such circumstances. Traditional theories have, in other words, failed to identify cultural forces that merge with pressures to engage in crime and further fuse with the patricentric components of male social character.

The use of Fromm's theories of social character, mothers' love as opposed to fathers' love, and his analysis of the social structural features of patriarchy provide a vehicle for exploration of the impact of culture on the male monopoly over criminal activity. For Fromm (1962), social character represents the shared values, ideals, responsibilities, and prevailing attitudes that result from factors present in the social structure, economic conditions, and social trends. The point of this essay has been to tie the theory of social character, as influenced by matricentric or patricentric values, to gender differences in criminal behavior. The importance of mothers' love, in particular, is presented as an instrumental force behind the lack of female involvement in the wide array of crime that crosscuts all social structural distinctions.

The relationship between mothers' love and women's typical embrace of socially responsible behaviors has been discussed in a wide variety of contexts in recent years.[15] This essay has extended Fromm's theories of mothers' love into what Gilligan (1982) calls the *ethic of care* and Ruddick (1989) calls *maternal thinking*, in an effort to articulate more fully the lack of female involvement in crime. For Fromm (1956, 1970) as well as Ruddick (1989), maternal thinking is decidedly different from other types of thinking and is an antithesis of the competitive, aggressive, destructive thinking endemic to either patriarchy or crime. That is, maternal thinking aims to preserve life, promote growth, shape behavior of children in positive directions, and to resolve conflict. For Ruddick, "these demands—for preservation, growth, and social acceptability—constitute maternal work: to be a mother is to be committed to meeting these demands" (Ruddick 1989:17). Fromm's (1970) discussion of matricentric versus patricentric values explains the relationship between dominant cultural forces of patriarchy and social institutions built upon adherence to authority and punishment. Societies oriented by matriarchal values hold support, nurturance, and love to be more important than patriarchal focus upon justice, punishment, and hierarchy.

It is true that many women adopt the patriarchal values of the larger culture—some women commit acts of violence against their children or others—and there has been a historical tendency to sentimentalize maternal values to unattainable levels. Nevertheless, Fromm (1970) and modern feminists such as Ruddick (1989) argue that the practice of mothering endures as a protection of the thinking that fosters peace, resolves conflict, and opposes violence or exploitation. The practice of mothering entails daily attention to conflict resolution, the development of strategies for achieving nonviolent resolution of differences, and maintaining strong ties among those who conflict with one another. Certainly some mothers do become violent, but as Held points out, the marvel is that mothers succeed as often as they do in avoiding violence and making peace: "Mothers seek a peace not of contending parties who then leave each other alone and go their separate ways but a peace with the human connections between persons restored and reconstituted" (Held 1993:154).

Fromm argues that principles of mothers' love extend beyond family to other symbols of the mother, such as country, nation, or the soil. Preservation of peace and promotion of growth constitute maternal thinking and set women apart from patricentric thinking. Ruddick (1989), Held (1993), Chodorow (1978), and others have argued that it is not the biological fact of being female that gives rise to maternal thinking, but it is the mother's practical engagement in the activity of caring for and raising children that promotes these values. Fromm (1970) argues that women's "practice" promotes an outlook on life that is at odds with the predominantly patriarchal culture. As with Fromm (1956, 1970), modern feminist theorists argue that mothers' love supports through forgiveness, protection, care, and attachment. The values promoted by mothers' love condition women to a different orientation toward aggression, competition, and violence than is typical of patriarchal society. Maternal thinking opposes the values that undercut virtually all types of criminal activity. Destruction of the environment for corporate profit, for example, is contrary to the ideals of growth, development, and future health that are components of maternal thinking. The metaphorical identification of nature with feminine qualities of birth, rebirth, and regeneration exemplifies the ideal of maternal thinking as protective and nurturing. The patriarchal exploitation of nature and destruction of the ecosphere for personal control of nature or corporate profit are, for many theorists, symbolically linked to more widespread patriarchal dominion (see Dinnerstein 1976). The point is that the values of maternal thinking about the earth and nature are different from the values of patriarchal thinking. Women are unlikely to engage in crimes that endanger the environment because the moral requirements of the ethic of care prohibit such exploitation. The same could be said about nearly any other crime within male offending patterns.

Men are not prohibited from the exercise of mothers' love or the expression of maternal thinking. In fact, activities of mothering are more open to men in contemporary American society than in any previous era, largely as a result of recently relaxed cultural requirements for male and female roles. Few men, however, avail themselves of the opportunities to mother, and thus rarely adopt maternal thinking or peacemaking as a means of either resolving conflict or controlling violence. Maternal thinking could be employed as a means of discerning better ways to restrain violent adults or to bring male violence under control within the practice of law enforcement and the use of state corrections. The prevailing practice, however, is to use what Fromm (1956) calls "fathers' love" and what Gilligan (1982) calls the *ethic of justice* as the means of control. The dominant point of view is that too much "coddling" of criminals will foster more crime. According to this view, the only appropriate response to criminal behavior is punishment and restriction. Underlying values of control, authority, domination, and justice prevail in the criminal justice system, just as they prevail throughout patriarchal capitalism, and as they prevail among those individuals who engage in criminal activities.

Conclusion

Among the many visions of feminism is to build a better life for all people. As Sheila Ruth (1989) has pointed out, this means not only that women want more jobs and a greater share of economic and political opportunities, but also that ignorance, misogyny, and violence must be taken into account as forces that denigrate the quality of human life and prohibit dignity, freedom, joy, and meaningfulness: "These are matters of the human spirit, spiritual matters. Feminists challenge the aggressiveness, stiffness, and uncaring character of masculinist culture because it is inhumane, that is, it lacks the quality of excellence humans may or ought to aspire to. How could we do that unless we had some vision . . . against which we measured present circumstances?" (Ruth 1989:171–72).

The point of this essay has been to illuminate some of the cultural forces that differentiate men from women, with particular attention to differences in involvement in crime. Ultimate opportunities for the reduction of crime in American society rest in our ability to redirect ourselves toward humanistic values that promote human harmony. If we want to reduce crime, we should emulate groups with very low incidence of criminal involvement. Women are among the demographic groups with the lowest offense categories in American society. If we want to reduce crime among men, we must be willing to adopt those values and characteristics that make women unique. *Mothers' love, maternal thinking,* and the *ethic of care* promote peace and disavow violence. Such values are an invaluable asset to reduction of crime.

Notes

1. Percentage is derived from doubling reported rapes, compared to new court commitments to prison for the crime of rape. The percentage cited is an estimate because not all offenders are arrested, tried, convicted, or sentenced in the same year in which the crime was committed.

2. There are numerous citations in the literature discussing the increases in women's crime in recent years. For a sample, see Adler 1975; James and Thornton 1980; Chilton and Datesman 1987; Simon 1975.

3. There are, of course, numerous economic, legal, and social factors that explain increased incarceration of black offenders, not the least of which is changes in the weighting of many offenses commonly committed by blacks to include longer prison sentences than are applied to crimes commonly committed by whites. For an excellent discussion of sentencing changes targeted particularly at increasing the amount of time black offenders stay in prison see "The Elusive Logic of Drug Sentences" (1995).

4. See Faludi (1991) for a discussion of the popular attack on feminism as the cause of many contemporary social problems.

5. For a discussion of the theories used to explain women's crime see Pollock-Byrne 1990 or Radosh 1990. For a discussion of moral thinking in women see Held 1993.

6. The theory of differential association (Sutherland 1939), for example, focuses upon the means by which people learn criminal behavior through association with others who know the techniques and subtle behavioral characteristics of the particular crime in question. See also: Merton 1968, or Kohlberg 1981. For an excellent discussion of the gendered nature of crime theories see Messerschmidt 1993.

7. There are, of course, traditionally gender-neutral toys such as checkers and other games, cards, and some educational toys. The point is, however, that boys are socialized to competition and occupations and girls are socialized to nurturance. Children's adult occupational choices reflect this early socialization.

8. Recent research has reaffirmed cultural patterns, which have been observable for centuries, that boys receive more attention, more rewards, more detailed instruction, and more opportunities for success in modern American schools (Sadker and Sadker 1985, 1994). Occupational roles have afforded males more choice at least since the industrial revolution. For example, the U.S. Census Bureau estimates that men are employed across 503 different occupations, while about one-third of women are employed in only ten occupations (U.S. Bureau of the Census 1992). Wage differentials between male and female workers have moved only slightly in the last fifty years, indicating that women generally must work ten days for every six or seven days that a man works to earn the same amount of money. See also Kimmel and Messner 1995.

9. Over 92 percent of congressional seats are held by men (see Lindsey 1994:345–47); three-quarters of Americans living in poverty are women and their dependent children (U.S. Department of Labor 1993; U.S. Bureau of the Census 1991); 99 percent of the highest paid officers and directors of the 799 largest industrial and service companies are men (Jacobs 1992:282); and men continue to outdistance women in all aspects of income, economic security, and social structural opportunities. There is considerable research on these issues. For an overview, see Sapiro 1994 or Lindsey 1994.

10. See Sampson and Groves 1989; Bonger 1969; Merton 1968; Vold and Bernard 1986.

11. While the stories of battered and abused women who murder are, indeed, sensational stories, they resound with themes consistently relayed in the case study research

on women convicted of crimes in all offense categories. Daly, for example, uses narratives to punctuate her statistical analysis of gender differences in sentencing (1994). Among
the most consistent themes in narratives relayed by Daly are economic marginality, physical
abuse throughout offenders' childhood, and patterns of adult assault by spouses and boy-
friends.

12. Gynocratic democracy refers to the ideals of matriarchal society in the practice of
democratic political participation.

13. While feminists have been divided about Gilligan's theory of moral differences,
the fact that cultural definitions of women characterize these traits as feminine is less
in dispute.

14. While some theorists have dismissed Fromm as simplistic (Farganis 1986:96), his
distinctions between mother's love and fathers' love resound in the theorizing of modern
feminists such as Gilligan (1982), Chodorow (1978), Ruddick (1989), and others.

15. For example, see Caldicott 1986 or Ruddick 1989.

References Cited

Adler, Freda. 1975. *Sisters in Crime: The Rise of The New Female Criminal.* New York:
McGraw-Hill.

Amos, Sarah M. 1898. "Prison Treatment of Women." *Contemporary Review* 73:803–13.

Baunach, Phyllis Jo. 1992. "Critical Problems of Women in Prison." In *The Changing Roles
of Women in the Criminal Justice System.* 2d ed. Ed. Imogene L. Moyer. 99–112. Prospect Heights, Ill.: Waveland.

Bonger, Willem. 1969. *Criminality and Economic Conditions.* Bloomington: Indiana University Press.

Browne, Angela. 1987. *When Battered Women Kill.* New York: Free Press.

Burston, Daniel. 1991. "A Profile of Erich Fromm." *Society* 28:84–89.

Caldicott, Helen. 1986. *Missile Envy: The Arms Race and Nuclear War.* Rev. ed. New York:
Bantam.

Chilton, Roland, and Susan K. Datesman. 1987. "Gender, Race and Crime: An Analysis
of Urban Arrest Trends, 1960–80." *Gender and Society* 1:152–71.

City of New York, Department of Corrections. 1929. *Annual Report.* New York.

Chodorow, Nancy. 1978. *The Reproduction of Mothering: Psychoanalysis and the Sociology
of Gender.* Berkeley: University of California Press.

Daly, Kathleen. 1994. *Gender, Crime, and Punishment.* New Haven, Conn.: Yale University Press.

Daly, Kathleen, and Meda Chesney-Lind. 1980. "Feminism and Criminology." *Justice
Quarterly* 5:497–538.

Dinnerstein, Dorothy. 1976. *The Mermaid and the Minotaur: Sexual Arrangements and
Human Malaise.* New York: Harper and Row.

"The Elusive Logic of Drug Sentences." 1995. *Chicago Tribune,* March 30, sec. 1, p. 12.

Faludi, Susan. 1991. *Backlash: The Undeclared War against Women.* New York: Crown.

Farganis, Sondra. 1986. *The Social Reconstruction of the Feminine Character.* Totowa, N.J.: Rowman and Littlefield.

Federal Bureau of Investigation. 1995. *Crime in the United States.* Washington, D.C.: U.S. Government Printing Office.

Feinman, Clarice. 1986. *Women in the Criminal Justice System.* New York: Praeger.

French, Marilyn. 1992. *The War against Women.* New York: Summit.

Fromm, Erich. 1955. *The Sane Society.* New York: Fawcett.

———. 1956. *The Art of Loving.* New York: Harper and Row.

———. 1962. *Beyond the Chains of Illusion: My Encounter with Marx and Freud.* New York: Simon and Schuster.

———. 1970. *The Crisis of Psychoanalysis.* New York: Holt.

———. 1973. *The Anatomy of Human Destructiveness.* New York: Holt, Rinehart and Winston.

———. 1976. *To Have or To Be?* New York: Harper and Row.

Gilliard, Darrel K., and Allen J. Beck. 1994. "Prisoners in 1993." *Bureau of Justice Statistics Bulletin.* 1–12. Washington, D.C.: U.S. Government Printing Office.

Gilligan, Carol. 1982. *In a Different Voice: Psychological Theory and Women's Development.* Cambridge, Mass.: Harvard University Press.

Greisman, Harvey. 1981. "Matriarchate as Utopia, Myth, and Social Theory." *Sociology* 15:321–36.

Harrell, H. 1900. "Women as Criminals." *Arena* 24:108–12.

Harris, Vernon. 1907. "The Female Prisoner." *Nineteenth Century and After* 61:780–97.

Held, Virginia. 1993. *Feminist Morality: Transforming Culture, Society, and Politics.* Chicago: University of Chicago Press.

Illinois Clemency Project for Battered Women. 1994. Petitions Presented to Governor James Edgar. February 21.

Jacobs, Jerry A. 1992. "Women's Entry into Management: Trends in Earnings, Authority, and Values among Salaried Managers." *Administrative Science Quarterly* 37:282–301.

James, Jennifer, and William Thornton. 1980. "Women's Liberation and the Female Delinquent." *Journal of Research in Crime and Delinquency* 17:230–44.

Kellor, Frances A. 1900. "Criminality among Women." *Arena* 23:516–24.

Kimmel, Michael S., and Michael A. Messner. 1995. *Men's Lives,* 3d ed. Boston: Allyn and Bacon.

Kohlberg, Lawrence. 1981. *The Philosophy of Moral Development.* San Francisco: Harper and Row.

Lindsey, Linda. 1994. *Gender Roles: A Sociological Perspective.* Englewood Cliffs, N.J.: Prentice-Hall.

Maguire, Kathleen, and Ann L. Pastore. 1995. *Sourcebook of Criminal Justice Statistics, 1994.* Washington, D.C.: U.S. Government Printing Office.

Merton, Robert K. 1968. "Social Structure and Anomie." In *Social Theory and Social Structure.* 185–214. New York: Free Press.

Messerschmidt, James W. 1993. *Masculinities and Crime: Critique and Reconceptualization of Theory.* Lanham, Md.: Rowman and Littlefield.

Milkman, Martin, and Sarah Tinkler. 1993. "Female Criminality: An Economic Perspective." In *Female Criminality: The State of the Art.* Ed. Concetta C. Culliver. 291–304. New York: Garland.

Mumola, Christopher J., and Allen J. Beck. 1997. "Prisoners in 1996." *Bureau of Justice Statistics Bulletin.* 1–17. Washington, D.C.: U.S. Government Printing Office.

Phillips, David P. 1983. "The Impact of Mass Media Violence on U.S. Homicides." *American Sociological Review* 48:560–68.

Pollock-Byrne, Joycelyn M. 1990. *Women, Prison, and Crime.* Pacific Grove, Calif.: Brooks/Cole.

Price, Barbara Raffel, and Natalie J. Sokoloff. 1982. *The Criminal Justice System and Women: Women Offenders, Victims, Workers.* New York: Clark Boardman.

Radosh, Polly F. 1990. "Women and Crime in the United States: A Marxian Explanation." *Sociological Spectrum* 10:105–31.

Reskin, Barbara, and Irene Padavic. 1994. *Women and Men at Work.* Thousand Oaks, Calif.: Pine Forge.

Rodgers, Harrell R., Jr. 1987. *Poor Women, Poor Families.* Armonk, N.Y.: Sharpe.

Ruddick, Sara. 1989. *Maternal Thinking: Toward a Politics of Peace.* Boston: Beacon.

Ruth, Sheila. 1989. "A Feminist World View." In *Radical Voices: A Decade of Feminist Resistance from Women's Studies International Forum.* Ed. Ranate D. Klein and Deborah Lynn Steinberg. 171–81. Oxford: Pergamon.

Sadker, Myra, and David Sadker. 1985. "Sexism in the Schoolroom of the '80s." *Psychology Today* 19 (March): 54–57.

————. 1994. *Failing at Fairness.* New York: Charles Scribner's Sons.

Sampson, Robert J., and W. Byron Groves. 1989. "Community Structure and Crime: Testing Social-Disorganization Theory." *American Journal of Sociology* 94:774–802.

Sapiro, Virginia. 1994. *Women in American Society: An Introduction to Women's Studies.* Mountain View, Calif.: Mayfield.

Simon, David R., and D. Stanley Eitzen. 1993. *Elite Deviance.* 4th ed. Boston: Allyn and Bacon.

Simon, Rita James. 1975. *The Contemporary Woman and Crime.* Washington, D.C.: National Institute of Mental Health.

Snell, Tracy L. 1994. "Women in Prison." *Bureau of Justice Statistics Special Report.* 1–12. Washington, D.C.: U.S. Government Printing Office.

Sutherland, Edwin. 1939. *The Principles of Criminology.* 3d ed. New York: Lippincott.

Taylor, Ian, Paul Walton, and Jock Young. 1973. *The New Criminology.* London: Routledge and Kegan Paul.

U.S. Bureau of the Census. 1991. "Money Income of Families and Persons in the United States: 1990." *Current Population Reports.* August. Washington, D.C.: U.S. Government Printing Office.

———. 1992. "Detailed Occupation and Other Characteristics from the EEO File for the United States." *Census of the Population: Supplementary Reports, 1990.* Washington, D.C.: U.S. Government Printing Office.

U.S. Department of Labor. 1993. *Employment and Earnings, October.* Washington, D.C.: U.S. Government Printing Office.

Vold, George B., and Thomas J. Bernard. 1986. *Theoretical Criminology.* 3d ed. New York: Oxford University Press.

"What Should Be Done for Women Offenders." 1916. *Survey* 35 (March 18): 723–24.

White, Garland F., Janet Katz, and Kathryn E. Scarborough. 1992. "The Impact of Professional Football Games upon Violent Assaults on Women." *Violence and Victims* 7:157–71.

6

Erich Fromm and the Frankfurt School Critique of Criminal Justice

Kevin Anderson

The young Erich Fromm's Freudian Marxist critiques of the criminal justice system seem to have disappeared into oblivion. Published in German in leading psychoanalytic journals in 1930 and 1931, Fromm's three scholarly articles on crime exhibit many of the problems common to the psychoanalytic criminology of that period. At the same time, however, these articles contain important and original discussions of how the fear of crime and the role of the state in repressing crime support and legitimate the existing capitalist social order. Except for a brief book review published in 1935, Fromm apparently never returned to these issues after 1931. Nor did he include any of his articles on criminal justice in a subsequently published collection in English that incorporated many of his early writings (Fromm 1970).

Given Fromm's importance as an intellectual figure in both left-wing and psychoanalytic thought, one might expect that these early articles would have been addressed somewhere in the scholarly literature. Yet I have found no mention of Fromm's early work in the criminological literature, nor have I found any reference to it in historical accounts of either the psychoanalytic movement or the early Frankfurt School.

With regard to the criminological literature, some accounts of psychoanalytic theories of crime mention Fromm's *Escape from Freedom* (1941) as a general source on Freudian psychology, but the authors seem unaware of these earlier articles pertaining directly to crime (Mannheim 1965; Gibbons 1982).

In the literature on the Frankfurt School, I have found no mention of the young Fromm's critiques of criminal justice, even though this literature often devotes considerable attention to Fromm's other writings before 1933. Those latter writings were crucial to the early Frankfurt School's attempt to develop a Freudian Marxism. Almost all of Fromm's writings during the early years of the Frankfurt

School, except those on crime, have been translated into English. Even studies of Fromm's life and thought fail to mention this material on criminal justice, except for a reference in a biographical sketch by Fromm's literary executor (Funk 1983).

In both the criminological literature and that on the Frankfurt School, Georg Rusche and Otto Kirchheimer's *Punishment and Social Structure* (1939) is usually viewed as the Frankfurt School's chief contribution to criminology. Yet *Punishment and Social Structure,* despite its originality, remains a fairly orthodox Marxist account of the history of the penal sanction in the West. The book gives no emphasis whatsoever to three issues that differentiate the Frankfurt School's Marxism from more orthodox versions: a renewed emphasis on the Hegelian dialectic, an attempt to combine Marx theoretically with Freud, and a critique of mass culture. In his 1930 inaugural lecture as the director of the Frankfurt Institute for Social Research, nearly a decade before the publication of *Punishment and Social Structure,* Max Horkheimer had already articulated these points when he stressed not so much the straight political economy that had dominated the work of the institute in the 1920s, but rather "important philosophical problems" such as "the connection between the economic life of society, the psychological development of its individuals and . . . changes within specific areas of culture" (1989 [1930]: 33). Unlike the Rusche and Kirchheimer book, Fromm's early work on criminology illustrates these distinctive features of Frankfurt School theory, with the exception of an emphasis on the dialectic. With regard to the latter issue, Fromm's work as a whole exhibits great respect for Hegel and the dialectic, but little direct grappling with these problems at a philosophical level.

Criminology in Pre-Hitler Germany: The Liberal Reformers Liszt and Aschaffenburg

In his early work on crime, Fromm drew from and critiqued previous scholarship in the field. In that work, Fromm addressed two schools of criminological thought: the German "modern" or liberal reform school of criminology as represented in the work of Franz von Liszt (1851–1919) and Gustav Aschaffenburg (1866–1944), and the Central European school of psychoanalytic criminology, whose main figures, besides Freud himself, included Franz Alexander (1891–1964), Hugo Staub (1886–1942), Fritz Wittels (1880–1950), and August Aichhorn (1878–1949).

Both Liszt and Aschaffenburg combined elements of biological, sociological, and pre-Freudian psychological positivism in their work. Both pioneered the use of statistical analysis for the study of crime in Germany. Liszt, a law professor, made a great effort to refute those who assumed that the criminal was a rational actor subject to regulation and deterrence by a series of well-calibrated sanctions. According to Liszt, the criminal's actions were determined, not by rational choice, but by any number of social factors beyond his or her control. Rusche and Kirchheimer summarized Liszt's general standpoint as follows: "Liszt, leader of the German reform school [of criminology], defined crime as a necessary product on the one hand of the society in which the criminal lives and on the other of the criminal's character, partly inherited and partly developed by his experience" (1939:141).

Liszt maintained that crime could be combated more effectively by state policies that worked to reduce poverty, alcoholism, divorce, and other social problems than by deterrence through the threat of punishment. Sometimes this perspective led him to some startlingly liberal, even radical views. As early as 1900, Liszt had stated in a famous lecture on juvenile crime: "If a juvenile or an adult commits a crime and we let him go, the probability that he will commit another crime is less in this case than if we punish him" (1905:339). This indictment of the correctional system led Liszt to advocate reform of the extremely harsh prison regimen common in Germany at the turn of the century.

Aschaffenburg, who studied psychology under the famous Richard von Krafft-Ebing, began his career as a prison psychiatrist. The founder in 1904 of the influential *Monatsschrift für Kriminalpsychologie,* a journal on which Liszt served as an associate editor (Parmelee 1913), Aschaffenburg became the preeminent German criminologist after Liszt's death in 1919 (Hentig 1972 [1954]). He was part of a younger group of researchers, mostly psychiatrists, who explored issues in social pathology such as crime, juvenile delinquency, and alcoholism. They used quantitative data fairly extensively in an attempt to create a positivist science of social pathology in which issues such as heredity versus environment could be studied (Schad 1972). Aschaffenburg's most important work, *Crime and Its Repression,* went through numerous editions.[1] In this work, Aschaffenburg, following Liszt, saw crime as a product of social forces: "In most criminals there is no inner impetus toward crime, but merely the inability to withstand the pressure of external driving forces" (1913:15).

It is not to his credit, however, that among these social "driving forces" Aschaffenburg included the "racial" characteristics of peoples, which, for example, he tied to the high homicide rate in Corsica.[2] He also stressed alcohol abuse, viewing it both as a direct cause of crime and violence and as a contributing factor to the delinquency of the children of alcoholics. The latter were, he wrote, "born candidates for the insane asylum and the prison" (1913:70). In the development of alcoholism, he saw both heredity and family socialization at work. While this stress on race and heredity was long ago refuted by mainstream liberal criminology, Aschaffenburg's dogged refusal to see crime and violence as unique to the poor and the working class places him closer to the spirit of contemporary criminology, as for example when he argued that alcohol abuse among university students can lead to behavior that "does not vary in the least from the rough acts that are committed by the less cultivated working population" (1913:82).

Economic themes are crucial to Aschaffenburg's explanation of the crime rate, a part of his work Fromm was to draw upon. Using statistics over several decades from both France and Germany, Aschaffenburg argued that fluctuations in grain prices could go a long way toward explaining the rate of certain types of crimes, particularly theft. The rate of theft rose sharply after a sudden rise in the price of grain, leading him to conclude that "theft is directly dependent on economic conditions" (1913:117). Rejecting forcefully Cesare Lombroso's theory of the criminal as a distinct physical type,[3] Aschaffenburg argued that most crime is caused by social not biological factors, and that most criminals "come out of classes in which poverty and wretchedness are common" (1913:178). At the same time, however, in keeping with his background as a psychiatrist, he held that, along with poverty, mental illness is a major factor that drives people to crime, and he advocated more frequent confinement in mental institutions as the solution to this problem. This is a typical example of another feature of Aschaffenburg's work, the medicalization of social problems.

Crime prevention should, he argued, center around two points, "the struggle against alcohol and against poor economic conditions" (1913:228). He was an especially forceful advocate of the state's role in developing "care of the sick and incurable, regulation of the aid given the poor, free employment offices, [and] insurance against disease, accident, and unemployment." During a severe economic crisis, he wrote, the state's responsibility increases even further, and it should provide "temporary employment, the distribution of bread and coal, and opening of stations where people can warm themselves, [and] lodgings for those without shelter" (1913:232).

With regard to punishment, a key issue in Fromm's work on crime, Aschaffenburg heaped scorn on what he regarded as the "pathetic" doctrine of retribution (1913:252). The only sphere in which punishment may actually achieve some of its avowed purpose, he wrote, is that of general deterrence, but even here we must remember that "fear of punishment is not sufficient to check crime," because "social causes" are the most important factor (1913:260). As to the notion of specific deterrence of the individual offender from future crimes, the policy of punishment "fails utterly," as could be seen in the high rate of recidivism among former prison inmates (1913:263). Because of the increasing crime rate, some advocated more frequent use of the death penalty or a return to corporal punishment, both of which he strongly opposed.

Aschaffenburg called for Germany to adopt the early-twentieth-century American system of reduced sentences for good behavior rather than long prison sentences where the offender is schooled in crime. Again following the American model of the period, and building directly on the writings of Liszt, he advocated a separate system of juvenile justice that would avoid the "stigma" of a public trial. Such a trial would, he noted in an early version of labeling theory, lead to a situation where "at school the child is despised by his mates, watched with suspicion by the teachers; perfectly excusable faults are regarded as signs of criminal tendencies" (1913:310). Even for an "incorrigible" youth, a public trial would backfire, making him or her into a hero or a martyr.

Psychoanalytic Criminology in the 1920s: The Work of Alexander and Staub

In addition to material from Liszt, Aschaffenburg, and other liberal-reform criminologists, Fromm appropriated and critiqued the work of the psychoanalytic school of criminology. He considered himself a member of this school, although as part of a Marxist minority. Today, Freudian theories of crime, which had a strong presence in American criminology from the 1930s through the late 1950s, have almost disappeared from the criminological literature. A recent textbook notes: "Applications of psychoanalytic theory to the study of crime causation are beginning to vanish" (Shoham and Seis 1993:23). But it is important to view them briefly in order to grasp another part of the background of Fromm's early work on crime.

From the perspective of a critical criminology, the psychoanalytic school represents an advance over the liberal reform school in that it posed an alternative to the prison and the execution chamber as the societal response to crime. This is evident, for example, in the title of a book published in German by Franz Wittels, one of the psychoanalytic school's prominent members, *A World without the Penitentiary* (1928), or in Aichhorn's classic discussion of juvenile delinquency, *Wayward Youth* (1935 [1925]). Fromm was to refer admiringly to both Wittels and Aichhorn in his work on crime. Important as it was to question the prison, however, the alternative proposed by the psychoanalysts was later found to be wanting as well.

That alternative was psychotherapy rather than punishment, for many criminals were now regarded as "sick" people, usually neurotics. Yet this approach, however humanistic its original intent, created several major problems. First, as psychoanalytic criminology took hold in the United States after its major proponents had emigrated, the procedure, especially for serious offenses, was not individual therapy but another form of institutionalization. In addition, as suggested by Erving Goffman (1961), Michel Foucault (1965 [1961]), and others, "healing" institutions such as asylums can exert as oppressive and destructive a power over the human person as can the penitentiary.

A second problem with the psychoanalytic school was that, at least in its American form, it represented a backward step, refocusing attention on the characteristics of the individual offender rather than on the broader social environment.

A third problem was the attempt by some of the school's members to use the term "neurotic" so indiscriminately or in so inconsistent a fashion that it became virtually meaningless. The sociological criminologist Michael Hakeem raised this point in the late 1950s in a debate with the psychiatrist Manfred Guttmacher (Hakeem 1958; Guttmacher 1958; see also Hakeem 1957–58).

Fourth, Freudianism has been critiqued by many feminists, who argue that it treats the male individual as normal and the female as abnormal (Shoham and Seis 1993). Some feminists, however, have used Freud frequently, albeit in modified form (Chancer 1992; Mitchell 1971; Benjamin 1988).

Despite these limitations, I would argue that Freud's work (along with that of one of his intellectual mentors, Friedrich Nietzsche) remains an important part of the theoretical grounding for criminology because it helps to elucidate the irrational motives that underlie so much of human behavior, especially with regard to crime. Unlike the earlier psychoanalytic school, criminological theory in recent years has tended to emphasize overall societal irrationality more than the irrationality of the individual offender. This, however, does not prevent a contemporary theorist of punishment, such as David Garland, from citing Freud when pointing to what he terms the persistence, in modern society, of "an emotionally laden fascination with crime and punishment and sometimes a deep susceptibility for the rhetorical appeals of authoritarian penal policies" (1990:238). As I recount below, Fromm differed from most other Freudians in his attempt at a broad social explanation of the role of crime and punishment in modern society. Before examining Fromm's work, however, let us glance briefly at the most important product of the psychoanalytic school of criminology that preceded Fromm's work, Franz Alexander and Hugo Staub's well-known book, *The Criminal, the Judge, and the Public* (1956 [1928]). Fromm both built upon this better-known work in psychoanalytic criminology and, I will argue below, moved decisively beyond it.

One of Alexander and Staub's most frequently discussed concepts is the criminal who is acting out of a sense of guilt: the person who commits a crime with the hope of being punished for a forbidden sexual feeling or desire, such as a son's attraction to his mother. Freud himself had originally developed this point in a discussion of "criminals from a sense of guilt," in which he grounded part of his argument in the work of Nietzsche (1970 [1916], pp. 332–33). Alexander and Staub's second type of criminal is the neurotic who, rather than acting out of guilt, "carries out in his actions his natural unbridled instinctual drives . . . he acts as a child would if he only could" (1956 [1928]: 30). Here they present the criminal as the repressed libido of bourgeois society. This second type of criminal is similar to the noncriminal, except that the criminal lacks a strong superego to control his or her antisocial impulses. These neurotic criminals "show the presence of an inner conflict between the social and the anti-social tendencies of their personality" (Alexander and Staub 1956 [1928]: 42). In Alexander and Staub's view, this second group comprises the largest percentage of criminals. A third group, the normal criminals, is larger than the criminals acting out of a sense of guilt but smaller than the neurotic criminals. It is composed to a great extent of professional criminals. Alexander and Staub argued that normal criminals exhibit no inner conflict, since they possess "a criminal superego" and live within "a special criminal morality" (1956 [1928]: 43). Fromm was to strongly contest this distinction between normal and neurotic criminals. Alexander and Staub used these ideas in testimony in several celebrated court cases in Weimar Germany, and in some of them the defendant was freed by reason of insanity.

Although these concepts would seem to focus mainly on the individual offender, Alexander and Staub also made a few broader societal applications of psychoanalysis to criminology. Some of these illustrate the social criticism underlying Central European psychoanalytic criminology in the 1920s. Alexander and Staub noted, for example, that in revolutionary times, the masses often develop a sense that frequent miscarriages of justice are taking place. In normal times, according to Freudian theory, the ego and the superego repress the libido, forcing it to abide by the "reality principle," thus holding unconscious desires in check. Once the masses lose their sense of social equilibrium, their sense that the justice system is in fact broadly "just," they may begin to feel they are getting nothing in return for this instinctual renunciation. As a result, "one rebels; there appears a spiteful determination to live out fully and unrestrainedly all those instinctual drives which are held heretofore in check" (Alexander and Staub 1956 [1928]: 9). They argued that Europe in the 1920s was in such a situation, wherein both ordinary crime and political rebellion were on the rise.

With regard to punishment, however, Alexander and Staub's policy suggestions are hardly radical. They recommended "abolition of all forms of punishment" for the neurotic criminal, but for the normal criminals, those who are psychologically healthy, they recommended deterrence through penal sanctions (1956 [1928]: 210). In a point Fromm was to pick up on, however, Alexander and Staub saw the criminal justice system as an institution expressing broad societal desires and goals, going far beyond crime control. They viewed modern forms of punishment as still based on "atonement and retaliation" rather than "a rational foundation" aiming solely at deterrence of crime (1956 [1928]: 211). The intense desire by some members of society to punish criminals masks the fact that these "respectable" members of society themselves have criminal inclinations. Among the general public, they wrote, "the louder a man calls for punishment of the lawbreaker, the less he has to fight his own repressed impulses" (Alexander and Staub 1956 [1928]: 215). With regard to the officials of the criminal justice system, "the underworld and its official prosecutors show not infrequently a sort of a subterranean affinity" (1956 [1928]: 216).

These broader social critiques and the demand to do away with punishment in favor of therapy for many offenders illustrate the liberal, even left-wing thrust of early Freudian criminology. Particularly in Weimar Germany, the intellectual classes had begun to question the roots of the capitalist system by the late 1920s. Discussions of crime became polarized between "law and order" demands by the far right and demands by the far left for radical changes, including scrapping the existing criminal justice system. Although the death penalty was still on the books in Germany, only four executions were carried out in 1932, compared to twenty-eight in 1921.

As in the United States in the 1960s, an ex-prisoner's autobiography, Georg Fuchs's *We Prisoners: Memories of Inmate No. 2911* (1994 [1931]), sparked much discussion by intellectuals. Fuchs wrote: "War, the death penalty, prison: these are the three moral issues of today, and even more of tomorrow! But basically these are the same problem: does the general public have the right to deprive another human being of his life? . . . The prisoner, whether serving a life sentence or a long-term one, is also deprived of his life, is buried alive" (Fuchs 1994 [1931]: 737). The prefatory material of Fuchs's book included a letter from Freud. Although he declined Fuchs's invitation to lead an international penal reform movement, Freud wrote that the prison system was "an expression of the brutality and lack of judgment that govern our civilization today." In a resigned tone, he concluded that even if the idea of "reform of the criminal justice system" were to gain enough support to become central to political debates, "capitalist society would not have the means to pay for this reform's requisite expenditure" (Freud 1994 [1931]: 738).

Fromm's Early Freudian Marxism

In the discussion below, I will first sketch briefly the young Fromm's more general theoretical work on Marx and Freud, since it forms a major part of the background to his writings on criminal justice from the same period. I distinguish between Fromm's more general early writings on Freudian Marxism and those on crime solely for analytical purposes. Although the former are fairly well-known and the latter virtually forgotten, all of these texts were written and published between 1929 and 1932.

Fromm was the first member of the Frankfurt School to write on Freud and Marx, and the only trained psychoanalyst among their leading lights. Even Martin Jay, in an account often considered more partial to Horkheimer than to Fromm, notes that it was "primarily through Fromm's work that the Institut [Frankfurt School] first attempted to reconcile Freud and Marx" (1973:88). In so doing, Fromm was building at least in part on work in the 1920s by two other Freudian Marxists, Wilhelm Reich and Siegfried Bernfeld. As Wolfgang Bonss has suggested, a complicated debate over Marx and Freud had developed in Central Europe, beginning in the early 1920s, that included "the eclectic adaptation of Freud by the Social Democrats, the dogmatic dissociation from Freud of the Communists, and the mediating positions of some practicing psychoanalysts" (1984 [1980]: 5). Although Reich's work on Marx and Freud has received more attention in the English-speaking world, Bernfeld's work on this topic, none of which has appeared in English,[4] probably exerted a greater influence on the young Fromm. Fromm made far more references to Bernfeld than to Reich in his published work during this period. In addition to the "materialist" character of Freud's concept of sexual drives, a point espoused by virtually all who attempted to synthesize Marx and Freud, Bernfeld discerned "dialectical" categories in key Freudian concepts. These categories, he argued, worked at "comprehending psychic polar opposites as identities." Bernfeld noted that categories such as "the sexual drives and the ego drives, narcissism and object relations, erotic drives and those toward death, each stand opposed to one another" (Bernfeld 1970 [1928]: 51–52). In this sense, Freud's core concepts, like those of Hegel and Marx, were often unities of opposites. A key difference not remarked upon by Bernfeld, however, was that Hegel and Marx posited conscious human subjects as social actors in a way that was undercut or denied by Freud's more deterministic social theory.[5]

Fromm's first publication on Marx and Freud was a brief article entitled "Psychoanalysis and Sociology," originally delivered as a lecture at the inaugural ceremony of the Frankfurt Psychoanalytic Institute, held on February 16, 1929. The Psychoanalytic Institute, now part of the University of Frankfurt as a "guest insti-

tute" of the Frankfurt School, was the first Freudian institute to gain official recognition from a German university (Funk 1983; Jay 1973). Thus, Freudianism
gained official status at a German university at the invitation of Germany's first
openly Marxist research institute, the Frankfurt School. Fromm, whose sociological
training included a 1922 doctoral thesis on Jewish law written under Alfred Weber, was only twenty-eight years old. By this time, he had moved away from his
earlier concerns with Jewish theology and toward a revolutionary Marxist position, a move that was later noted by Fromm's former theology teacher, Gershom
Scholem, who described Fromm as "an enthusiastic Trotskyite" by 1926 (1980:156).[6]

In his 1929 lecture, which could more accurately have been entitled "Psychoanalysis and Marxism," since Marxism was the only form of sociology that Fromm
addressed, he argued, on the one hand, that Freudian psychology would help
sociology remember "that the subject of sociology, society, in reality consists of
individuals" (1989c [1929]: 37). On the other hand, psychoanalysis needed to be
connected to the work of Marx, whom Fromm termed "the greatest sociologist
of all" (1989c [1929]: 39). With the help of Marxism, Fromm wrote, social psychology could move beyond the limits of studying only the individual or the family
and could begin to examine issues such as "to what extent the family is itself the
product of a particular social system" (1989c [1929]: 38), that is, capitalism.

Connecting individual concerns to larger social and economic forces was not
the sole contribution of Marxism, however. Although Fromm had not yet read
Marx's *Economic and Philosophical Manuscripts* (1844), first published in German
in 1932, he interpreted Marx in a humanist, subject-centered manner rather than
in terms of a deterministic materialism. He ended his article with a well-known
quote from Marx and Engels's *The Holy Family:* "History does nothing, it pos-
sesses no immense wealth, it fights no battles. It is instead the human being, the
real living person, who does everything, who owns everything, and who fights
all battles" (1989c [1929]: 39). Thus, grounding psychoanalysis in Marxism not
only brings the social to the fore at a more global level, but Marxism adds its own
humanist and subjective factors to the otherwise more scientistic conceptions of
psychoanalysis. Here Fromm anticipates the broad humanist themes of his later
work on Marx (see Fromm 1961, 1965).

In 1930, Horkheimer appointed Fromm to a tenured position at the University
of Frankfurt, that of director of the Social Psychology Section of the Frankfurt
School (Wiggershaus 1994 [1986]). That same year, Fromm's nearly book-length
article "The Dogma of Christ" appeared in *Imago,* the world's most prestigious
psychoanalytical journal, which listed Sigmund Freud as editor-in-chief. Also in
1930, two of Fromm's articles on crime, "Oedipus in Innsbruck" and "The State
as Educator: On the Psychology of Criminal Justice" (to be discussed below),

appeared in other psychoanalytic journals. In the following year, Fromm published his third article on criminal justice, "On the Psychology of the Criminal and the Punitive Society," also in the renowned *Imago*.

Fromm's second general essay on Marx and Freud, "Politics and Psychoanalysis," appeared in another psychoanalytic journal, also in 1931. As with the 1929 piece on sociology and psychoanalysis, Fromm's discussion of politics was within the Marxian tradition. In "Politics and Psychoanalysis," Fromm, writing a year after the publication of Freud's most sociological work, *Civilization and Its Discontents* (1930),[7] began by suggesting that, just as psychoanalysis had determined that individuals' irrational feelings and actions "are the result of certain instinctual impulses," so it "seemed to follow that psychoanalysis could also provide the key to an understanding of similarly conditioned social action, of similarly irrational political events" (1989b [1931]: 213). Some think naively that mass psychoanalysis might eliminate social aggression and violence. But in order to address societal aggression and violence, Fromm argued, we must look to the economic system as the key to understanding the collective situation of individuals who compose a given society. This brings social psychology into contact with historical materialism. Fromm then cited Marx and Engels's *The German Ideology* to the effect that understanding how individuals produce and reproduce themselves materially is the key to grasping social life and, therefore, "Life is not determined by consciousness but consciousness by life" (1989b [1931]: 214).

While both Marx and Freud thus "depose consciousness from the throne" (Fromm 1989b [1931]: 214), some crude conceptions of the Marx-Freud relationship—here he included "even an author like Bertrand Russell" (1989b [1931]: 215)—hold that they are totally incompatible because Marxism stresses material interests while psychoanalysis stresses sexuality. Fromm argued to the contrary, making a point that he would continue to develop in different ways for the rest of his life. He wrote that with regard to Freud, this apparent incompatibility is belied by the fact that "Freud ascribed a major role to the instinct of self-preservation, alongside the sexual drives" (Fromm 1989b [1931]: 215). Since economic motivations could be considered as a significant part of the drive toward self-preservation, Freud was also a materialist. As to Marx's work, Fromm once again emphasized the subjective alongside the materialist side, writing that Marxism "has one single psychological presupposition, specifically that it is people who make history and that people act from the necessity to gratify their needs" (1989b [1931]: 215).

In a point developed more empirically in his articles on criminal justice, Fromm wrote that although economic factors are certainly crucial, ideology operates somewhat independently of those factors. Here psychoanalysis can become central for a Marxist analysis of society "because the coherence and stability of society are by no means formed and guaranteed only by mechanical and rational factors (compulsion by state power, mutual egoistic interests, etc.) but also by a series of libidinous relations within society and particularly among the members of the various classes (for instance, the infantile attachment of the petty bourgeoisie to the ruling class and the related intimidation)" (1989b [1931]: 216). Thus, Fromm maintained, some forms of attachment to the dominators by the dominated cannot be explained solely by rational economic or political motives. In this regard, the categories of psychoanalysis can have great explanatory power.

Fromm vehemently rejected, however, any notion that psychoanalysis alone could "cure" the "quasi-neurotic behavior of the masses," which in any case is much of the time "an appropriate reaction to current and real, though harmful and unsuitable, living conditions." The solution to these deep-seated social problems, he wrote, is not individual therapy but the "transformation and elimination of those very living conditions" through social action (1989b [1931]: 218). Further, he wrote, social revolts should not be dismissed as neurotic, as some psychologists had tended to do: "It is not neurotic for a repressed class to rise up against its oppressors and activate strong sadistic impulses in this struggle" (1989b [1931]: 217). Psychoanalysis can, however, assist Marxist advocates of social transformation in understanding and then helping to overcome ideological illusions, which persist even when their original economic foundations have disappeared.

At the level of general theory, Fromm's pre-1933 studies of Marx and Freud culminate in his lengthy essay, "The Method and Function of an Analytical Social Psychology: Notes on Psychoanalysis and Historical Materialism" (1932), originally published in the Frankfurt School's organ, the *Zeitschrift für Sozialforschung*. Freudian psychology is "materialistic," wrote Fromm, because it shows "that our 'moral' and idealistic motives are in some measure the disguised and rationalized expression of instinctual drives" (1970:138). Fromm listed these drives as those of hunger and love, self-preservation and the libido—in short, the reality principle and the pleasure principle.

Here Fromm explicitly differentiates his position from that of the later Freud in *Civilization and Its Discontents* (1930), especially from the notion of a death instinct. According to Fromm, aggression and violence spring up not through a drive toward death or destructiveness but by way of sadism. Sadistic impulses grow, he argued, when the basic instinctual drives toward sex and self-preservation are repressed or sublimated and when "instinctual satisfactions of a more positive nature are ruled out on socio-economic grounds." In an apparent reference to fascism and militarism, he wrote: "Sadism is the great instinctual reservoir, to which one appeals when one has no other—and usually more costly—

satisfactions to offer the masses; at the same time, it is useful in annihilating 'the enemy'" (1970:141). In drawing these broad social implications from Freudian theory, Fromm rejected what he considered to be Reich's more restrictive view, whereby Freud's usefulness for Marxism was limited to "the sphere of individual psychology" (1970:142). He continued, however, to refer to Bernfeld's work only in positive terms.

Then, citing earlier work on the family by both Bernfeld and Reich, Fromm argued that the family needs to be seen as a social institution in a particular context. Thus, "the emotional relationships between father and son are quite different in the family that is part of a bourgeois, patriarchal society than they are in the family that is part of a matriarchal society" (Fromm 1970:145).[8] The family not only differs from society to society, however, it is also an active agent on behalf of society, "the medium through which the society or the social class stamps its specific structure on the child" (Fromm 1970:145). Most previous social psychology, Fromm argued, had ignored these issues and "turned bourgeois, capitalist society into an absolute," viewing it as "normal" and as containing the general form of the family. These non-Marxist social psychologists also tended to absolutize Freud's concept of the Oedipus complex, "even though sociological and ethnological studies indicated that this particular emotional relationship was probably typical only of families in a patriarchal society" (Fromm 1970:147).

With regard to Marx, one also needs to cast aside many simplistic popular interpretations, Fromm wrote, taking issue once again with Bertrand Russell. He also attacked the leading social-democratic theorist Eduard Bernstein for holding that in Marxist theory, although psychological motivations for human behavior may be important, "economics is always the decisive factor," a proposition Fromm termed "muddy." Additionally, he critiqued another leading social democrat, Karl Kautsky (Fromm 1970:151),[9] before offering his own interpretation of the implications of Marxism for psychology:

> The idea that the "acquisitive drive" is the basic or only motive of human behavior is the brainchild of bourgeois liberalism, used as a psychological argument against the possibility of the realization of socialism. Marx's petit-bourgeois interpreters interpreted his theory as an economistic psychology. In reality, historical materialism is far from being a psychological theory; its psychological presuppositions are few and may be briefly listed: *men* make their own history; *needs* motivate men's actions and feelings (hunger and love); these needs increase in the course of historical development, thereby spurring increased economic activity. In connection with psychology, the economic factor plays a role in historical materialism only to the extent that human needs—primarily the need for self-preservation—are largely satisfied through the production of goods. (Fromm 1970:151)

Fromm argued further that, for Marx, a situation wherein acquisitive drives hold an overwhelming position in society is not a universal feature of human society, but a situation particular to capitalism.

Fromm concluded this essay by arguing that insofar as Marxism needed a psychology, Freudian theory was the first psychology "that historical materialism can really use." Psychology could be of enormous assistance to Marxism in describing "empirically the process of the production of ideologies" (1970:155). It could also help Marxism overcome some of its theoretical problems. One of these problems was how to account for the persistence and even the relative stability of class society. With the aid of Freudian theory, the state and the dominant classes could be seen to operate toward the masses similarly to how a father acts toward a child in a bourgeois patriarchal family:

> Exploring the roots of the majority's libidinal ties to the ruling minority, social psychology might discover that this tie is a repetition or continuation of the child's psychic attitude toward his parents, particularly toward his father, in a bourgeois family. We find a mixture of admiration, fear, faith, and confidence in the father's strength and wisdom, briefly, an affective conditioned reflection of his intellectual and moral qualities, and we find the same in adults of a patriarchal class society vis-à-vis the members of the ruling class. Related to this are certain moral principles which entice the poor to suffer rather than to do wrong, and which lead them to believe that the purpose of their life is to obey their rulers and to do their duty. (Fromm 1970:159)

In this regard, not only the family but also the "cultural apparatus" of society propagates ideologies that legitimate the existing system of domination. At this point, Fromm refers in passing to institutions other than the family, "the educational system and other systems (such as the penal system)" (1970:159–60). In an accompanying footnote he mentions one of his studies of criminal justice (Fromm 1931).

As Douglas Kellner reminds us, these considerations by Fromm in the period just before 1933 have a specific political context: "In light of the failure of the German and European revolutions in the post–World War I period and in view of the emergence of fascism, it was obvious that an adequate radical psychology was needed to deal with the subjective conditions of revolution (or fascism) as an issue of both central political and theoretical importance" (1989:36). Thus, by 1932, the ideological illusions among the masses to which Fromm referred were primarily those that were drawing many toward fascism, with its defense of fatherland and the traditional patriarchal family, its attacks on and scapegoating of Jews, and its call for a war on the rampant crime and "immorality" of Weimar Germany.

During this same period, Fromm directed a major empirical study of the psycho-social attitudes of the German working class. This study, which had to be broken off as he and his colleagues fled Germany, was not published until half a century later (Fromm 1984 [1980]). At the same time, as Joel Kovel rightly stresses, what distinguishes Fromm's work in this period and later is "the introduction of Marx's humanism—the humanism of the *1844 Manuscripts*" into psychoanalysis. This gave him a yardstick from which to measure and critique the alienated human relations of capitalist society. This underlying radical humanism, writes Kovel, separated Fromm not only from liberal mainstream psychologists, but also "from the other psychoanalytic Marxists of the time, notably Wilhelm Reich" (1994:xi).

Fromm's Three Articles on Criminal Justice

Fromm's first publication on crime, "Oedipus in Innsbruck," was written in the tradition of previous psychoanalytic criminology, focusing on the psychology of the individual offender. It differs from his other two articles on crime because of the absence of the theoretical issues developed in his general writings on Marx and Freud. Also, Fromm's subsequent critique of Freud's Oedipus complex is not yet found in this article. Here, he relies uncritically on it.

The article appeared early in 1930 in a leading Freudian journal, *Psychoanalytische Bewegung.* Apparently building on Alexander and Staub's notion of the criminal acting out of a sense of guilt, Fromm discussed a well-known Austrian murder case: A young student, Philipp Halsmann, when interrogated by police, stuck stubbornly to the story that his father had died accidentally while the two of them were hiking without a guide in the mountains, even when he was confronted with physical evidence that seemed to prove that his father had died in a violent en-counter and then had fallen down the mountainside. Halsmann, although ini-tially found guilty of murder, was later pardoned. His defense lawyers had at-tempted to introduce into evidence a garbled version of Freud's notion of the Oedipus complex.

In an apparent attempt to influence the outcome of the appeal in Halsmann's favor, Fromm published an initial version of this article in a newspaper in Janu-ary 1930. In this article, Fromm asked, "On what grounds does the accused rep-resent things which are false as facts, obstinately holding fast to such 'facts'?" (1930a:76).[10] Court-appointed psychiatrists claimed that Halsmann was mentally ill because he was stricken with the Oedipus complex and "therefore" may have killed his father. Fromm refuted such a view, arguing that the Oedipus complex, with its intense father-son hostility, "is not abnormal . . . but it does not normally end with actual murder." Normally it is repressed; otherwise "most men would become murderers of their fathers" (1930a:77). In the case of the Halsmanns, the father's brusque behavior, rooted in part in his experiences as a physician in the military, created much tension with his shy and self-absorbed son. Some of this underlying hostility, Fromm wrote, was illustrated by a joke the father told just before they left for their risky mountain-climbing trip. The father reportedly joked that if an accident were to happen, his son would become his heir sooner rather than later. In a typically Freudian manner, Fromm commented that this joke was more than just a joke; it was "a sign, even if an unconscious one, of a hostile tension" between father and son (1930a:78).

Fromm hypothesized that the shock of hearing the father fall to his death after a violent encounter (apparently with someone other than the son) called forth two types of feelings in the young Halsmann. On the one hand, due to the shock of his father's sudden demise, a feeling of triumph over the father welled up from his unconscious, the expression at the conscious level of the deep-rooted, aggressive, Oedipal wish. On the other hand, strong feelings of guilt followed almost immediately, when he became conscious of his Oedipal wish to see his father killed. Philipp Halsmann was stricken with severe guilt, especially now that his father was dead. To assuage these intense guilt feelings, Fromm hypothesized further, young Halsmann repressed the memory of what had really happened on the mountain. He concocted for himself and then came to believe the story of an "accidental" death. The young man repressed all memory of the violent encounter that apparently had caused his father's death, not because he himself had killed his father, but because in this way "all guilt, including the guilt of another party, is wiped away" (1930a:79).

Whereas Alexander and Staub had detected the criminal acting out of a sense of guilt, here Fromm discerned a variation on this theme: One who denies, out of a sense of guilt, that a crime has taken place. Although this article broke no new ground in terms of Freudian Marxism, it used psychoanalytic categories with some effectiveness to call into question a common assumption: that a defendant's demonstrably false account of how the crime took place should be considered part of the proof used to convict that defendant. In this sense, Fromm's article questioned and undermined the normal workings of the legal system.

In a brief note published in *Psychoanalytische Bewegung* some months later, Freud himself took up the Halsmann case, but without referring to Fromm's earlier piece. Proceeding more cautiously than Fromm, Freud argued that the Oedipus complex probably had little effect on whatever did or did not happen on the mountain: "Precisely because it is always present, the Oedipus complex is not suited to provide a decision on the question of guilt" (Freud 1961 [1930]: 252). In contrast to Fromm, Freud concluded that if Halsmann had repressed the memory of his father's violent death because of guilt feelings, this would be "a rarity of the first order" in "an adult who gives no indication of severe neurosis" (1961 [1930]: 253).

Had Fromm's work on crime stopped here, there would be no reason to consider it as anything more than a footnote, written by a subsequently famous psychologist, to the better-known writings of figures such as Alexander and Staub. Fromm's second article on crime, however, also published in 1930, is highly original on two counts. First, it extended the categories of Freudian Marxism (not merely Freudianism) to the study of crime for the first time. Second, rather than focusing on the individual offender or even on criminals as a social group, it centers on crime as an issue in society as a whole: Fromm concentrated on how the dominant classes use the threat of punishment and the public preoccupation with crime for their own purposes of social control over the mass of the population.

This second article, "The State as Educator: On the Psychology of Criminal Justice," appeared in the psychology of education journal *Zeitschrift für psychoanalytische Pädagogik*. This journal, whose chief editors were the prominent Freudians Heinrich Meng and Ernst Schneider, also included on its masthead the well-known names August Aichhorn, Siegfried Bernfeld, Marie Bonaparte, Sándor Ferenczi, Anna Freud, Jean Piaget, and Fritz Wittels. A year earlier, in a 1929 call for papers, the journal had listed the psychology of punishment as one of several topics of interest, referring especially to the relationship between punishment and the psychoanalytic concept of repression.

In "The State as Educator," Fromm began his discussion of criminal justice by referring to the growing interest in psychoanalytic approaches to the understanding of crime and criminals. Even though much of the educated public had embraced psychoanalytic concepts, the legal system itself had shown little inclination to change from its older punishment-oriented approaches centering around deterrence and rehabilitation after punishment. Fromm briefly reviewed the discussion around psychoanalysis and crime. Then he wrote that, despite the merits of the new proposals to do away with punishment, in many cases, in favor of therapy, there was "considerable skepticism regarding the prospects for such efforts in contemporary society" (Fromm 1930b:6 and this volume, p. 124).[11]

At this point, Fromm moved away from the issues that had preoccupied the psychoanalytic criminologists and began to develop a Marxist social psychology focusing on those forces and groups that support and maintain the criminal justice system in its present form:

Modern criminal justice thinks of itself as a type of pedagogy. It officially renounces the thought of revenge and maintains that its intention is to reform or correct the criminal, and that on the whole its methods are a useful means toward reform or correction of the offender. It tries to achieve this reform or correction in two ways: negatively, it believes that it can intimidate and deter through punishment, so that henceforth the offender will be a quiet, well-behaved citizen; positively, it creates a system of finely-calibrated rewards for good behavior through mandatory work, or through "uplifting" words of encouragement from a clergyman as well as other devices, all in order to educate the criminal on how to become a socially useful person. (1930b:6 and this volume, p. 124)

Such methods, he wrote, "are having little success." This was not a temporary aberration, however: "theoretical analysis shows that these methods *can* have little success" (1930b:6 and this volume, p. 124).

The criminal justice system, wrote Fromm, fails to carry out its stated goals for two reasons. First, crimes committed to fulfill the offender's elementary survival needs cannot easily be deterred by legal means alone: "In these instances the only possibility is an improvement in the economic situation of the 'criminal' to the point where his situation is so secure that committing a crime to gratify elementary needs is unnecessary" (Fromm 1930b:6 and this volume, p. 124). Second, the more expressive types of crimes are, he argues in the tradition of the Freudian school, rooted in unconscious motives. Here "the contemporary penal system on the whole may be considered to have just as little effect" because behavior rooted in unconscious drives cannot "be prevented by influencing people at the conscious level" (1930b:6 and this volume, p. 124).

At this point, he asked a profound question that broke new ground in the criminological thought of his time: If the criminal justice system has so little effect on the crime rate, and if this is well known to both policy makers and social scientists, why then does society maintain "these ineffective measures with so much determination" (1930b:7 and this volume, p. 124)? More is at stake here than the deterrence and punishment of offenders or the more general deterrent effect of the criminal justice system on "the potential criminal" (1930b:7 and this volume, p. 125). The criminal justice system in fact has a far broader social significance.

Here Fromm began to use some of the theoretical insights he had also elaborated in his more general discussions of Marx and Freud, written in the same period. He stated that the social system does not survive only through the raw exercise of power by institutions such as the police and the military. "As the history of revolutions shows," these repressive bodies are not omnipotent; they can successfully defend and prop up the system only if an "additional factor" is present, "the psychic readiness of the great majority to adjust to the existing society and to subordinate themselves to the ruling powers" (Fromm 1930b:7 and this volume, p. 125). Bernfeld had already raised this point in discussing how educational

institutions legitimate existing social structures, but Fromm now wished to include the criminal justice system as another important agent of legitimation.

One aspect of this process is the way in which the state projects itself through
the criminal justice system as a father figure to the mass of the population. In
this way, the belief is instilled in the population that "existing social relations are
necessary; specifically, that they are grounded in the superior insight and wisdom
of the rulers." The child fears and resents the father's physical and mental superiority, which leads to tension and conflict, but "frequently the child makes the
best of his situation when he succeeds in transforming into admiring worship
his aversion" for the father (1930b:7 and this volume, p. 125).[12]

This is the attitude "that the state desires and considers necessary among the
great mass of its citizens" (1930b:7 and this volume, p. 125). The state attempts
to project itself as a "father image in the unconscious of the masses" (Fromm
1930b:7–8 and this volume, p. 125), and does so in various ways. In a monarchy,
the king is simply revered as the father of the nation. The criminal justice system is another way of projecting such a father image into the unconscious of the
masses.

A key aspect of the father role is the father's physical superiority, his ability to
threaten punishment and to carry out this threat if necessary: "Moreover, as in
the case of the masses with regard to the state authority, it is of little importance
in principle whether the threat of punishment is carried out. The ability to threaten
and to punish is decisive. It is precisely this ability that constitutes, for the child,
a father as the father in the specific psychological sense that is under discussion
here, and [for the masses it] constitutes the state, or the class ruling in and by it,
as a reflection of the father" (Fromm 1930b:8 and this volume, p. 126). A prime
example of the state's projecting itself as a father image is its use of the death penalty. In modern political systems, the head of state usually has the power to pardon those sentenced to death and is therefore "the symbolic embodiment of paternal authority" (Fromm 1930b:8 and this volume, p. 126). Thus the criminal
justice system legitimates state power as a whole. Fromm concluded: "It is clear
therefore why there must be a criminal justice system, independent of its effect
on criminals" (1930b:8 and this volume, p. 126).

Fromm illustrated his argument about the criminal justice system's legitimating role by referring to a second unstated function: In carrying out punishment,
the state "provides the masses with a form of gratification of their sadistic impulses." Alexander and Staub had already made this point, but they did not take
the step that Fromm now took, namely connecting this notion with the Marxian concept of class conflict. Fromm remarked that these sadistic impulses among

the masses are thus "diverted" from a possible targeting of the state itself.[13] Instead, the criminal becomes the target of the masses' pent-up rage stemming from the forced renunciation of their instinctual drives for sexual and economic well-being and fulfillment. In applauding the severe "justice" carried out against the criminal by the state, the masses can gratify their sadistic impulses "in a manner that is harmless for the state" (1930b:8 and this volume, p. 126). Such a display of anger and hatred at the time of executions or notorious public trials is not only harmless for the state, but actually legitimates it. War, Fromm wrote, serves a similar function in legitimating the state.

Therefore, Fromm concluded, exposés of the criminal justice system's failure to carry out its stated goals of controlling or stopping crime will not necessarily lead to changes in the system, even if such critiques were to become widely accepted. This is because the modern state needs a punishment-centered criminal justice system "for purposes that have nothing to do with effective approaches toward the criminal" and everything to do with "influenc[ing] the masses psychologically in the sense desired by the rulers" (1930b:9 and this volume, pp. 126–27).

Fromm's third and last criminology article, "On the Psychology of the Criminal and the Punitive Society," was published in 1931 in a special issue of *Imago* devoted to criminology. This issue also included articles by Alexander, Staub, and Bernfeld. Fromm's article, which ran some twenty-five printed pages, was probably related to a course of the same title that he taught in the fall 1930 semester at the University of Frankfurt (Funk 1983:59). In the article, Fromm surveyed critically a large amount of contemporary criminological theory and research before setting out, in the concluding pages, his own Freudian Marxist perspective.

In the discussion below, I will focus mainly on the parts of this article that develop further the arguments already elaborated in "The State as Educator." This is where I believe Fromm is at his most original. In other parts of the 1931 article, he often simply repeated, or even magnified, many of the problematic features of psychoanalytic criminology, especially the notion that most criminals are neurotic. At times, Fromm also took positions that are, from a psychological standpoint, extremely deterministic with regard to the propensity to commit crime. Most problematic of all is his notion, found in the article's penultimate paragraph, that "dangerous" repeat offenders who could not be "changed" through therapy might need "preventive detention." The indefensibility of this proposal is not, in my view, undercut completely by the fact that Fromm immediately qualified it by arguing, in Marxist terms, "that 'dangerous' is a relative term whose meaning depends on the social system and the assessments it produces" (1931:251 and this volume, p. 149).

Fromm began by quoting Liszt to the effect that "every crime is the product of the individual characteristics of the criminal on the one hand, and, on the other, of the social conditions and environment of the criminal at the moment of his deed" (1931:226 and this volume, p. 129). Then he discussed economic data on crime causation, drawn from Aschaffenburg and others, who had found a strong correlation between hard economic times and property offenses. Next, he took up the theories of Alexander and Staub.

Early on in this article, Fromm argued that Alexander and Staub's psychoanalytic perspective on crime needed to be "turned around":

> One could ask why a group of people whose economic situation does not permit them to gratify essentially normal needs commits offenses that are intended to gratify these needs. However, it would be better to turn the question around and ask: Why do most people in precisely this economic situation commit *no* offenses to gratify needs that other people can obtain legally? The answer to this question is very simple. By means of a certain kind of education and a series of other institutions, society succeeds in implanting ideals in the propertyless masses that enable most of them to prefer poverty to dishonesty. Criminals are people in whom such a superego formation succeeded not at all or only partially. (1931:231 and this volume, pp. 132–33)

This turning-around of the way in which psychoanalytic criminology asked questions seemingly brings us back to the Marxist themes of Fromm's earlier article, "The State as Educator," which focused on the legitimating functions of the criminal justice system for the capitalist state. Fromm, however, did not yet refer to any Marxist categories. Instead, pushing psychoanalytic criminology's characterization of most criminals as neurotic to its logical conclusion, he challenged the Freudian school's typology, which recognized two main types of crime: unconsciously motivated crimes and crimes of economic necessity. The former involved neurosis, according to the standard psychoanalytic interpretations. Both types of crime, Fromm now argued, involve the rejection of social norms such as honesty and obedience to law. Both involve unconscious factors. Therefore, instead of rushing to create categories of criminals, psychoanalytic criminology must examine "the specific mixture of irrational instinctual motives and rational ego-motives" that is characteristic of modern society (1931:232 and this volume, p. 133). All crimes, he implied, even those seemingly committed for economic reasons, need to be looked at in terms of neurosis. This of course goes far beyond even Alexander and Staub, who had viewed most, but not all, crimes as based in neurosis. Here Fromm seems to have attempted to be more Freudian than the leading Freudians!

This did not prevent him from bringing in a Marxist focus on class, which he

proceeded to intertwine with psychological factors. Even social and class differences, wrote Fromm, have not only economic but also psychological implications.
The inclination toward crime can be blocked by renunciation, repression, or sublimation of the instinctual drives toward sex and self-preservation. To be sure, the
propertied classes have many more ways available by which to sublimate their
unconscious impulses, since they have far greater access to cultural and economic
goods. Historically, however, the masses have also received opportunities to sublimate their unconscious drives: "The *circenses* [circus games] that the Roman emperors donated to the masses, and the burning of heretics in the Middle Ages, also
belong here, as do soccer matches and movie theaters" (1931:237 and this volume,
p. 138). Fromm developed at some length a theory of the different psychological
motivations toward crime among the contemporary upper and lower classes. He
argued "that the question of whether crime is to be explained mainly by economic
or instinctual causes is posed wrongly" (1931:239 and this volume, p. 139).

Toward the end of his article, Fromm moved away from a focus on the psychology of the offender. As in "The State as Educator," he began to make a Freudian Marxist critique of the criminal justice system as a whole, asking: "What is
the goal of punishment?" Then, footnoting Liszt, he answered: "It is supposed
to serve the purposes of deterrence, correction or reform of the criminal, and
societal security" (1931:242 and this volume, p. 142). Fromm proceeded to discuss each of these points. He cited a sharp denunciation by Liszt in 1905 of a situation in which "the inclination toward crime increases with each sentence." This
situation, Liszt had continued, proves "the ineffectiveness of our contemporary
system of punishment" (1931:243 and this volume, p. 142). Fromm also cited
supporting empirical data on recidivism from Aschaffenburg.

What about deterrence, whether specific or general, the second stated purpose
of the criminal justice system? In answering this question, Fromm cited Aschaffenburg at some length, who had written with regard to general deterrence that "if we
examine the statistics objectively," we are drawn to conclude "that the expected result
has not occurred, or has occurred only to a minimal extent" (1931:243–44 and this
volume, pp. 142–43). On specific deterrence, Fromm again quoted Aschaffenburg,
who had written that the high rate of recidivism refuted this notion.

On the third stated purpose of the criminal justice system—protecting the
public against crime—Fromm notes that if the penal system simply produces
recidivists, this obviously does nothing to protect the public.

Fromm then moved into a discussion similar to that in "The State as Educator," but in a more pointed manner: "What can it mean that society holds on to
measures whose inefficacy with regard to the intended purpose has been clearly
demonstrated? Appparently the criminal justice system also has another, as it were

hidden function, that it performs satisfactorily and with precision" (1931:245 and this volume, p. 144).

At this point, Fromm noted that both Liszt and Aschaffenburg, despite their critiques of its ineffectiveness, nonetheless supported the overall continuation of the existing criminal justice system. Liszt had written that because "the strength and depth of an unsullied and clear popular consciousness of law are invaluable for law and order," the legal system needs to take account of punitive sentiments in the population. Liszt concluded that, in lawmaking, "the more accurate scientific conclusion" should be "sacrificed for the sake of the traditional legal and moral views of the people" (Fromm 1931:245 and this volume, p. 144). Fromm also cited similar passages from Aschaffenburg, who had written of the "didactic value" of the present system for the "overall orientation of the people" (Fromm 1931:246 and this volume, pp. 144–45). What then were these functions of the criminal justice system that necessitated its continuation despite its ineffectiveness in carrying out its stated goals?

The first of what Fromm termed these hidden functions is the legitimation of the state in the eyes of the population:

> Every class society is characterized by the domination of one class over another, more specifically, by the small stratum of the propertied over the great mass of the propertyless. The means by which this domination is exerted are quite varied. The most visible are the means of physical violence represented by the police and the military. These means are certainly not the most important, however. In the long run, domination over the masses could not be carried out by them alone. A psychological means is added that is much more important, for it makes the use of open violence necessary only in exceptional cases. This psychological means consists in the fact that the masses are put in a situation of psychic attachment and dependence on the ruling class or its representatives so that they will obey it and subordinate themselves to it without the use of violence. (1931:246 and this volume, p. 145)

The criminal justice system, stated Fromm, is an important factor in this process. It helps the dominated classes "transfer" their infantile attitudes of obedience toward their fathers, forming similar attitudes toward the rulers. Just as the child, fearing the father, makes a mental adjustment and internalizes that fear as a sense of duty and obligation toward the father, so the transference of these feelings toward the "ruling class and its representatives" is "one of the most important requirements for the social stability of class society" (1931:247 and this volume, p. 145). The criminal justice system is one means of achieving this, "and not the most unimportant," because it reproduces both physically and psychologically the father's punitive role. Here Fromm cited his earlier article, "The State as Educator."

In addition, Fromm wrote, the criminal justice system has a second hidden function. Citing Alexander and Staub as his source, Fromm wrote: "Punishing the criminal provides a form of gratification for the aggressive and sadistic drives of the masses" (1931:247 and this volume, p. 146). Seeing criminals punished compensates for the instinctual deprivation that the masses suffer daily. This point helps explain why the modern criminal justice system operates so often in a vengeful, retributive manner, despite its rationalist talk of deterrence and rehabilitation.

Thus a twofold process is at work in the way the criminal justice system influences the masses. On the one hand, the state assumes the role of a punishing father figure to the masses. On the other hand, through its punishment of criminals, the state allows the sadistic drives of the masses to be gratified in a manner harmless to the state. Fromm concluded: "Criminal justice is an indispensable psychological requirement for a class society. Only from this point of view can we understand the contradiction that has appeared between the ineffectiveness of the criminal justice system and the holding on to it both by eminent experts in criminal law and by politicians concerned with crime" (1931:248–49 and this volume, p. 147). Because of this situation, Fromm argued, the new insights into criminals' motivations developed by psychoanalysis will not have a major effect on the workings of the criminal justice system. Future work in criminology, however, needed to build on the previous work of the progressive school of criminology, as exemplified by Liszt.

Rusche and Kirchheimer's Alternative Marxist Analysis

While Fromm was developing his critiques of the criminal justice system, Georg Rusche was beginning his own work on crime. Rusche's first article on this topic, "Prison Revolts or Social Politics: On the Events in America," was published on the front page of Germany's leading newspaper, the *Frankfurter Zeitung,* in 1930. It was this article that probably brought him to the attention of the Frankfurt School, resulting in their financial support over several years for his work on what would become *Punishment and Social Structure,* with Otto Kirchheimer later brought in as co-author.

Like Fromm, Rusche argued that the true purpose of the modern criminal justice system was other than its stated goals of deterrence and rehabilitation. Rusche believed that the system's true purpose was control over the labor force. Thus, whereas Fromm stressed the criminal justice system's role in generating cultural and psychological support for the capitalist system among the masses, Rusche emphasized economic factors. In this sense, Rusche's work tended to follow the lines of an orthodox, economistic Marxism. This may account for his surprising failure to cite Fromm, even after joining the Frankfurt School.

The hard-hitting radicalism of Rusche's analysis of crime and punishment in the early 1930s was greatly muted by the circumstances in which his work was subsequently published in English in 1939. Under the cautious direction of Max Horkheimer and on the advice of several American criminologists such as Thorsten Sellin, Kirchheimer, who had been assigned in Rusche's absence to rework the manuscript for publication, removed the latter's critical references to the U.S. penal system from the 1939 published version of *Punishment and Social Structure* (Wiggershaus 1994 [1986]). This was a particularly ironic and serious distortion of Rusche's perspective, because the American situation had originally been the starting point for his critique of the criminal justice system. Rusche's original 1930 article, "Prison Revolts or Social Politics," in fact began with a description of uprisings in American penitentiaries that were suppressed with great harshness. In combination with the 1930 fire in Columbus, Ohio, in which more than three-hundred prisoners were killed, Rusche argued that these events pointed to a move away from earlier approaches to crime in America. Those approaches had stressed parole, juvenile courts, and other measures, which had given American criminal justice the status of "the unsurpassed model of humanitarianism" (1930:1). This shift toward harsh repression was rooted in "certain changes in the social structure of America" (1930:1), including the catastrophically high unemployment rates of the Great Depression combined with a lack of social welfare programs on the same scale as in Europe. The American public, wrote Rusche, is not so much conscience-stricken as "of the opinion that those who honestly want to work can find work." He added: "The public reacts to the rising crime rate with indignation, and demands more severe punishment for criminals. Propaganda concerned with these issues denounces immigrants and Negroes, and right-thinking nationalism recalls the 'un-Americanness' of criminals. So originates the agitation against those at the bottom of society and attention is turned away from the real causes" (1930:2). The results were newer, harsher sentencing policies, prison overcrowding, and even recommendations of a return to physical punishment. The economic crisis, wrote Rusche, created a sense of "hopelessness and despair" that "has led to this series of prison revolts" (1930:1).

The 1930 article also developed in preliminary form some of Rusche's arguments regarding economic conditions and penal policy, which he stated more fully in his 1933 article, "Labor Market and Penal Sanction." The latter appeared in the Frankfurt School's *Zeitschrift für Sozialforschung,* where Rusche wrote that criminal justice is a fertile field for Marxist approaches because the underlying "brutality" of capitalist social relations is exhibited more openly here than in other spheres, where "mystification and cover-up" are the rule (Rusche 1978 [1933]: 2). He briefly mentioned psychoanalytic criminology as having made some innovations, but said that it lacked economic and historical grounding. Had he examined Fromm's articles, however, he might have modified his view that the criminal justice system operated in a manner that was free of mystification.

Rusche's key point was that penal sanctions vary according to economic conditions—the general level of prosperity, the unemployment rate, and the type of labor needed by the dominant classes—but he also implicitly adopted some elements of a fairly traditional deterrence model. Criminal law, he said, is aimed almost exclusively at the lower classes, and one constant appears in various types of economic structures: "If penal sanctions are supposed to deter these strata from crime in an effective manner, they must appear even worse than the strata's present living conditions" (1978 [1933]: 3). Rusche reached the chilling conclusion that there is a social and economic ceiling above which penal reform cannot go: "One can also formulate this proposition as follows: all efforts to reform the punishment of criminals are inevitably limited by the situation of the lowest socially significant proletarian class which society wants to deter from criminal acts" (1978 [1933]: 4). Therefore, in a modern capitalist society that relies on prison as its principal means of punishment, prison life must be below that level if it is to have a deterrent effect.

Citing the radical journalist Agnes Smedley's reports on China, he referred to the harsh physical punishments and frequent executions of criminals there during the 1930s. He argued that poverty, unemployment, and starvation were so severe among large sections of the population that prison became impractical: "The mere fact of being given food would make prison an enticement, not a deterrent" (1978 [1933]: 4). In societies where labor is scarce, however, it is more common to lock up criminals and use their labor to benefit the state, since this is sufficient deprivation to keep crime below a certain level.

In the rest of this article, Rusche sketched in abbreviated form the central arguments of what would become *Punishment and Social Structure*. Crime control in Europe, he stated, had passed through several historical stages. First, there was the system of penance, fines, and the relatively mild punishments of the early medieval period. Second, in the later Middle Ages, as the development of capitalist agriculture drove peasants off the land, vast unemployment and poverty among the masses necessitated extremely harsh physical punishments if criminal sanctions were to have a meaningful deterrent effect. Third, in the early colonial period, emigration to the colonies reduced the number of unemployed, resulting in a system of workhouses in which scarce labor was forced into service. Finally, the industrial revolution created dislocations once again and, by the middle of the nineteenth century, vast unemployment and poverty. The result was a return to frequent executions and severe punishment, this time by making the new penal institution, the penitentiary, harsher. Physical punishment was not restored, but only because "hard-earned humanitarian ideals hindered it and political wisdom kept the ruling classes from overstraining an already revolutionary situation with such open provocation" (1978 [1933]: 6). Recapitulating his 1930 article, Rusche also discussed briefly the turn toward harsh punishments in the United States.

In the published version of *Punishment and Social Structure*, Rusche and Kirchheimer followed this basic outline, although with the radicalism of Rusche's earlier language substantially toned down. There are once again a few passing references to psychological factors in punishment such as "sadism" in their discussion of physical punishment in the early modern era, but these are very rare (Rusche and Kirchheimer 1939:21). Even such extreme cruelty, they wrote, must be understood in social and economic terms. Whether in the early modern period or during the period of mercantilism, when punishment became lighter, their central thesis is that "purely ideological viewpoints took second place to economic motives" (1939:52).

Dario Melossi critiqued the economism of *Punishment and Social Structure* in 1978, arguing that it limited the authors' effort to "account for the adoption of imprisonment per se by the new society arising from the ruins of feudalism" (1978:75). Unlike Fromm, Rusche and Kirchheimer played down the ideological dimension. Whereas Fromm viewed the whole spectacle of crime and punishment as a means of "educating" the masses into the values of the capitalist system, and of diverting their resentment into a direction harmless to the state, Rusche and Kirchheimer showed the rational economic purposes that the structures of punishment served, at least for the dominant classes, while also providing a needed historical perspective on these issues. A more adequate Marxist theory of punishment might have combined elements from Fromm and from Rusche and Kirchheimer in keeping with Horkheimer's notion of an interdisciplinary Critical Theory, but this apparently was never attempted.

Foucault's Alternative to Rusche and Kirchheimer

The most notable and sustained attempt to overcome the one-sidedness of Rusche and Kirchheimer is of course that of Michel Foucault, who was almost certainly unfamiliar with Fromm's early work on crime.[14] Although Foucault's *Discipline and Punish* (1978 [1975]) contains only a few references to Rusche and Kirchheimer, the references are significant. In addition, he made several key references to their earlier work in his other writings during the 1970s. As in the 1920s in Germany, the 1960s and 1970s saw an outpouring of personal testimonies by prisoners in the United States, France, and other Western countries. In addition, a number of highly politicized prison revolts occurred, most notably at Attica in 1971. Foucault began his work on the prison in this atmosphere.

Marxists such as Rusche and Kirchheimer viewed the prison ultimately as a superstructure resting on an economic base, the developing capitalist mode of production. From the beginning of his work on the prison, Foucault, in contrast, regarded it as much more: "I don't think that the penal system forms part of the superstructures. In reality, it is a system of power which penetrates deeply into the life of individuals and which bears on their relationship to the apparatus of production. In this way, it is not at all a superstructure. In order for individuals to constitute a labor force available to the apparatus of production, a system of constraints, coercion, and punishment, a penal system and a system of penitentiaries are needed" (1994 [1973]: 430). Here prison becomes almost a necessary condition for a capitalist economy, rather than a product of the rise of capitalism.

With *Discipline and Punish* in 1975, Foucault distanced himself even further from Marxism, especially from what he viewed as Marxism's primacy of the economic. His critique of Marxism also flowed from his political commitments at that time. Foucault was active in the Prison Information Group, an organization that expressed solidarity with prisoners' revolts and worked closely with prisoners. In 1972, he complained that even groups to the left of the Communist Party failed to recognize, as he put it, that the prisoner is "the marginal [element] of capitalist society" and that "today, in our system, marginalization is achieved by the prison" (1994 [1972]: 306). He implied that the prisoners, not the workers, were the truly exploited and potentially revolutionary group in modern capitalist society. David Macey, a sympathetic biographer, wrote that during this period "Foucault himself was at times prepared to describe criminality as a form of political revolt and to quote Victor Hugo's *Les Misérables:* 'Crime is a coup d'état from below'" (Macey 1993:265; see also Foucault 1974:161). At that time, such notions were not unique to Foucault. They were common among many members of the New Left, who viewed the Attica prisoners or groups such as the Black Panthers, themselves composed in part of former prisoners, as the revolutionary vanguard.

Toward the end of *Discipline and Punish,* Foucault noted that almost from its inception in the early nineteenth century the penitentiary was attacked "as the great failure of penal justice," adding that "the critique of the prison and its methods appeared early on, in . . . 1820–45" (1978 [1975]: 264–65). Citing a wealth of data from those early years, Foucault showed that it had been frequently argued that prison did not lower the crime rate, and that it actually produced delinquency. Yet he also noted that, instead of leading to a questioning of prison itself, these attacks, even when successful, have led to oscillations between punitive and rehabilitative functions of the prison. Thus, "for the past 150 years, the proclamation of its failure has always been accompanied by its maintenance" (1978 [1975]: 272).

As with Fromm as well as Rusche and Kirchheimer, Foucault then asked what the hidden, unstated functions of the modern prison might be. One of its functions, he wrote, is to isolate criminals from the social classes from which they have emerged, in order to forestall wider social rebellions. Another is the use of ex-convicts as informers, helping the police to control and administer illegal industries such as prostitution. A third, closely related function is the use of criminals against revolutionary and labor organizations—as informers, as agents-provocateurs, and as thugs and goons employed in repressing strikes and demonstrations. Not only state power but also social scientific knowledge is crucial here because, more generally, prison sets up a mechanism of surveillance, "producing the delinquent as pathologized subject" (1978 [1975]: 272). The disciplinary techniques developed by the state in the surveillance of criminals lead in turn to "perpetual surveillance of the population" by the police and the criminal justice system (1978 [1975]: 281). Curiously, however, and perhaps because he rejected the Marxist concept of ideology, Foucault here gave little attention to what Fromm considered central, the ways in which the criminal justice system is used ideologically to legitimate the social order in the eyes of the masses.

Throughout *Discipline and Punish,* and in numerous other works published during the 1970s, Foucault argued that prison is only one example of a certain type of disciplinary power that has arisen since the early modern period; other examples include the mental asylum, the educational system, and the modern military with its Prussian-style discipline. These institutions operate through "a technique of constituting individuals as correlative elements of power and knowledge" (1978 [1975]: 194). In an often-cited passage, he wrote: "We must cease once and for all to describe the effects of power in negative terms: it 'excludes,' it 'represses,' it 'censors,' it 'abstracts,' it 'masks,' it 'conceals,' In fact, power produces; it produces reality; it produces domains of objects and rituals of truth" (1978 [1975]: 194).

Implicit here is a critique of both the Marxist and the Freudian concepts of repression, as well as the Marxist concept of ideology. The notion of repression, Foucault argued, implies some type of human essence that is yearning to be liberated, whereas he held that human needs and desires are almost entirely socially constructed, and hence highly variable and flexible. Elsewhere, Foucault argued that the whole notion of ideology is problematic because it implies that we know or can know the truth: "Like it or not, it always stands in virtual opposition to something else which is supposed to count as truth" (1980:118).

As with poststructuralist thought more generally, Foucault, despite all of his criticisms of the prison and other repressive modern institutions, could not provide any solid answer as to why these institutions should be changed or abolished. (I employ the term *repressive* deliberately since I do not share his rejection of the concepts of repression and ideology.) This is true even though Foucault, unlike Fromm or Rusche and Kirchheimer, looked at the repressive institutions of criminal justice from the standpoint of those subjected to them, such as the prisoner or the mental patient. Foucault's direct concern with the prisoner included conducting clandestine surveys of French prisoners and organizing meetings and publications where their voices could be heard. Yet because Foucault rejected another humanist concept, that of the subject, he had insufficient philosophical grounds on which to pose alternatives.[15]

The Continuing Relevance of Fromm

For his part, as we have seen, Fromm argued in his early essays on crime that the criminal justice system functions in an ideological manner to divert the population's anger against the exploitative social and economic system toward crime and the criminal, and thus away from the dominant classes that have created and perpetuated that system. In this way, mass resentment can be expressed in a manner harmless to the state. Fromm compared this process to the effects of war-fever in shoring up political support for the status quo. Today, in fact, such state measures are often explicitly termed a "war on crime." Using Freud's concept of sadism as well as Marxian class analysis, Fromm argued that the masses derive an alienated form of gratification from seeing criminals suffer. Foucault, who rejected the Marxist concept of alienation because it would imply what he regards as an essentialist view of human needs and capacities, had weaker grounds from which to make such a critique.

Fromm's second argument regarding the unstated functions of the criminal justice system in class society was that it binds the masses to the state and the social system. It does so because, in carrying out its roles of punishment and clemency toward offenders, the state projects itself as an overarching father figure to the population as a whole.[16] This notion included father-like behavior by the head of state, such as protection of the population from criminals, punishment of criminals, and, on occasion, mercy toward repentant offenders. Here, wrote Fromm, the masses have a more or less masochistic attitude toward the rulers.

Combining the first attitude, sadism, with this second more masochistic attitude, allows us to discern an early version of what was to become Fromm's thesis of the sadomasochistic authoritarian personality, first elaborated in his *Escape from Freedom* (1941), and later in a somewhat different manner by his erstwhile Frankfurt School colleague Theodor Adorno (1950).[17] To Fromm and even Adorno, such a sadomasochistic attitude is an expression of human alienation. To Foucault, it is simply an utterly normal example of power producing certain attitudes among those subjected to it, attitudes that in turn help to produce and reproduce from below hierarchical relations of power and domination.

One need not accept the orthodox Freudian psychoanalytic apparatus underlying Fromm's youthful writings on criminal justice to see some major advantages to his conceptualization of the ideological role of the criminal justice system. Fromm's formulations, rooted in a dialectical and humanist perspective, point beyond the existing state of affairs toward a more peaceful, humanist society, one free of repression, in which social relationships would be transparent rather than masked by ideology, and in which human beings could exercise freely their creative capacities. It was from this vantage point that he mounted a radical critique of the criminal justice system under a class society. During the hard-nosed and cynical last decades of the twentieth century, Foucault's antihumanist perspective has had to many a certain resonance. For this reason, however, Foucault's perspective should be questioned, since its wide acceptance may indicate an attitude of resignation by critical intellectuals in the face of a rotten and retrogressive social reality.

Yet even if we do not wish to use Fromm to question Foucault and poststructuralism, I believe that we still need to rediscover Fromm's early critiques of the criminal justice system as an important part of the heritage of critical criminology. Fromm, like Foucault and like Rusche and Kirchheimer, asked "What are the real functions of a criminal justice system that clearly has little or no effect on crime itself?" At a time when the United States is incarcerating people on an unprecedented scale, and when African-American males in particular are being demonized and targeted for imprisonment and execution, we must examine closely how this cruel, irrational system not only perpetuates itself, but also serves as a major source of legitimation for the overall social system. Today, throughout the industrialized world, highly ideological "wars" against crime, immigration, single motherhood, welfare dependency, and homosexuality are major themes in political and cultural debate. These "wars" help to cover up the fact that the dominant classes have no clue as to how, under the present economic system, the wrenching structural changes in the world economy can result in an adequate standard of living for the population of the industrially developed lands, much less those of the Third World or the former Communist bloc. It is a sobering fact that Fromm wrote his critiques of the criminal justice system on the eve of Hitler's coming to power, especially when we recall that "law and order," the cry so beloved of our politicians today, was also a central feature of Nazi propaganda.

Notes

Research for this chapter was supported by grants from the German Academic Exchange Service (DAAD) and the Northern Illinois University Graduate School. I would like to thank Rainer Funk of the Erich Fromm Archives in Tübingen, Germany, for his help with source materials. I received helpful comments on earlier drafts from Janet Afary, Piers Beirne, Bonnie Berry, George Uri Fischer, Charles Herr, Douglas Kellner, Joel Kovel, Lauren Langman, Marilyn Nissim-Sabat, and Heinz Osterle, as well as research assistance from Marc Rittle and Michelle Sierzega. An earlier, abbreviated version of this essay was published in *Justice Quarterly* (15:4) 1998:667–96. I also presented parts of it at annual meetings of the American Society of Criminology, held in Miami in 1994 and in Boston in 1995, and of the American Sociological Society, held in Toronto in 1997.

1. Although Aschaffenburg is seldom mentioned by criminologists today (one exception is Quinney 1970), when his book appeared in an English translation in 1913 it was one of the first works by a German criminologist to be published in the United States. It was published as part of a prestigious series on crime under the auspices of the American Institute of Criminal Law and Criminology, a translation series that also included books by the well-known European scholars Cesare Lombroso, Gabriel Tarde, Enrico Ferri, and Willem Bonger.

2. In his otherwise erudite study of the history of the death penalty in Germany, Richard Evans (1996) unfortunately focuses exclusively on race and heredity in his discussion of Aschaffenburg.

3. Aschaffenburg was seemingly unaware of the shift by Lombroso toward a more multicausal model of the etiology of crime. For a discussion, see Beirne (1993).

4. In the United States, Bernfeld's theoretical work on Marx and Freud has not been given much emphasis, even when his other work on education (Bernfeld 1973 [1925]) has been discussed (Ekstein 1966; Paret 1973), but in postwar Germany, the New Left gave great prominence to this aspect of his work (see for example Jörg Sandkühler's introduction to Bernfeld [1970]).

5. For a recent sociological appreciation of Freud's notion of the coexistence of opposites, albeit from a very different theoretical tradition than Marxism, see Smelser (1998).

6. Scholem, who was obviously upset by this development in his former pupil, was surely at least partially in error here, since no Trotskyist groupings existed yet in 1926. But his remark might at a broader level reflect Fromm's far-left political views in those days, which may well have included some critiques of the Soviet Union. One does find very sharp attacks on the Soviet system as "state capitalism" or "totalitarianism" in Fromm's later work on Marx (1961:vii).

7. It should be noted, however, that Fromm in this essay passes over in silence one argument Freud had made in *Civilization and Its Discontents* (1989 [1930]). Freud now placed a death instinct bound up with aggressiveness and destruction alongside a life instinct bound up with self-preservation and sexuality. In Freud's new formula, first presented in *Beyond the Pleasure Principle,* sexuality and self-preservation were now part of the same overall set of drives and they stood opposed to the aggressive and destructive drives. For good overviews of Fromm's more explicit critiques of Freud in the 1930s and 1940s, see Funk (1982 [1978]) and Burston (1991). See also Fromm (1941, 1962). In his last years, in *Anatomy of Human Destructiveness* (1973), Fromm returned to and critically appropriated Freud's notion of a death instinct. Here Fromm also dealt with the question of crime at the level of Nazi and Stalinist mass murder, rather than the ordinary crimes of theft and assault that he took up in his 1930–31 writings. However, the issues he raised in 1973 are beyond the scope of this essay.

8. Here Fromm foreshadowed some of the themes of his later work on matriarchy, gender, and social psychology, such as his 1934 essay, "The Theory of Mother Right and Its Relevance for Social Psychology" (included in Fromm 1970). This and other writings by Fromm on gender have recently been collected and reprinted by Funk (Fromm 1997). For discussions of this aspect of Fromm's work, see Burston (1991) and Kellner (1992).

9. Fromm's polemic against the mechanical materialism of Bernstein and Kautsky was probably colored by his sympathy for the Bolshevik Revolution, which they had opposed. Later in this essay he refers to but does not attack *Historical Materialism,* an equally mechanistic materialist book by a leading Bolshevik theorist, Nikolai Bukharin, a work that was criticized strongly by the Hegelian Marxists Georg Lukács and Antonio Gramsci.

10. Although I am citing the original versions of Fromm's three articles on crime, I have also consulted the new editions published in Fromm's German-language collected works (Fromm 1989a), which contain editor's notes by Rainer Funk.

11. I am citing both the German original and the English translation in part 3 of this volume.

12. Here and elsewhere in these essays on crime, Fromm appears to treat the father-son Oedipal conflict as the norm, as if crime were entirely a male issue. He might have overcome this serious limitation in his writings on crime had he been able to incorporate his later critiques of Freud's Oedipus complex and his own writings on gender and matriarchy, referred to above. As previously noted, however, Fromm never wrote directly on criminal justice after 1931.

13. It is doubtful that Fromm implied here a general disparagement of the masses as sadistic because, as noted above in the discussion of Fromm's writings on Marx and Freud, he regarded the sadistic impulses of oppressed groups toward their rulers as a normal and ubiquitous phenomenon.

14. Foucault discussed his lack of familiarity with the Frankfurt School until late in his life in a series of interviews on Marxism (1991 [1981]), but even then did not seem to be aware of Fromm's early work on crime.

15. See Fraser (1989) for a good although somewhat hesitant critique of these limitations in Foucault's thought.

16. As noted above, Fromm often assumes male roles as universals in these early writings.

17. In a recent essay on the intellectual legacy of *Escape from Freedom,* Neil McLaughlin concludes that Fromm's "insights into the often irrational roots of human motivation demand our renewed attention" (1996:259). See also the discussions of Fromm in Bronner (1994) and Kovel (1994). For an interesting elaboration of Fromm's theory of sadomasochism by a feminist criminologist, see Chancer (1992). For a perceptive discussion of the differences between Fromm's position and that of Adorno and Horkheimer, see Smith (1992).

References Cited

Adorno, Theodor, et al. 1950. *The Authoritarian Personality.* New York: Harper and Bros.

Aichhorn, August. 1935 [1925]. *Wayward Youth.* New York: Viking Press.

Alexander, Franz, and Hugo Staub. 1956 [1928]. *The Criminal, the Judge, and the Public.* Trans. Gregory Zilboorg. Glencoe, Ill.: Free Press.

Aschaffenburg, Gustav. 1913. *Crime and Its Repression.* Trans. Adalbert Albrecht. Boston: Little, Brown.

Beirne, Piers. 1993. *Inventing Criminology: Essays on the Rise of "Homo Criminalis."* Albany: SUNY Press.

Benjamin, Jessica. 1988. *The Bonds of Love: Psychoanalysis, Feminism, and the Problem of Domination.* New York: Pantheon.

Bernfeld, Siegfried. 1970 [1928]. "Sozialismus und Psychoanalyse." In *Psychoanalyse und Marxismus: Dokumentation einer Kontroverse.* Ed. Hans Jörg Sandkühler. 46–55. Frankfurt: Suhrkamp Verlag.

———. 1973 [1925]. *Sisyphus or the Limits of Education.* Trans. Frederic Lilge. Berkeley: University of California Press.

Bonss, Wolfgang. 1984 [1980]. "Introduction: Critical Theory and Empirical Research—Some Observations." In Fromm 1984 [1980]: 1–38.

Bronner, Stephen Eric. 1994. *Of Critical Theory and Its Critics.* Boston: Basil Blackwell.

Burston, Daniel. 1991. *The Legacy of Erich Fromm.* Cambridge, Mass.: Harvard University Press.

Chancer, Lynn. 1992. *Sadomasochism in Everyday Life.* New Brunswick, N.J.: Rutgers University Press.

Ekstein, Rudolf. 1966. "Siegfried Bernfeld, 1892–1953: Sisyphus or the Boundaries of Education." In *Psychoanalytic Pioneers.* Ed. Franz Alexander, Samuel Eisenstein, and Martin Grotjahn. 415–29. New York: Basic Books.

Evans, Richard J. 1996. *Rituals of Retribution: Capital Punishment in Germany, 1600–1987.* New York: Oxford University Press.

Foucault, Michel. 1965 [1961]. *Madness and Civilization.* Trans. Richard Howard. New York: Random House.

————. 1974. "Michel Foucault on Attica: An Interview." *Telos* 19 (Spring): 154–61.

————. 1978 [1975]. *Discipline and Punish: The Birth of the Prison.* Trans. Alan Sheridan. New York: Pantheon.

————. 1980. *Power/Knowledge: Selected Interviews and Other Writings, 1972–77.* Ed. Colin Gordon. Trans. Colin Gordon, Leo Marshall, John Mepham, and Kate Soper. New York: Random House.

————. 1991 [1981]. *Remarks on Marx: Conversations with Duccio Trombadori.* Trans. R. James Goldstein and James Cascaito. New York: Semiotext(e).

————. 1994a [1972]. "Le grand enfermement." In Foucault, *Dits et écrits, 1954–1988.* 4 vols. Ed. Daniel Defert and François Ewald. 2:296–306. Paris: Éditions Gallimard.

————. 1994b [1973]. "Prisons et révoltes dans les prisons." Pp. 425–32 In Foucault, *Dits et écrits, 1954–1988.* 4 vols. Ed. Daniel Defert and François Ewald. 2:425–32. Paris: Éditions Gallimard.

Fraser, Nancy. 1989. *Unruly Practices.* Minneapolis: University of Minnesota Press.

Freud, Sigmund. 1961 [1930]. "The Expert Opinion in the Halsmann Case." In Freud, *Complete Psychological Works, Standard Edition.* 24 vols. 21:251–53. London: Hogarth Press.

————. 1970 [1916]. "Some Character-Types Met with in Psycho-Analytic Work." In Freud, *Complete Psychological Works, Standard Edition.* 24 vols. 14:311–33. London: Hogarth Press.

————. 1989 [1930]. *Civilization and Its Discontents.* Ed. and Trans. James Strachey. New York: Norton.

————. 1994 [1931]. "Response to Fuchs." In *The Weimar Republic Sourcebook.* Ed. Anton Kaes, Martin Jay, and Edward Dimendberg. 738. Berkeley: University of California Press.

Fromm, Erich. 1930a. "Ödipus in Innsbruck." *Psychoanalytische Bewegung* 3:75–79.

————. 1930b. "Der Staat als Erzieher: Zur Psychologie der Strafjustiz." *Zeitschrift für Psychoanalytische Pädagogik* 4:1 (January): 5–9. (English translation in this volume, pp. 123–28)

————. 1931. "Zur Psychologie des Verbrechers und der strafenden Gesellschaft." *Imago: Zeitschrift für Anwendung der Psychoanalyse auf die Natur- und Geisteswissenschaften.* 17 (2): 226–51. (English translation in this volume, pp. 129–56)

————. 1941. *Escape from Freedom.* New York: Holt, Rinehart and Winston.

————. 1961. *Marx's Concept of Man.* New York: Frederick Ungar.

————. 1962. *Beyond the Chains of Illusion: My Encounters with Marx and Freud.* New York: Simon and Schuster.

————. 1970. *The Crisis of Psychoanalysis: Essays on Marx, Freud, and Social Psychology.* New York: Holt, Rinehart and Winston.

————. 1973. *The Anatomy of Human Destructiveness.* New York: Holt, Rinehart and Winston.

————. 1984 [1980]. *The Working Class in Weimar Germany: A Psychological and Sociological Study.* Cambridge, Mass.: Harvard University Press.

————. 1989a. *Gesamtausgabe.* 10 vols. Ed. Rainer Funk. Munich: Deutscher Taschenbuch Verlag.

————. 1989b [1931]. "Politics and Psychoanalysis." Trans. Mark Ritter. In *Critical Theory and Society: A Reader.* Ed. Stephen Eric Bronner and Douglas MacKay Kellner. 213–18. New York: Routledge.

————. 1989c [1929]. "Psychoanalysis and Sociology." Trans. Mark Ritter. In *Critical Theory and Society: A Reader.* Ed. Stephen Eric Bronner and Douglas MacKay Kellner. 37–39. New York: Routledge.

————. 1997. *Love, Sexuality, and Matriarchy: About Gender.* Ed. Rainer Funk. New York: Fromm International.

————, ed. 1965. *Socialist Humanism.* New York: Doubleday.

Fuchs, Georg. 1994 [1931]. "We Prisoners: Memories of Inmate No. 2911." In *The Weimar Republic Sourcebook.* Ed. Anton Kaes, Martin Jay, and Edward Dimendberg. 737–38. Berkeley: University of California Press.

Funk, Rainer. 1982 [1978]. *Erich Fromm: The Courage to Be Human.* New York: Continuum.

————. 1983. *Erich Fromm.* Reinbek bei Hamburg: Rowohlt Taschenbuch Verlag.

Garland, David. 1990. *Punishment and Modern Society.* Chicago: University of Chicago Press.

Gibbons, Don C. 1982. *Society, Crime, and Criminal Behavior.* 4th ed. Englewood Cliffs, N.J.: Prentice-Hall.

Goffman, Erving. 1961. *Asylums.* New York: Doubleday.

Guttmacher, Manfred S. 1958. "A Psychiatric Approach to Crime and Correction." *Law and Contemporary Problems* 23:4 (Autumn): 633–49.

Hakeem, Michael. 1957–58. "A Critique of the Psychiatric Approach to the Prevention of Juvenile Delinquency." *Social Problems* 5 (3): 194–206.

————. 1958. "A Critique of the Psychiatric Approach to Crime and Correction." *Law and Contemporary Problems* 23:4 (Autumn): 650–82.

Hentig, Hans von. 1972 [1954]. "Gustav Aschaffenburg, 1866–1944." In *Pioneers in Criminology.* 2d ed. Ed. Hermann Mannheim. 421–28. Montclair, N.J.: Patterson Smith.

Horkheimer, Max. 1989 [1930]. "The State of Contemporary Social Philosophy and the Tasks of an Institute for Social Research." In *Critical Theory and Society: A Reader.* Ed. Stephen Eric Bronner and Douglas MacKay Kellner. 25–36. New York: Routledge.

Jay, Martin. 1973. *The Dialectical Imagination: A History of the Frankfurt School and the Institute for Social Research, 1923–1950.* Boston: Little, Brown.

Kellner, Douglas. 1989. *Critical Theory, Marxism, and Modernity.* Baltimore: Johns Hopkins University Press.

————. 1992. "Erich Fromm, Feminism, and the Frankfurt School." In *Erich Fromm und die Frankfurter Schule.* Ed. Michael Kessler and Rainer Funk. 111–30. Tübingen: Francke Verlag.

Kovel, Joel. 1994. "Foreword to the English Edition." In *The Erich Fromm Reader.* Ed. Rainer Funk. vi–xi. Atlantic Highlands, N.J.: Humanities Press.

Liszt, Franz von. 1905. *Strafrechtliche Aufsätze und Vorträge*. Vol. 2. Berlin: J. Guttentag.

Macey, David. 1993. *The Lives of Michel Foucault*. New York: Vintage.

Mannheim, Hermann. 1965. *Comparative Criminology*. Boston: Houghton Mifflin.

McLaughlin, Neil. 1996. "Nazism, Nationalism, and the Sociology of the Emotions: *Escape from Freedom* Revisited." *Sociological Theory* 14 (3): 241–61.

Melossi, Dario. 1978. "Review of Georg Rusche and Otto Kirchheimer: *Punishment and Social Structure*." *Crime and Social Justice* 9 (Spring–Summer): 73–85.

Mitchell, Juliet. 1971. *Woman's Estate*. New York: Vintage.

Paret, Peter. 1973. "Preface: *Sisyphus* and Its Author." In Siegfried Bernfeld, *Sisyphus or the Limits of Education*. ix–xxvii. Berkeley: University of California Press.

Parmelee, Maurice. 1913. "Preface." In Gustav Aschaffenburg, *Crime and Its Repression*. xi–xv. Boston: Little, Brown.

Quinney, Richard. 1970. *Criminology*. Boston: Little, Brown.

Rusche, Georg. 1930. "Zuchthausrevolten oder Sozialpolitik: Zu den Vorgängen in Amerika." *Frankfurter Zeitung* 403 (June 1): 1–2.

———. 1978 [1933]. "Labor Market and Penal Sanction." Trans. Gerda Dinwiddie. *Crime and Social Justice* 10 (Fall–Winter): 2–8.

Rusche, Georg, and Otto Kirchheimer. 1939. *Punishment and Social Structure*. New York: Columbia University Press.

Schad, Susanne Petra. 1972. *Empirical Research in Weimar Germany*. The Hague: Mouton.

Scholem, Gershom. 1980. *From Berlin to Jerusalem: Memories of My Youth*. Trans. Harry Zohn. New York: Schocken.

Shoham, S. Giora, and Mark C. Seis. 1993. *A Primer in the Psychology of Crime*. New York: Harrow and Heston.

Smelser, Neil J. 1998. "The Rational and the Ambivalent in the Social Sciences: 1997 Presidential Address." *American Sociological Review* 63 (1): 1–16.

Smith, David Norman. 1992. "The Beloved Dictator: Adorno, Horkheimer, and the Critique of Domination." *Current Perspectives in Social Theory* 12:195–230.

Wiggershaus, Rolf. 1994 [1986]. *The Frankfurt School*. Trans. Michael Robertson. Cambridge: MIT Press.

Part 3

Two Essays by the Young Fromm on Crime and Criminal Justice

Translators' Note

Fromm published these two essays on crime in leading psychoanalytic journals in 1930 and 1931, during the same period as his better-known early essays on Marxism and psychoanalysis, several of which he collected and translated into English in *The Crisis of Psychoanalysis* (1970). These two essays on crime, which develop for the first time anywhere a Freudian Marxist critique of the role of the criminal justice system in modern capitalist society, have not been published previously in English. They have not been widely discussed, even in German. We would like to thank Rainer Funk, Eric Plaut, and Jürgen Rojahn for their helpful suggestions, especially on the translation of psychoanalytic terms.

7

The State as Educator:
On the Psychology of Criminal Justice (1930)

Erich Fromm

Translated from the German and Annotated by Heinz D. Osterle
and Kevin Anderson

An increasing interest has developed recently in the psychology of criminals, judges, criminal law, and punishment. This probably has three major explanations. First, this interest probably originated from the growing diffusion of psychoanalytic insights and especially from the publications on the psychology of criminals and of judges by F. Wittels[1] (1928) and by Alexander and Staub[2] (1956 [1928]). Another reason for this increased interest probably lies in the fact that a series of criminal trials has occurred (one is reminded of the Friedländer, Halsmann, and Husmann cases[3]), in which the psychopathological basis [*Grundlagen*] of the crimes was so obvious that they stimulated reflection on the theoretical problem of the psychology of crime. To these more superficial explanations could be added the fact that current social, political, and cultural developments as a whole are necessarily accompanied by increasing insight of the progressive parts of society into the problematic features of such venerable established [*autoritätsgetragen*] institutions as the judicial system [*Justiz*], leading in turn to efforts toward a theoretical solution to these problems. It has often been believed that theoretical insight into the unconscious background of crime and into unconscious feelings about punishment and its effects could have great practical significance. It was believed that if it were possible to persuade the court that a criminal acted out of unconscious, instinctual motives, then it would be also possible to prove definitively that punishment for this sexual criminal [*Triebverbrecher*] could have no rehabilitative effect, because he is not conscious of the motives for his actions, and consequently has no control over them. It was expected that a reasonable court would draw the appropriate [*entsprechend*] consequences from this insight, and that it would resort only to measures that have a useful healing effect on the psychopathic criminal, instead of foolishly resorting to punishment. Up to now, there has been little experience with such efforts to bring about, through a psychoanalytic understanding of the criminal, a different and more useful procedure than the previous one, so that no judgment can yet be made from the standpoint of practical knowledge about the viability of these efforts. There are, however, a few theoretical considerations that lead to considerable skepticism regarding the prospects for such efforts in contemporary society. Since these considerations touch on pedagogical problems in many respects, they may perhaps be of interest to the readers of this journal.

Modern criminal justice [*Strafjustiz*]⁴ thinks of itself as a type of pedagogy. It officially renounces the thought of revenge and maintains that its intention is to reform or correct [*bessern*]⁵ the criminal, and that on the whole its methods are a useful means toward reform or correction of the offender. It tries to achieve this reform or correction in two ways: negatively, it believes that it can intimidate and deter through punishment, so that henceforth the offender will be a quiet, well-behaved citizen; positively, it creates a system of finely-calibrated rewards for good behavior through mandatory work, or through "uplifting" words of encouragement from a clergyman as well as other devices, all in order to educate the criminal on how to become a socially useful person. Experience has shown that these methods, which are no different from the usual methods of intervention (threat of punishment, promise of rewards, and compulsion to work), are having little success. In addition, theoretical analysis shows that these methods *can* have little success. Insofar as people disobey the laws of society because they are pushed to do so by hunger, thirst, and other elementary needs, punishment cannot be an effective [*zweckmässig*] means to deter them. In these instances the only possibility is an improvement in the economic situation of the "criminal" to the point where his situation is so secure that committing a crime to gratify elementary needs is unnecessary. Insofar as we are concerned not with the "economic criminal" [*Notverbrecher,* "criminal motivated by economic factors"] but with the "sexual criminal" [*Triebverbrecher*], the contemporary penal system on the whole may be considered to have just as little effect. Psychoanalysis has given us sufficient data to show that few actions that are in reality caused by unconscious impulses can be prevented by influencing people at the conscious level of their personality, and the data indicates that this is true for criminal as well as noncriminal neurotics.

If, however, both the present criminal justice system and even the modern penal system [*Strafvollzug,* "treatment of prisoners"] are ineffective and unsuitable for the attainment of their own goals, then there must be other reasons as to why society holds on to these ineffective measures with so much determination.

From an examination of these motives, one is led to consider that the criminal justice system has not only the actual criminal as its object, nor only the person with a clean record [*unbescholten*] who might become a criminal unless deterred by example, i.e., the potential criminal. Rather, one of the essential functions of the criminal justice system is its significance for the great mass of non-criminals.

What does this mean?

In no way does the stability of the social structure depend solely on the strength of the external instruments of power, which are meant to guarantee the continued existence of the society. To be sure, the police and the military are strong supports for society, but they can—as the history of revolutions shows—only fulfill their duties when an additional factor comes into play. This additional factor is the psychic readiness of the great majority to adjust [sich einzufügen] to the existing society and to subordinate themselves [sich unterzordnen] to the ruling powers. We cannot discuss here, in all of its detailed ramifications, the question of which psychic and especially libidinal tendencies and impulses cause this social submissiveness [Gefügigkeit], and the question of how these tendencies are induced [provoziert]. (See the instructive discussion of these issues by Bernfeld [1928]).[6]

Here the problem will only be touched upon insofar as it connects to criminal justice.

Contemporary society, like all previous ones, is grounded in severe instinctual renunciation [Triebverzicht] on the part of the masses, on the subordination of the masses to the ruling strata, and, from the psychological side, on the belief that existing social relations are necessary [Notwendigkeit]; specifically, that they are grounded in the superior insight and wisdom of the rulers. These psychic attitudes have their model and their source in the attitude of the child to the father. The real situation, in which the child is confronted by the father, makes it necessary to fear his physical superiority, to admire and to worship his mental superiority, and frequently the child makes the best of his situation when he succeeds in transforming into admiring worship his aversion toward the forbidding father, who demands instinctual renunciation.

This psychic attitude [seelische Einstellung] of the child toward the father is the same one that the state desires and considers necessary among the great mass of its citizens. The state must use every possible means to present itself to the masses as a father image [Vaterimago],[7] and in this way to make it possible for the individual to transfer his former attitude toward his father to the rulers. The means and methods by which the representatives of the state try to present themselves as a father image in the unconscious of the masses are very diverse. (In a monarchy they culminate in a very primitive and simple way in the veneration of the kaiser's person.) Criminal justice is one of these methods. What is, for the child, one of the essential qualities of the father, that instills in him such fear but also deep respect? It is the fact that the father can punish, that the child is defenseless because of the father's physical superiority. It is, in short, the threat of castration by the father and his undeniable power [*Potenz*] to carry out this threat, should he so desire. Moreover, as in the case of the masses with regard to the state authority, it is of little importance in principle whether the threat of punishment is carried out. The ability to threaten and to punish is decisive. It is precisely this ability that constitutes, for the child, a father as the father in the specific psychological sense that is under discussion here, and [for the masses it] constitutes the state or the class ruling in and by it, as a reflection of the father.

It is clear therefore why there must be a criminal justice system, independent of its effect [*Einwirkung*] on criminals. It is an institution through which the state imposes its will as a father image on the unconscious of the masses, in which it repeats an important function of the father, his power to punish and to threaten. This is most clearly visible in the death penalty. The central factor in the father's power is the power to castrate, to cause serious bodily injury. It is no accident that the kaiser or the president is legally empowered to pardon those sentenced to death, that he therefore is allowed to make the final judgment about life or death. He is the symbolic embodiment of paternal authority, and he proves himself as such through his right to decide about life and death.

Another function of the criminal justice system should also be mentioned briefly. It provides the masses with a form of gratification of their sadistic impulses—it is very important to the rulers that these impulses be diverted from them and onto another object—and at the same time provides the masses with a certain equivalent for their instinctual renunciation. What is commonly termed a sense of justice [*Gerechtigkeitsgefühl*] or consciousness of justice [*Rechtsbewusstsein*] in the masses is nothing but an expression of certain libidinal impulses of a sadistic or aggressive type, and it is understandable that the state likes to appeal to this popular sense of justice [*Rechtsgefühl*], because it can gratify these impulses in a manner that is harmless for the state. (Part of the function of war lies in the same direction.)

Therefore, we see that the significance of criminal justice lies not only in the fact that it is intended to protect society from the criminal and to reform or correct him; rather, one of its essential functions is to influence the masses psychologically in the sense desired by the rulers. Criminal justice is like the rod on the wall, which is supposed to show even the well-behaved child that a child is a child, and a father a father.

The result of these considerations is that all insight into the ineffectiveness of the contemporary criminal justice system with regard to the criminal will hardly lead to basic changes in the system, as long as the peculiar [*Eigenart*] structure of the existing society prevails. Society needs the criminal justice system for purposes that have nothing to do with effective approaches [*zweckmässiges Verhalten,* "suitable behavior"] toward the criminal. The criminal justice system is an instrument for "educating" [*Erziehung*] the masses in the sense of fixating them artificially to the situation where a person is "educated" [*erzogen*]. It is the situation of the child who reveres the father.

Notes

Translators' note: "Der Staat als Erzieher. Zur Psychologie der Strafjustiz" originally appeared in *Zeitschrift für psychoanalytische Pädagogik* (Vienna) 4:1 (1930): 5–9 and was reprinted in Erich Fromm, *Gesamtausgabe,* vol. 1, ed. Rainer Funk, 7–10 (Munich: Deutscher Taschenbuch Verlag, 1989). The *Zeitschrift* included on its masthead several internationally known psychologists, such as Marie Bonaparte, Anna Freud, and Jean Piaget. In the original, authors and dates are given in the text but more specific references are lacking; these have been provided here by the translators.

1. Translators' note: Fritz Wittels (1880–1950) was a medical doctor who became an early follower of Freud. He practiced psychoanalysis first in Vienna and, from 1928, in New York. In addition to the book on crime and prison to which Fromm refers here, Wittels published a number of other books, including the early biographical study, *Sigmund Freud, His Personality, His Teaching, and His School* (New York: Dodd, Mead, 1924).

2. Translators' note: Franz Alexander (1891–1964) was among the most prominent of the Freudians who emigrated to the United States, and was also the best-known psychoanalytic criminologist. Educated at the Berlin Psychoanalytic Institute, Alexander first came to the United States in 1930, and soon established the Chicago Psychoanalytic Institute, which he headed from 1932 to 1956. His writings on crime include, in addition to the book Fromm cites, *The Roots of Crime,* co-authored with William Healy (New York: Knopf, 1935). Hugo Staub (1886–1942), a well-established liberal Berlin lawyer, was drawn to psychoanalysis in the mid-1920s, and soon began conducting seminars on psychoanalytic criminology at the Berlin Psychoanalytic Institute. He left Germany in 1933, enlisted in the French army to fight Hitler in 1939, and then emigrated to the United States, where he continued to study delinquency.

3. Translators' note: Fromm analyzed this case of an apparently false confession to the murder of his father by a young Austrian student, Philipp Halsmann, in his article "Oedipus in Innsbruck: Zum Halsmann-Prozess" [Oedipus in Innsbruck: on the Halsmann trial], *Psychoanalytische Bewegung* 2:1 (1930): 75–79. Friedländer was a young man whose double murder of his brother and his brother's friend was discussed by Alexander, who saw unconscious homosexual motivations at work. We were unable to obtain information on the Husmann case.

4. Translators' note: The term *Strafjustiz* carries the literal meaning of "punitive justice." An alternate translation might be "penal system" or "penal justice." Here and elsewhere, we have translated it as "criminal justice" or "criminal justice system," in keeping

with contemporary criminology's use of these terms to designate the police, the courts, and the correctional system as a whole. However, Fromm is speaking primarily of the latter two functions, paralleling the way this term was used in pre–World War II American criminology, with "law enforcement" considered as a separate entity.

5. Translators' note: The notion of "reform" or "correction" [*Besserung*] of the criminal is related to rehabilitation and corrections. *Besserung* carries the literal meaning "change for the better."

6. Translators' note: Siegfried Bernfeld (1892–1953) was, along with Wilhelm Reich and Fromm himself, a pioneer in the attempt to link the theories of Marx and Freud. Bernfeld's influential essay, "On the Question of Psychoanalysis and Marxism," appeared in the Austro-Marxist journal *Der Klassenkampf* in 1925. Born in Austria, he became a socialist Zionist, led a Jewish self-defense force in Vienna during the 1918 revolution, and came a bit later to psychoanalysis. In his scholarly work, he wrote widely on child psychology and the psychology of education. His *Sisyphus or the Limits of Education* (1925) eventually appeared in English (Berkeley: University of California Press, 1973), but his more explicitly Marxist work from the 1920s did not. During the late 1920s, Bernfeld exercised a considerable influence on Fromm. Bernfeld left Germany in 1933 and, after a short time in Austria and France, came to the United States in 1937. Settling in San Francisco, he began to write on Freud's life and thought. Ernest Jones drew extensively on these writings for his biography of Freud. Fromm, in addition to referring here to Bernfeld's book on how the school system inculcated social submissiveness, reviewed it in the same issue of *Zeitschrift für psychoanalytische Pädagogik* in which the present article appeared.

7. Translators' note: This term could also be translated as "representation of the father."

References Cited

Alexander, Franz, and Hugo Staub. 1956 [1928]. *The Criminal, the Judge, and the Public.* Trans. Grigory Zilboorg. Glencoe, Ill.: Free Press.

Bernfeld, Siegfried. 1928. *Die Schulgemeinde und ihre Funktion im Klassenkampf.* Berlin: E. Laub Verlagsbuchhandlung.

Wittels, Fritz. 1928. *Die Welt ohne Zuchthaus.* Stuttgart: Hippokrates Verlag.

8

On the Psychology of the Criminal and the Punitive Society (1931)

Erich Fromm

Translated from the German and Annotated by Heinz D. Osterle and Kevin Anderson

---

More than thirty years ago, Franz von Liszt[1] formulated the following definition of the causes of crime: "Every crime is the product of the individual characteristics of the criminal on the one hand, and, on the other, of the social conditions and environment of the criminal at the moment of his deed" (Liszt 1905e [1898]: 234). The psychoanalyst can also agree with this general description of the causes of crime if he emphasizes at the same time that the "specific characteristics of the criminal" are for the most part based on the criminal's constellation of drives, which are found predominantly at the unconscious level. The difficulties and conflicts begin with regard to determining the individual factors constituting the specific characteristics of the criminal, as well as the qualitative and quantitative relations of these factors to socioeconomic factors.

Socioeconomic Factors and Crime

Crime statistics have long taught us to see a connection between economic factors and criminality: property offenses [*Eigentumsdelikte*][2] are dependent on the economic situation of the population. This is expressed in how the number of property offenses is dependent on the rise and fall of grain prices and on the change of seasons. The connection between grain prices and criminality has been proven without any doubt in a series of studies (cf. Fuld 1881; Berg 1902; Müller 1899; Herz 1905). To illustrate this connection we quote the figures for Austria-Hungary from 1905, which were found by H. Herz.

Herz summarizes these statistics as follows: "Food prices do not affect the entire area of property offenses equally. Atavistic crimes, such as theft and robbery, expressing themselves mostly in the raw exploitation of opportunity and in violence, are directly dependent on food prices. Offenses better adapted to modern

Table 8.1. Crime Rate per 100,000 Adults by Type of Crime for Austria-Hungary

Year	Price of a Combined Hectoliter (2.84 bushels) of Grain, in Shillings	Theft	Embezzlement	Crimes against Persons	Crimes against the State	Aggravated Assault and Battery
1862–65	10.11	60.0	9.4	14.6	9.7	5.3
1866–70	11.83	74.2	10.7	22.4	15.9	6.7
1871–75	13.75	76.5	12.5	26.5	18.3	8.3
1876–80	13.23	84.1	16.3	28.2	19.7	8.3
1881–85	11.93	79.3	15.2	28.2	19.8	8.9
1886–90	9.81	62.6	13.9	29.1	20.3	8.7
1891–95	10.01	58.8	14.5	27.0	18.5	9.7
1896–99	11.25	57.2	15.3	29.1	20.0	11.9

Source: Herz 1905.

conditions . . . that replace violence with lying and counterfeiting, overcome this primitive kind of dependence" (Herz 1905:292). Earlier studies of conditions in Germany arrive at the same result in principle, the dependence of property offenses on grain prices. What matters is the rise and fall of the prices, not their absolute level. In contrast, morals offenses and violent offenses [*Sittlichkeits- und Aggressionsdelikte*] lack such a direct connection with food prices (cf. Aschaffenburg 1923:114ff.).[3]

Statistics on the frequency of crime in different seasons show the same connection between criminality and economic conditions.[4] The German statistics in table 8.2 offer a clear picture:

The increase in sexual crimes begins in Germany in March . . . ; the maximum is quickly reached in July, after which the number quickly decreases again below the computed yearly average; the months of October and March lie considerably below the computed average. A very similar curve is shown by "obscene acts," except that in this case the maximum is reached in June. The fluctuations are tremendous. July exceeds the winter months by more than double the number of sexual crimes. (Aschaffenburg 1923:16, 1913:19–20)[5]

The yearly distribution of offenses against property presents an entirely different picture, with malicious mischief alone forming an exception. Psychologically, these latter offenses are much closer to assault and battery than to property offenses, to which the categories of our penal code assign them. They therefore show a pattern that is quite similar to assault and battery even though the variations between summer and winter are a little less marked. Theft and fraud, on the contrary, never reach the computed average of one hundred from March to September. But, from then on, there is a rapid increase in their frequency, which continues through the whole winter. (1923:30, 1913:28)[6]

Table 8.2. Crime in Germany According to the Year and Month When the Crimes Are Committed

("Statistics of the German Empire," N.F. LXXXIII, II, p. 52)
If there are 100 offenses per day in the year, there are per day in the month:

Kinds of Crimes and Offenses	Jan.	Feb.	March	April	May	June	July	Aug.	Sept.	Oct.	Nov.	Dec.
Crimes and offenses against national laws	95	97	90	92	99	103	105	**109**	105	103	103	98
Resisting officer	89	94	89	94	97	104	109	**117**	112	104	99	90
Breach of peace	94	99	96	100	98	101	105	**110**	106	102	100	89
Rape	64	66	78	103	128	144	**149**	130	108	90	68	69
Obscene acts, distribution of obscene literature	62	74	83	101	130	**150**	141	133	109	84	69	64
Insult (*Beleidigung*)	83	89	85	93	108	115	120	**122**	113	99	93	80
Infanticide	89	**127**	**127**	121	118	102	95	80	91	86	82	87
Simple assault and battery	76	80	79	95	108	116	124	**134**	121	102	88	74
Aggravated assault and battery	75	78	78	95	108	113	118	**133**	124	106	93	78
Crimes against property	109	108	96	90	93	93	92	93	93	104	113	**117**
Petit larceny, also when repeated	113	115	98	85	87	88	88	92	92	106	117	**121**
Grand larceny, also when repeated	102	107	92	89	94	98	98	94	96	106	**112**	111
Embezzlement	100	97	94	94	98	100	103	101	98	104	105	**108**
Fraud, also when repeated	112	108	95	88	92	92	92	93	90	88	102	**121**
Malicious mischief	88	92	98	108	**109**	106	104	104	103	101	99	88

Source: Aschaffenburg 1913.

Statistics therefore offer a very clear picture here as well. Crimes in which libidinal motives play a decisive part (sexual and violent offenses) are most frequent during spring and summer, whereas crimes in which economic necessity is a decisive factor occur primarily during the time of greatest economic need, i.e., in winter. Particularly instructive is the fact, noted by G. Aschaffenburg (1923:18, 1913:21), that the highest number of marital and extramarital pregnancies in Germany, and in Europe as a whole, occurs in May, the highest number of suicides in June, and the highest number of sexual crimes in June as well.

Statistics show a rough empirical relationship [*Erfahrungszusammenhang*] that seems theoretically self-evident to us: For property offenses, economic motives are—on average—decisive, as are sexual motives for sexual and aggressive offenses. Statistics, however, by their nature reveal only averages, and offer no clues with regard to the relationship between rational and irrational factors in an individual crime. It is one of the tasks of the analytical psychology of crime [*Kriminalpsychologie*] to examine the relationship—both qualitative and quantitative—between rational-egoistic and irrational-sexual factors in an individual crime, particularly the indirect influence of sexual factors on property offenses as well as the indirect influence of economic factors on sexual offenses [*Triebdelikte*]. The following presentation will be mainly concerned with the second question, i.e., the direct impact of the socioeconomic situation on sexual impulses that lead to crimes.

The Relationship of Economic and Psychological Causes

The most useful point of view with regard to grouping crimes according to their motives is probably to see them as a *continuum* [*Ergänzungsreihe*]. At one end are extreme cases of "economic crimes" ["*Notverbrechen*"] caused by dire need and driven by the instinct of self-preservation; at the other end is the purely "sexual crime" ["*Triebverbrechen*"], which is independent of the real economic situation and motivated only by the sexual impulses of the offender [*des Handelnden*].

Grouping the various crimes in a continuum is probably more useful than the criminological diagnosis set up by F. Alexander and H. Staub (1956 [1928]).[7] In its use of groups that are more mutually exclusive, their diagnosis is certainly adapted to the categories of contemporary penal law and therefore seems to promise greater possibilities of practical application.[8] But it also runs the danger of assuming different and separate groups of crimes when what is really at play is a continuous series in which nothing but the increase and decrease of certain tendencies can be determined.

Just before one of the endpoints of the continuum, the "economic crime," is the large number of ordinary property offenses that do not serve to rectify the most extreme and elementary needs and therefore are not (or are not exclusively) motivated by the instinct of self-preservation. The motive for these offenses is rather the wish to avail oneself of the possibility of a more or less enhanced enjoyment of life, i.e., in the libidinal component of the egoistic strivings, in narcissistic needs. These needs are actually quite normal, and are also completely conscious. Here the property offense does not have a primarily symbolic character, and the motive of the crime is not pathological. One could ask why a group of people whose economic situation does not permit them to gratify essentially normal needs commits offenses that are intended to gratify these needs. However, it would be better to turn the question around and ask: Why do most people in precisely this economic situation commit *no* offenses to gratify needs that other people can obtain legally? The answer to this question is very simple. By means of a certain kind of education and a series of other institutions, society succeeds in implanting ideals in the propertyless masses that enable most of them to prefer poverty to dishonesty. Criminals are people in whom such a superego formation succeeded not at all or only partially. Obviously, the fear of social reprisal supplies an essential reason against eating forbidden fruit. The more the offense contributes to the gratification of conscious egoistic-narcissistic needs, and the less it is the veiled symbolic expression of unconscious, purely sexual impulses, the greater the role of this motive of fear.

It would be one-sided, however, to fail to recognize that one particular motive still plays an important part even in these ordinary offenses, insofar as they exceed the gratification of elementary needs of self-preservation. For this motive plays, along with other motives, a *decisive* part in *all* offenses. We are thinking of the hostile impulses of appropriation and destruction [*Wegnehmen und Zerstören*]. We encounter them with great regularity in the analysis of children and adults. The difficult issue of the quality and the genesis within an individual of these impulses to rob and to destroy will not be discussed here. We would like to confine ourselves to the remark that in all offenses they form a *decisive motive, which is frequently unconscious as regards its strength.*

The offenses at the other end of the continuum are also relatively easy to understand. There are the purely sexual crimes in which only individual character [*individuelle Konstitution,* "specific constitutional factors"], or rather individual childhood experience, is decisive for crime causation and development [*Verbrechensbildung,* "formation of crime"]. The most extreme cases, at the very end of the series, are the insane, those criminals whose mental and emotional life is disturbed by organic malfunctions. Harder to understand are the offenses at the center of the continuum, i.e., property offenses that go beyond the gratification of egoistic-narcissistic needs, and that express unconscious sexual impulses, but also the sexual and aggressive offenses in whose origin socioeconomic factors play a role, if only indirectly.

All explanations that seek to apply what is valid only at the ends of the continuum to all cases within the series are evidently wrong. Neither can all offenses be explained by economic causes alone. (This is demonstrated both by crime statistics and by the fact that the great majority of the poor does not become criminal.) Nor can all offenses be explained by instinctual causes. Otherwise, relatively speaking, most criminals would not be recruited from the propertyless masses.

Psychoanalytic research has already given the first and decisive insight into the specific mixture of irrational instinctual motives and rational ego-motives.

Even the apparently rational actions of the criminal, based on egoistic motives, are usually determined by instinctual impulses of which he is not conscious. The wishes and interests of the ego are amalgamated with those of the primitive drives (the id), and thus prove the strong tendency inherent in the psychic apparatus to bring about such amalgamations and to make even irrational and instinctual actions seem rational and intelligible to the ego.

All of that and especially the unconscious sexual motives, which are conditioned by the life experience [*Lebensschicksal,* "life and fate"] of the individual, have been so well presented by F. Alexander and H. Staub (1956 [1928]; cf. Wittels 1928)[9] that we need not go into greater detail here.

It seems necessary, however, to contradict a view that makes a distinction between mentally healthy and neurotic criminals, designating one group as healthy and normal, in whom the pursuit of pleasure [*die Lusttendenz*] is largely in the service of expediency, and thus is rationalized, while only those individuals who have preserved the pleasure-seeking of childhood in a relatively unmodified form are to be considered neurotic (cf. F. Alexander 1931).

In our view, this approach does not appear to be very useful. The fact of extensive rationalization says nothing about the strength of unconscious libidinal motives, and therefore nothing about the more or less compulsive nature of criminal activity. We also find, with regard to a great many neurotic symptoms, that they are put into the service of ego-interests (secondary gains from illness). Consequently, we consider these symptoms to be no less neurotic, although, if the rationalizations are successful, they are more difficult to cure. It should not be forgotten that the concept of a crime that has been put completely into the service of expediency is a contradiction in terms, for as a crime it shares an attribute of the neurotic symptom or behavior, that of being badly adapted to social reality. In evaluating the psychic structure of both the criminal and the neurotic, we cannot take the rationalization as our starting point, but rather only the underlying unconscious drives, their strength and their characteristics. An unconscious wish can be largely rationalized, and yet it can coexist with a total inability to be influenced by punishment or to be motivated in a normal way. Conversely, the lack of rationalization, or its rudimentary character, says nothing about the strength and uniqueness of the unconscious instinctual motives or about the "capacity for reform or correction" [*"Besserungsfähigkeit"*], i.e., the ability of the criminal to be cured.

An example will illustrate the whole problematic. Let us take two female department store thieves, one wealthy and one poor. In both cases, analysis can perhaps show that the motive of their activities lies in the unconscious, e.g., in certain fixations of the oral phase or in the context of a wish for a child. The wealthy female thief does not have a rationalization. It is absent because she lacks the *possibility* to rationalize. Conversely, the other thief *must* rationalize the theft. She can hardly help putting it in the service of her ego-interests. Yet it would be a basic error to term the wealthy thief a neurotic kleptomaniac and the poor one a normal, psychologically healthy criminal. It is of course possible that the poor female thief steals not from libidinal motives at all, but out of necessity. However, only the study of the criminal personality at the unconscious level, not the presence of a rationalization, can elucidate such a problematic. This is the issue here.

The Fallacious Distinction between the Healthy and the Neurotic Criminal

This question is not only of theoretical but also of practical importance, because people have tried to draw conclusions concerning punishment from the distinction between "healthy and neurotic criminals." The healthy one is supposed to be punishable, i.e., also capable of reform or correction through punishment, while the neurotic criminal is considered to be sick and in need of treatment. The reflections of a leading criminologist [*Kriminalist*], Heindl,[10] show what basic errors and psychological absurdities can occur if the emphasis is put on the moment of rationalization. He writes with regard to the professional or career criminal:

> If one looks at monsters such as Hering, Grossmann, and Haarmann,[11] one finds in them an aspect of their behavior that is characteristic of every professional, business-like, or trading activity. One project is followed by another in rapid sequence. This phenomenon is connected with the motive for the crimes. With professional crimes, in contrast to occasional ones, profit seeking always is the motive, or at least the dominant motive. . . . With many professional criminals, a search of their home reveals that they kept an extremely precise record of their misdeeds and profits. Take Hering for example. His record books, which leave no doubt about the motive and frequency of his crimes, offer the best proof that these people considered crime a pure business matter. . . . Bichel, Bishop, and Dumollard[12] also committed one murder after another because they wanted to have a continuous source of income from them. In recent years, all mass murderers that have committed a whole series of murders tried to gain their livelihood from them, and made killing people a job that sustained them. Haarmann sold the clothes, Grossmann the flesh of his victims. Business, nothing but business! This is making a living, but in the most disgusting way. When one victim was not yet cold, sales-devoted businesspeople like Williams[13] and Haarmann were already looking for a new one. They even had to look for a victim right away because the cash profit of the previous murder was small or negative. (1926:140–41)

While Heindl considers passion, love, hatred and anger, sexual impulse, or economic necessity as motives for the occasional crime, he looks "in vain for such motives" with regard to professional criminals, especially professional murderers:

They are cut from different cloth. They belong to the second class of the mentally healthy criminals that we would like to term professional criminals. Of course, they also become delinquent only when the opportunity arises, but—and this is their characteristic feature—they look for it. They seek it systematically like a traveling salesman looks for customers. They have no inner conflict before committing the crime. *Les affaires sont les affaires!* [Business is business!].[14] They see in crime an activity like any other occupation. (1926:139)

We would like to point out briefly the extent to which Heindl contradicts himself with this thesis of the mentally healthy criminal. He points out the stereotypical character of the offenses committed by the professional criminal, which certainly do not occur for rational reasons, and which are frequently revealing. He purports to see in them the symptoms of mental or moral poverty [*Armutszeugnis,* "certificate of poverty"], the result of intellectual and physical inferiority. To be sure, he emphasizes the facts of the case that are psychologically important; but he does not recognize their cause, the compulsive repetition in the crime of an identical, unconscious impulse. He soon moves away from such a possible starting point for psychological reflection: "But perhaps we need not engage in such subtle psychology. Perhaps it simply is the tendency toward inertia innate in all people, the inclination to trot always on the same track that they share with herds of cattle and with carriage horses. They commit their offenses like a job, like others who glue the same shopping bags on a daily basis, make the same motions on a lathe, or administer the same knife thrusts to calves and swine" (1926:155).

Heindl completely overlooks an essential fact that reveals the psychological absurdity of his thesis of the mentally healthy mass murderer. When Haarmann commits a series of murders in order to sell the almost worthless rags of his victims, it is evident that the rational purpose of the crime has no clear relationship whatsoever to the crime itself. He could have achieved the same economic effect with an incomparably smaller risk to himself if he had stolen some old clothes from a second-hand clothing dealer. The most basic psychological analysis shows that the decisive motive for his crimes lies in instinctual impulses more or less unconscious to him, and that the use of the crime to achieve certain economic goals is only a superficial rationalization of the underlying instinctual impulses.

This confrontation with the psychologically superficial position of Heindl seems important to us. It shows the theoretical and practical consequences that a psychological position may entail in the evaluation of the psychic structure of the criminal when it proceeds from rationalizations, especially in the distinction between healthy and sick criminals.

The Psychological Underpinnings of Crime and the Class Structure of Contemporary Society

Up to now we have demonstrated that the majority of crimes, i.e., all that are located between the endpoints of the continuum, are characterized by a mixture of mostly unconscious, irrational instinctual motives [*Triebmotive*] and mostly conscious, rational purposive motives [*Zweckmotive*]. In other words, the instinctual situation, conditioned by individual development, is the motive for the crimes, in conjunction with the socioeconomic situation. After this fact has been stated, the question arises as to why crime plays such an important part in gratifying specific libidinal impulses in specific *social* strata.

The question must be raised as to what other forms of release or adjustment could be found for such overpowering instinctual impulses, conditioned as they are by early childhood development. The simple release or adjustment through the ego's rejection of those impulses coming from the lower depths (the id), i.e., through control and renunciation of instinctual gratification, is impossible for such criminal personalities. This is so because of the strength of the impulses or because of the inability of the ego to handle them. In the criminal, a type of repression (in relation to the impulse to be realized in the offense or perversion) that would lead to neurotic manifestations does not take place either, due to certain individually determined aspects. There is a third possibility of handling such instinctual impulses, sublimation. Undoubtedly, this possibility is conditioned to a rather large extent by individual psychological structure. The perversions show that for many people, the possibility of simple renunciation or repression, as well as that of sublimation, does not exist because of their individual development. On the other hand, there can be no doubt that the possibility of sublimation depends not only on individual factors of instinctual development but also on the social, specifically the economic, situation of the individual. The participation of the individual in the enjoyment of cultural assets, i.e., the sum total of the available instinctual gratifications, is largely dependent on his economic situation. This situation is of decisive influence on the individual's ability to sublimate because this ability is largely dependent on an adequate childhood education. The type and extent of one's education, which strongly affects the ability to sublimate, is primarily an economic problem. The occupation of a person is no less significant with respect to the potential for sublimation. This is clear with regard to proletarian occupations [*Beruf des Proletariers*]. Such occupations must be chosen early and under much stronger pressure, i.e., less according to individual needs. Later on, they offer far less in content, and generally provide far more limited opportunities for sublimation than middle class [*bürgerlich*] occupations. For the latter, there are numerous other possibilities of sublimation that are primarily passive [*rezeptiv,* "receptive"], and not based on creative achievement. They can be directly purchased and are therefore directly dependent, both qualitatively and quantitatively, on one's economic situation.

Of course, a whole range of similar possibilities for gratification are also available for free, or at low cost, to the great masses. The *circenses* [circus games][15] that the Roman emperors donated to the masses, and the burning of heretics in the Middle Ages, also belong here, as do soccer matches and movie theaters. But it cannot be denied that the propertied have far more possibilities in this regard than do the propertyless, inasmuch as property offers an unmatched freedom to structure one's life and to make good use of one's time.

These reflections show that the possibilities for sublimation depend not only on the psychological characteristics of the individual, but also on his economic situation. In many cases, sublimation founders, not because of a lack of individual psychic capacity to sublimate, but because of economic conditions.

Nor should it be overlooked that, in advantageous economic situations, a great number of instinctual gratifications become available that are denied to the propertyless. These gratifications draw part of the libido away from the overly developed partial or component impulse [*Partialtrieb*], i.e., they weaken the urgency of its gratification. What do these reflections mean with regard to crime causation [*Verbrechensmotive*]? They show that the economic situation exerts an indirect as well as a direct influence on criminality, to the extent that in many crimes instinctual impulses are realized that, in a different economic situation, could be released in a socially acceptable fashion.

However, the more limited possibility of sublimation is not the only factor through which the social situation has an indirect influence on crime causation and development. A second essential factor is the reinforcement of individual hostile or aggressive impulses that a member of the oppressed class receives from his hatred of the ruling class and its laws. This hatred is intensified by feelings of social disadvantage, whether glaringly conscious or massively suppressed in a given individual ego.

A further motive, often important in crime causation and development, is the gratification of narcissistic needs. The particular strength of such needs is once again rooted in individual development. With the proletarian, however, often the problem is not the particular strength of these needs, but rather a form of narcissistic "malnutrition." It is quite clear that the propertied person—in addition to the possibilities of gratification that can be purchased directly, such as beautiful clothes, good food, beautiful houses, etc.—has far greater opportunities for narcissistic gratification than does the propertyless one. Certainly, with regard to the latter, those without property are not completely lacking. Activities in associations and political parties, admiration from wife and child, and many other things offer possibilities for narcissistic gratification. But these are much more limited than those available to the propertied. In particular, one should again ponder the issue of class situation. A member of the subordinate class experiences a repetition of the narcissistic humiliations that he received as a child. Crime offers far-reaching gratifications—being named in the news, appearing in court, the attention of so many people who otherwise would not care about him—but only until the moment when the prison gates close behind him.

A fourth, essentially socially conditioned motive is the fact that the member of an oppressed class, who feels that he is being exploited and mistreated by society, easily succeeds in "bribing" his superego. In other words, he represents to himself as permissible his antisocial attitude because in his mind it is nothing more than an adequate reprisal for the injustice done to him (cf. Alexander and Staub 1956 [1928]).[16]

For property offenses, a further socially conditioned motive is added to everything that has been mentioned. The gratification of the irrational motives originating from the id can at the same time be put in the service of justified, natural, and rational ego-needs. Frequently, if libidinal motives alone do not suffice to make the crime psychologically possible, their amalgamation with ego-motives will become a compelling and insurmountable motor for criminal behavior.

These reflections will help to clarify the relationship between individual and social components in crime causation. It appears that the social component works in a double sense. It works *directly* because the economic situation supplies, to crime causation and development, the important addition, in property offenses, of ego-interests. But more importantly, it also works *indirectly* with regard to certain libidinal motives, inherited biologically, and conditioned by childhood experience. Because of one's social position,[17] these libidinal motives find little legitimate release, or they are reinforced to such an extent that crime becomes the most likely form in which all impulses can be released. In this latter case, the gratification of certain sexual urges is combined with that of hatred against the father or against society, and also with narcissistic gratifications.

Therefore, the question of whether crime is to be explained mainly by economic or instinctual causes has been posed wrongly. Instead, there is a specific relationship between the two groups of motives, in which the economic situation is of decisive importance for the development of the instinctual situation. In this sense, many crimes can be defined as gratifying libidinal impulses that are individual in their origin but developed under certain socioeconomic conditions.[18]

On Soundness of Mind and Legal Responsibility

The insight that most criminals—especially professional and habitual criminals—act and must act under unconscious impulses yields important consequences for the question of *accountability* [*Verantwortlichkeit*], and for the possibilities of punishment and reform or correction.

The school of jurisprudence that rejected the fiction of free will answered the question of accountability even before the discovery that unconscious motives are present in the criminal. It did so purely on the basis of experience and in a manner quite satisfactory even today.

F. von Liszt states:

The criminal . . . therefore is, for us human beings, absolutely and completely un-free. His crime is the necessary, inevitable result of the prevailing conditions. For criminal law there is no other basis than determinism. (1905b [1893]: 39)

I see . . . the essence of a sound mind [*Zurechnungsfähigkeit*], which is the prerequisite for accountability before the law [*strafrechtliche Verantwortlichkeit*],[19] in the normal receptivity to motives [*Bestimmbarkeit durch Motive*].[20] (1905b [1893]: 43)

Whoever is motivated [*reagiert*] in a normal way, is of sound mind and legally responsible. This condition disappears with every disturbance of emotional life, be it in the areas of imagination, emotion, or volition, through which one's motivation becomes abnormal, atypical. . . . Responsibility before the law and being of sound mind therefore mean receptivity to the creation of motivation as intended by the punishment. (1905c [1896]: 219–20)

Starting from the standpoint of determinism, Liszt's definition of the mental health of a person *who is motivated in a normal way and therefore can be influenced by the creation of motives,* is just as opposed to Paragraph 51 of the German Penal Code[21] (which is based on the theory of free will) as it is in agreement with the insights of psychoanalysis.[22] The criminal who *must* act as he acts under the influence of instinctual impulses *unconscious* to him is therefore a person who is not motivated in a normal way. He cannot be reformed by punishment and consequently is, in the sense of F. von Liszt, not of sound mind and not legally responsible.

Liszt saw this most clearly with regard to habitual criminals. He says:

The normal person therefore is thought to be of sound mind and responsible before the law. . . . But what is a normal reaction? Is not every crime a deviation from the normal behavior of the average person? . . .

A second question is added to it . . . . If the ineradicable tendency toward crime defies every attempt at reform or deterrence [*Abschreckung*], if it is only a problem of protecting society from the incorrigible [*unverbesserlich*] person by means of execution, banishment, or permanent incarceration, and if it is no longer a question any more of influencing behavior [*Motivsetzung*] through punishment, what is the meaning of the state of mind [*Motivierbarkeit*] of the offender as a prerequisite for sentencing? (1905c [1896]: 220–22)

If a person with diminished soundness of mind has demonstrated his danger to the community by committing a crime, his incarceration in an institution is necessary for the security of society. The convict must not be released from custody until the danger to the community has ended. The designation used for the institution is not relevant . . . . But we must not speak of punitive institutions. What we want is a cure for the patient [*Heilung des Kranken*], and if this can no longer be hoped for, care for the incurably ill patient [*Verpflegung des Siechen*]. . . .

But just this combination of punishment and custody [*Verwahrung*] suggests the second of the above-mentioned questions: Can the hard and fast line between a penitentiary [*Zuchthaus*] and an insane asylum [*Irrenanstalt*], between crime and insanity, be maintained, and especially, can the concepts of soundness of mind and legal responsibility provide the line of demarcation? . . .

The incorrigible criminal is not of sound mind. . . . What is lacking here is the normal process of motivation, and with it the receptivity of the criminal to the new state of mind intended by the punishment. . . .

The distinction between the incarceration of incorrigible criminals for the protection of society and the confinement of mental patients dangerous to the public is not only impractical but also to be rejected in principle. (1905c [1896]: 224–27)

F. von Liszt derived his thesis that the habitual criminal is sick and belongs in a mental institution, not in a penal institution, from a well-known fact. By resorting to crime again and again despite having been repeatedly subjected to legal sanctions, the habitual criminal proves that he is not a normal, healthy person, if one regards the latter, as Liszt does, as a person motivated in a normal way. Psychoanalysis need not add anything to these statements. However, it is able to explain why the unreformed criminal cannot help acting the way he does and why all punitive and educative measures directed at his conscious intent [*an seinen bewussten Willen*] are bound to fail. Only an insight into the unconscious and irrational motives of his actions can provide the key to understanding the facts that Liszt saw very clearly.

Let us now ask whether punishment, even if it is not interpreted as retribution and revenge, i.e., the instinctual gratification of those carrying out the punishment [*die Strafenden*, "punitive ones"], can achieve these goals and can be understood as a rational social measure. On theoretical grounds, one can be very skeptical about the effectiveness of punishment.[23] However, experience turns this theoretical skepticism into a full and complete rejection.

The Failure of the Criminal Justice System

What is the goal of punishment? It is supposed to serve the purposes of deterrence, correction or reform of the criminal, and societal security.[24]

How does the established penal law fulfill these three goals? We will first be concerned with the goal of correction and reform of the criminal. Let us again listen to F. von Liszt:

> Imperial crime statistics demonstrate in an irrefutable manner that the increase in recidivism is far greater than the overall increase in the number of criminals who have been sentenced, and is far greater than the number sentenced for the first time. . . .[25] The inclination toward crime increases with each sentence. . . . The harsher the type and length of the previous sentence, the faster recidivism follows. This not only demonstrates the ineffectiveness of our contemporary system of punishment with regard to professional criminality, but one may also assert without exaggeration that each instance of punishment must be considered a factor in the development of criminality. (1905f [1900]: 324–25)

In summation, Liszt states: "Our punishments have neither a corrective nor a deterrent effect. They do not prevent or hinder crime. On the contrary, they have the effect of strengthening the inclination toward crime."[26] This conclusion is confirmed by experience: "All penitentiary prisoners who had served at least three sentences (penitentiary, prison, or house of correction), of which one or more amounted to six months and over, were counted on the first of October 1894, and to these were added also all those who were committed between then and March 31, 1897. A conference of officials reported what in their judgment was to be expected of each of these 15,539 men and 2,510 women in the future" (Aschaffenburg 1923: 224, 1913:202; see also table 8.3).

We see therefore that punishment does not achieve the goal of reforming or correcting criminals who are dangerous to society. The same facts that prove the complete failure of the goal of correction or reform also show that the second goal of punishment, deterrence, is not achieved either, or hardly so. A distinction is made between two kinds of deterrence, i.e., specific and general. The former is intended to deter the previously convicted person from further criminal acts; the latter is to prevent the mass of people that have not yet become criminals from committing a first offense. With regard to the deterrent effect of punishment, G. Aschaffenburg states:

> In normal times one may perhaps hope for some effect from the threat of punishment; but this effect cannot of course be expressed in numbers. On the contrary, if we examine the statistics objectively, the impression strongly suggests itself that the

Table 8.3. Recidivism of the Convict after Release

	Probable	Incorrigibility	Physical or Mental Defects	Other Reasons	Doubtful	Improbable
			Probable Because of			
Men	14,726	14,441	163	122	440	373
Women	2,319	2,217	38	64	123	68
Total	17,045	16,658	201	186	563	441
[1894–97]						
Men	8,369	8,357	10	2	225	92
Women	1,132	1,128	4	—	30	26
Total	9,501	9,485	14	2	255	118

Source: Aschaffenburg 1913.

expected result has not occurred, or has occurred only to a minimal extent. For many years, the number of people punished for the first time has increased rather than decreased, and with juveniles it has increased decisively. . . . Hence it follows that the fear of punishment is not enough to stop crime. We must not forget, however, that causes external to the individual largely explain this increase. We must therefore limit our opinion with regard to general deterrence to the point that it is not strong enough compared to the growing social danger. . . . At the moment that a crime is decided on or, as in the case of a crime of passion, suddenly committed, the idea of punishment has very little effect as a countermotive. The threat of punishment can be seen only as a remote contingency, because of the excitement in the one case and the hope to remain undetected in the other. Every crime committed by someone not previously punished is a proof of the failure of general deterrence. (1923:292ff.)

With regard to specific deterrence, Aschaffenburg states in the same context: "As regards the effects of specific deterrence, the statistics on recidivism are extraordinarily instructive. They prove that, generally speaking, it fails utterly." In summation, Aschaffenburg thinks he can state with regard to the efficacy of punishment: "Our statistics leave no doubt that our penal system is ineffective" (1923:316).

Finally, the above-cited material shows with great clarity that the third goal of punishment, societal security from crime, is also a failure. Societal security from the recidivist cannot be achieved by a subtly calibrated dose of punishment following each criminal act, but only by his incarceration for the entire period of his danger to the public. Considering the present social conditions and the present state of our methods of influencing the criminal, this usually means incarceration for life. Precisely this has often been demanded by politicians who concern themselves with crime [*Kriminalpolitiker*], and who emphasize the rational character of punishment (cf. Heindl 1926).

Hence, we see that both statistics and the conclusions of leading experts of criminal justice confirm that punishment is an almost complete failure as an effective measure for reform and correction of the criminal, deterrence, and societal security.[27]

The Hidden Purposes of Criminal Justice in a Class Society

Punishment should not gratify the drive for revenge and retribution, but should constitute instead an effective and rational policy. What does it mean then that experts in criminal justice and penal law who advocate the latter point of view generally support the continuation of the prevailing system, albeit with a variety of minor modifications? What can it mean that society holds on to measures whose inefficacy with regard to the intended purpose has been clearly demonstrated? Apparently the criminal justice system also has another, as it were hidden function, that it performs satisfactorily and with precision. It is because of this hidden function that the system is not being abandoned even though it is manifestly incapable of fulfilling its officially stated purposes.

F. von Liszt offers a hint about this additional goal of criminal justice. How does he justify his own inconsistency in sending the habitual criminal to a correctional facility instead of a mental institution, in spite of his insight into the habitual criminal's unsoundness of mind? He states:

> The value judgments of the people [*Volk*], however, are primarily determined not by the anti-social meaning of the criminal act, but by their traditional individual-ethical views. The more the legislator is imbued with the conviction that the strength and depth of an unsullied and clear popular consciousness of law are invaluable for law and order, the more cautiously he will guard against destroying willfully those deeply rooted moral views before being able to replace them with new ones. The popular legal and moral views prevalent today indubitably demand the distinction between crime and insanity, between the maximum security prison and the mental institution. The legislator must take this into account. . . . I therefore demand of the legislator that the more accurate scientific conclusion [*bessere wissenschaftliche Überzeugung*] be sacrificed for the sake of the traditional legal and moral views of the people. (1905c [1896]: 227–28)

The real and hidden purpose of punishment is expressed with the same clarity by G. Aschaffenburg: "A critical examination of general prevention demands the regrettable conclusion that it certainly does not fulfill the great expectations connected with it. I believe it works rather quietly . . . and more in an educational than in a directly deterrent manner. Greater and perhaps also more important than the value of the individual sanction is the didactic value [*erziehliche Wert*] of the idea of general prevention for the overall orientation [*Gesamtanschauungen*] of the people" (1923:294; only partly in 1913:262).

What then is the importance of this "didactic value" of criminal justice "for the overall orientation of the people"?

First of all, it is clear that the object of criminal justice in this respect is no longer the criminal, not even the potential criminal who is to be deterred from a criminal act, but the great mass of the people. Criminal justice has then a sociopsychological function that no longer has anything at all to do with crime and its prevention. We see that even in the mind of some politicians concerned with crime, the criminal justice system is an educational institution that is intended to have an effect on the great mass of the people. A few psychoanalytical considerations may demonstrate how and on the basis of what mechanisms this effect takes place.

Every class society is characterized by the domination of one class over another, more specifically, by the small stratum of the propertied over the great mass of the propertyless. The means by which this domination is exerted are quite varied. The most visible are the means of physical violence represented by the police and the military. These means are certainly not the most important, however. In the long run, domination over the masses could not be carried out by them alone. A psychological means is added that is much more important, for it makes the use of open violence necessary only in exceptional cases. This psychological means consists in the fact that the masses are put in a situation of psychic attachment and dependence on the ruling class or its representatives so that they will obey it and subordinate themselves to it without the use of violence.

How does this happen?

Psychoanalysis has shown to what extent it is possible even with healthy adults to reactivate [*wiederholen*] psychic attitudes from childhood and to transfer the infantile attitude toward the father onto other persons. Characteristic of the child's attitude toward the father is the belief in his physical and mental superiority, or the fear of him. It is one of the most important requirements for the social stability of class society that the masses transfer this infantile attitude of the child toward the father onto the ruling class and its representatives. Through the reactivation of these infantile and very intense emotional bonds, the individual member of the masses is made to accept such a degree of voluntary subordination, even reverence and love, that in the normal course of social life, violent measures are superfluous. The means by which the ruling class imposes itself on the masses as a father figure are quite varied. One of them, and not the most unimportant, is criminal justice. It demonstrates one of the most essential attributes of the father, his power to punish, and it generates the fear that makes an attitude of loving reverence preferable to rebellion. For the child, the power to punish is one of the most essential and constitutive qualities of the father. Therefore, the state, as the representative of the ruling class, must attribute to itself this power to punish. The state must also demonstrate this power, because in it lies an important means by which to force itself on the unconscious of the masses as a father figure. Criminal justice is as it were the rod on the wall, which is supposed to show even the well-behaved child that a father is a father, and a child a child (cf. Fromm 1930 and this volume, pp. 123–28).

In addition to this "educational purpose" [*erzieherischer Zweck*], punishment has another sociopsychological function (cf. Alexander and H. Staub 1956 [1928]: 209ff.). Punishing the criminal provides a form of gratification for the aggressive and sadistic drives of the masses, which are thereby compensated for the many renunciations forced upon them. Punishment makes it possible for them to transfer their natural aggression against the oppressive and ruling class onto the criminal, and thereby to find release for this aggression.[28]

The "sense of justice" [*Gerechtigkeitsgefühl*] of the people, their legal-moral views, are to a large extent nothing but the expression of an unconscious need for revenge and retribution. Therefore what is termed a "just" punishment is often in irreconcilable conflict with rational and effective policies. It is always more or less adapted to the principle of retaliation [*Talionsprinzip*],[29] and its ineffectiveness in deterring and intimidating the criminal consists precisely in the matching [*Angleichung*, "equalization"] of the punishment to the impulses motivating the crime. Consequently, the "just" punishment serves the unconscious need for punishment in the criminal himself and thus frequently does not work to prevent but to stimulate [*Förderung*, "help, support"] the crime. Experience shows that punishment remains useless with regard to certain overpowering instinctual impulses. A murderer is not deterred by the threat of capital punishment. The threat usually founders because of the strength of the drives causing the murder. Viewed from a rational [*zweckrational*] standpoint, one could expect that an "unjust" punishment, i.e., a punishment that threatens the perpetrator of an offense with a disproportionately severe sanction, would be rather more successful than a "just" punishment that is mild and proportionate to the offense, if the offender is conditioned more by egoistic than by strong libidinal motives. A murderer will rarely be prevented from carrying out his crime by the threat of capital punishment. Unless motivated by the most dire emergency, an action based on selfishness [*Eigennutz*], i.e., less on compelling instinctual drives, would more likely be prevented by the threat of capital punishment. In real life [*in der Praxis*], apart from a state of national emergency, such unjust punishments will fail because the masses, seeing in them the expression of a hostile and repressive tendency, would resist such a punitive system with every means at their disposal.

Moreover, the history of penal law shows a development not only away from draconian punishments, but also from "just" punishments derived from a generalized principle of retaliation, and toward the increasing subordination of tendencies gratifying instinctual drives to those gratifying purposive ones. It has been a long road from the burning, quartering, or castration of the criminal as a sought-after popular amusement to the almost secret execution, or to the abolition of capital punishment. For the time being, social conditions necessitate the education of the masses in the sense of fixing infantile attachments and their subsequent transfer to the rulers. They also necessitate instinctual compensation both for exaggerated instinctual renunciations and the release of aggression against the rulers, by transferring them to the criminal. As long as such conditions prevail, the Janus face of criminal justice—one turned toward the criminal, one toward the masses—cannot be removed. Criminal justice is an indispensable psychological requirement for a class society. Only from this point of view can we understand the contradiction that has appeared between the ineffectiveness of the criminal justice system and the holding on to it both by eminent experts in criminal law and by politicians concerned with crime.[30]

The Future of Psychoanalysis and Criminal Justice

Can psychoanalytical insight into the causes and motives of crime be of any practical use under these circumstances? Is there any chance in the near future for psychoanalysis to conquer the courtroom and prevail with its insights?

We consider the chances of this, *de lege lata* [under the established legal system],[31] to be quite small. The reasons are easily understood from the foregoing. The chances would without doubt be great if the criminal justice system would actually and exclusively pursue the goals of fighting crime and reform or correction of the criminal as purposefully and effectively as possible. But as long as the system does little of what it officially asserts [*vorgibt*] it is doing, there is little prospect that it will be guided by the demands of effectiveness, and equally little hope for the practical application of psychoanalytical insights. We were able to show that the criminal justice system is intended to have quite different functions, educating the masses in the sense of subordination and attachment to the rulers, and compensating the masses for their instinctual renunciation. Since criminal law is a product of specific social conditions, and its unspoken function emerges precisely from these social conditions, we will have to remain quite skeptical about the victory of psychoanalytical insights in the existing society.

However, we need not be quite so skeptical about the use of psychoanalysis in the courtroom, also *de lege lata*. This is especially true in cases where the issues are not personal guilt, responsibility, and the effective punishment or correction of the criminal, but revolve around establishing the facts of the case [*Tatbestandsfeststellung*], i.e., in instances where psychology can serve to establish those facts and assist in determining whether a defendant committed a crime or not. In these cases, psychology plays a role similar to that of chemistry or medicine, for example. There is a fairly large number of cases in which psychological considerations play an important role in determining whether a defendant has committed the crime. These are mainly cases in which a confession by the defendant is not forthcoming and the discovery of a plausible motive is decisive for an attribution of guilt. There are also cases in which it is not the crime that is in doubt, but its classification under a certain paragraph of the penal code. This is true if it contains psychological aspects, as for example the distinction between murder and manslaughter. Here psychological considerations are often necessary for clarifying a legal situation [*juristischer Tatbestand*].

In all of these cases, psychoanalysis could also be useful *de lege lata,* because here it is not opposed to the present criminal justice system because of its own, quite different ideas [*Auffassungen,* "conceptions"] about guilt, accountability, and reform or correction. Psychoanalysis can carry out the same function within this system as does chemistry, for example, when it provides information on whether a bloodstain comes from human or animal blood, or as does graphology, when it determines the identity of a person by examining two different types of handwriting. However, one cannot be too optimistic in this regard either. The resistance to psychoanalysis is for the most part socially conditioned (cf. Freud 1961 [1925]). This resistance is so great that we must not be surprised if the most anachronistic psychological views are frequently used in interpreting the facts of a case. This demonstrates a retrograde point of view that would be unthinkable with regard to matters of medicine or chemistry.

However, the chances of using psychoanalysis will be quite different for penal law and criminology *de lege ferenda* [in the legal system of the future].[32] Small as they are at present, they will be great in the future. Psychoanalytic research on crime is still in its infancy, and its further development will be tied to the investigation of many individual criminals as well as groups of criminals. However, it will be able to demonstrate that crimes are conditioned by unconscious motives, and precisely which ones. It will also demonstrate that rational motives provide only one component, and not the decisive one, in the generation of most crimes. As a result of its insights, this research will be able to make decisive contributions to the problem of the reform and correction of the criminal. It will assist in making a diagnosis instead of a "verdict," which will include psychological factors, above all unconscious ones, as well as economic factors. Cases in which the improvement of the criminal's economic situation is enough to end his criminality would be eliminated. This would apply to cases of pure economic emergency or to cases in which the possibility of sublimation, or the substitution of other instinctual gratifications, would lead to the cessation of criminal behavior. This research will also cooperate in the creation of methods through which the easily curable criminals could be corrected in a suitable form of reeducation [*Nacherziehung,* "post-education"] (cf. Aichhorn 1935 [1925]).[33] For criminals who cannot be corrected by such methods, psychotherapy, i.e., the discovery of the unconscious motives of their actions, would be the only effective form of influencing them. However, for those whose constellation of drives cannot be changed even by analytical therapy, in other words, for the incurable, even psychoanalysis would not be able to give any other advice than preventive detention [*Sicherungsverwahrung*] as long as they are dangerous. It must not be forgotten, however, that "dangerous" is a relative term whose meaning depends on the social system and the assessments it produces.

Consequently, the essential contribution of psychoanalysis must remain a theoretical one for the time being, namely the continuation of research into the psychology of criminals and the critique of the existing criminal justice system. This research and critique can be based on the best traditions of the study of penal law, building on the insights and demands for change put forth decades ago by F. von Liszt and his school. We can secure these foundations from a scientific point of view and continue in this direction only if we are careful not to follow Liszt in one point, "that the more accurate scientific conclusion be sacrificed . . . for the sake of the traditional legal and moral views of the people" (1905c [1896]: 228).

Notes

Translators' note: The German version of this essay was reprinted in Erich Fromm, *Gesamtausgabe,* vol. 1, ed. Rainer Funk (Munich: Deutscher Taschenbuch Verlag, 1989), 11–30. All subheadings have been added by the translators. The essay originally appeared in 1931, in a special issue devoted to crime of *Imago: Zeitschrift für Anwendung der Psychoanalyse auf die Natur- und Geisteswissenschaften* (17:2), the leading psychoanalytic journal, which listed Freud as editor in chief. This special issue contained the following contributions: Franz Alexander, "Psychische Hygiene und Kriminalität" (145–73); Franz Alexander, "Ein besessener Autofahrer" (174–93); Hugo Staub, "Psychoanalyse und Strafrecht" (194–216); Hugo Staub, "Einige praktische Schwierigkeiten der psychoanalytischen Kriminalstatistik" (217–25); Erich Fromm, "Zur Psychologie des Verbrechers und der strafenden Gesellschaft" (226–51); Siegfried Bernfeld, "Die Tantalussituation" (252–67); Friedrich Haun, "Strafe für Psychopathen?" (268–302).

1. Translators' note: Franz von Liszt (1851–1919), a cousin of the composer with the same name, was the paramount leader of the liberal reform wing of German criminology and jurisprudence from the 1890s until his death. In 1899, Liszt became a professor of law at the University of Berlin, where he conducted a seminar in criminology. In 1902, he founded the Preparations Committee for the Reform of Criminal Law and, in 1908, the journal *Kritische Beiträge zur Strafrechtsreform*. Although not a Freudian, Liszt was especially concerned with the psychology of the individual offender. He strongly critiqued the concept of general deterrence, as well as the notion that criminal behavior is motivated primarily by rational choice. His earlier writings were published in a massive two-volume collection (Liszt 1905a), in which he subjected the criminal justice system to withering critiques for attempting to control crime through harsh sanctions. His other notable works include an influential textbook and a study of international law.

2. Translators' note: We have usually translated *Delikt* as "offense," although other possible renderings would include "violation" and "crime." We have translated *Verbrechen* as "crime," although it also carries the meaning of "felony."

3. Translators' note: Gustav Aschaffenburg (1866–1944), the leading reform-oriented German criminologist of the early twentieth century after Liszt, studied psychology and neurology under Richard von Krafft-Ebing in Vienna and Jean Charcot in Paris. From 1904 to 1934, he was a professor of psychiatry at the University of Cologne and the director of the Lindenberg Clinic for Nervous and Mental Diseases. In 1905 he founded an influential journal, the *Monatsschrift für Kriminalpsychologie und Strafrechtsreform*. His major work, *Crime and Its Repression,* first published in 1903, went through three German editions, and was translated into English in 1913. Aschaffenburg saw crime as the product of social factors, including poverty and alcoholism, but he gave some weight to supposedly hereditary factors as well. He also concluded that mental illness is a major factor in crime causation. Aschaffenburg critiqued the failure of the German criminal justice system to control crime through its policies of harsh sentences and executions. By the 1920s he came out against the death penalty. After Hitler came to power in 1933, Aschaffenburg did not immediately emigrate, apparently hoping that the Nazis would moderate their policies, despite the fact that, although he had been baptized as a Lutheran, both of his parents were Jews. In 1939, he emigrated to the United States, where he briefly held positions at Catholic University of America and Johns Hopkins University.

4. Translators' note: Here, rather than "criminality," Fromm should have written "property offenses," given the data in table 8.2 and the passage he cites from Aschaffenburg. We would like to thank Jürgen Rojahn for bringing this to our attention.

5. Translators' note: Fromm is using the 1923 third German edition of Aschaffenburg's book. Here, as in many cases, the passage Fromm quotes was already contained in the 1903 edition, which was translated into English in 1913; hence we also give a reference to that 1913 translation, even though we have sometimes translated the passage slightly differently.

6. Translators' note: In fact, according to table 8.2, these crimes reached their highest level in December, and began to decline during the rest of the winter. Once again, we would like to thank Jürgen Rojahn for pointing this out.

7. Translators' note: For background on Alexander and Staub, see notes to the previous chapter.

8. Translators' note: Alexander and Staub, in a chapter of their book entitled "A Psychoanalytical Table of Criminological Diagnosis," delineate several types of crime. Their first large category, "chronic criminality," has four subcategories: (1) "Criminal behavior of those individuals whose Ego . . . is considerably damaged or totally paralyzed" and who are therefore "considered by legal and forensic medicine as not responsible" (1956 [1928]: 119). Examples include those inflicted with "idiocy" or "organic mental diseases," as well as "alcoholics" and "drug addicts." (2) "Criminal behavior conditioned by neurosis," which "is prompted first of all by unconscious motives." These unconscious motives "loosen the Ego from the influence of the inhibitory Superego, or the Ego is deceived by means of various disguises and therefore it fails to appreciate the meaning of the criminal act." One set of examples would include "compulsive or symptomatic crimes" such as "kleptomania" or "pyromania." Another more common example is the "neurotic acting out of criminal tendencies." Here, "the Ego is won over to the crime by means of psychological mechanisms involving suffering, or by means of rationalizations" (1956 [1928]: 120). (3) "Criminal behavior of the normal, non-neurotic criminal whose Superego is criminal." This group includes, but is not limited to, the professional criminal. Here the criminal is part of "a special community that functions on the basis of a special moral code which is different from the usual; it is a special moral code of criminals ('honesty among thieves'). The whole personality of the individual belonging to such a community identifies itself with the crime. His antisocial acts are totally acceptable to his Ego as well as to his Superego. Tramps, beggars, gangsters (primacy of the pleasure principle), professional criminals like pickpockets, burglars, receivers of stolen goods, all belong to this diagnostic group." (4) "The genuine criminal" is a purely theoretical construct, an ideal or "imaginary type." This individual "is not adjusted at all to social life" and would tend to "carry out in action any of his primitive drives as soon as he would perceive them," without "any inner inhibition" of a moral nature (1956 [1928]: 121). Their second large category, "accidental criminality," has two main subcategories: (1) "Crimes resulting from 'mistakes'" would include manslaughter in cases where, under severe strain to the ego, "an unconscious criminal trend may break through" and be acted upon, even though such a course of action is completely rejected by the ego. (2) "Situational crimes," in which an especially severe life crisis leads to crime, because "the inhibitory power of the Superego . . . is put out of commission." These latter crimes are "usually understood and forgiven by the community" (1956 [1928]: 123).

9. Translators' note: For background on Wittels, see notes to previous chapter.

10. Translators' note: Robert Heindl (1883–1958) was a leading government lawyer and criminologist. His early work included a study of British, French, and Spanish penal colonies. In 1912 he wrote a critique of the policy of deportation of criminals, which led the German government to abandon its plans to begin such measures. Heindl held a number of positions in police administration, and was appointed editor of Germany's oldest criminology journal, *Archiv für Kriminologie,* in 1917. After World War I, he was

appointed legal counselor [*wirklicher Legationsrat*] to the Foreign Office [*Auswärtiges Amt*]. His major work, a widely circulated book on the professional criminal (Heindl 1926), took up a number of issues, including penal colonies, fingerprinting and graphology, types of criminals (from petty thieves to serial killers), and crime causation. This book is not without its curiosities, such as photos of nude and tattooed prisoners or of the bodies of criminals who had been beheaded in China. It also exhibits occasional anti-Semitism, as when Heindl writes that most professional criminals "throw their money to the wind" and that "only a few Jewish receivers of stolen goods are careful savers" (1926:141). Pensioned off from his government position in 1933 at age fifty, Heindl resumed his government career after 1945. (The entry in the 1968 edition of *Neue deutsche Biographie* is silent about the years 1933–45.) He served from 1946 to 1949 as president of the Central Office for Criminal Identification, Police Statistics, and Police Communication Systems of the State of Bavaria, before retiring a second time.

11. Translators' note: Fritz Haarmann, "the Werewolf of Hanover," was executed in 1925. He had been convicted of thirty murders, mainly of young men, although the true number may have been more than fifty. Many of the victims, with whom he had sex, were bitten in the throat. Subsequently he sold their flesh as meat and their clothing to second-hand dealers. His crimes became legendary, especially after he made a lurid and detailed confession. His case also became the topic of much political debate, with leftists suggesting that it took so long to arrest him because of his connections to the police, for whom he was a paid informer. Even at his trial, Haarmann, who apparently knew the Hanover police chief, was treated in a deferential manner by the judge, who allowed him to crack jokes and interrupt witnesses. For its part, the far right argued that homosexual murderers like Haarmann were being protected by a Jewish conspiracy. His crimes also became a staple of popular songs, and were referred to in films and literary works in the 1920s. Artistic works of the period, such as expressionist painter Otto Dix's "Sexual Murder" (1922), show a preoccupation with serial killers and sexual violence against women. Wilhelm Grossmann, "the Bluebeard of the Silesian Railway," was arrested in 1921 for killing and cannibalizing some fourteen women and girls in his apartment near the Berlin terminus of the Silesian railroad. He had sex with his victims, whom he also killed and dismembered, usually selling their flesh as meat. He later hanged himself in his cell. We were unable to obtain additional information about Hering, the third serial killer listed by Heindl.

12. Translators' note: Andrew Bichel was executed after apparently killing several young women in Bavaria in 1807–8. Martin Dumollard confessed to a series of murders of young women in a town outside Lyon, and was executed in 1861. We could not find additional information on Bishop.

13. Translators' note: John Williams was arrested in 1811 for two cases in the East End of London in which entire families had been murdered with great brutality, including slashed throats and decapitations. He committed suicide in jail before his trial.

14. Translators' note: French in the original.

15. Translators' note: Latin in the original.

16. Translators' note: Alexander and Staub had written: "The psychological situation in the case when the sense of justice is injured . . . leads to rebellion and to the breaking through of primitive anti-social drives; one feels threatened by the very authorities whose business it is to uphold the law. . . . The ego at once loses its dependence on the inner representative of authority—the superego. . . . This lifts the moral inhibitions" (1956 [1928]: 83–84).

17. Translators' note: in the sense of being economically disadvantaged.

18. The same is probably true of prostitution. Here also certain instinctual needs are gratified that would have other possibilities of release under different socioeconomic conditions.

19. Translators' note: *Zurechnungsfähigkeit* refers to a defendant's ability to stand trial or even to comprehend the punishment to be meted out. It carries three meanings which are relevant here: (1) accountability for one's actions, (2) soundness of mind, and (3) responsibility before the law. We have usually opted either for 2 or 3, and sometimes both. We have usually translated another related, but more legal and less psychological term, *strafliche Verantwortlichkeit,* as "accountability before the law."

20. Translators' note: Here the term "receptivity" indicates different motivational tendencies, i.e., sexual desire, greed, anger, or revenge.

21. Translators' note: Alexander and Staub summed up Paragraph 51 as follows: "This paragraph admits that those who commit a crime while in a state of unconsciousness or in a state of general psychic disorganization, are not [legally] responsible; this principle is applicable only to the comparatively rare cases of epileptic or hysterical twilight states, or to cases of severest intoxications. . . . Thus it is clear that only borderline cases of severe mental diseases are covered by the article mentioned above; yet these cases play a relatively unimportant part in practical criminology" (1956 [1928]: 64).

22. We will only point out briefly that we cannot share F. Alexander and H. Staub's (1956 [1928]) position on the problem of [legal] accountability. The two authors want to see the participation of the ego in the criminal act as a measure of accountability. [Translators' note: Alexander and Staub had written that "the practical concept of responsibility can thus be replaced by a *scientific* concept of the degree and mode of *participation of the ego in the given act*" (1956 [1928]: 62).] However, they forget that the ego in its content is just as determined, unfree, and unaccountable as any other psychic agency [*seelische Instanz*]. It is therefore not acceptable to emphasize the participation of the ego in the commission of an offense, in order to ground punishment in legal philosophy. In this way, the doctrine of free will is readmitted into penal law through the back door, after Liszt and his school had already expelled it through the front door decades ago. Another assumption by the two authors seems to originate from the same tendency of adaptation to the prevailing criminal law. It is the notion of the "normal criminal," i.e., the criminal with a normal superego who is adapted to the community of criminals. It seems to us that this ethic of criminals is more the result of romantic notions than an empirical fact. Both this phenomenon of an ethic of criminals and the element of community that supposedly impresses itself on us as something essential [*bei denen das Gemeinschaftsmoment*

as wesentlich imponiert] are secondary formations. Instead, criminal behavior is based on the actual life needs of criminals, which are antisocial and hostile to any sense of community.

23. In this context, the unconscious feeling of guilt and the unconscious need for punishment come to mind. They were particularly emphasized by Theodor Reik (1959 [1925]).

24. Cf. Liszt (1905d [1896]).

25. Translators' note: In the article Fromm is citing, Liszt presents data from Germany for the years 1882–96. During this period, the overall population increased by 15.8 percent, while the number of people receiving criminal sentences increased by 38.5 percent. When this latter figure was broken down, reported Liszt, there was, on the one hand, an increase of a mere 13 percent in the number of first-time offenders sentenced during those sixteen years, roughly keeping pace with the increase in population. On the other hand, however, during the same sixteen-year period the number of recidivists sentenced increased by a staggering 116 percent (Liszt 1905f [1900]: 324–25).

26. Translators' note: Fromm does not give a specific reference for this citation from Liszt, and we could not locate it.

27. There can be no doubt that such presently popular penal reforms as gradated sentencing must remain just as ineffective as the old methods. This is true in part because of the inability and incompetence of the people entrusted with the administration of punishment, but mainly because even this gradated punishment merely intends to influence the minds of the criminals with educational measures that obviously had failed even before those criminals had been sent to the correctional facility. The inefficacy of these reform measures, which was to be expected in theory, was confirmed by Heindl in an illuminating way on the basis of the empirical data up to now. Concepts such as personality profiling [*Persönlichkeitserforschung*], which are used especially in the Prussian decree on penal reform, demonstrate goodwill, but do not go beyond the framework of the psychology of consciousness [*Bewusstseinspsychologie*], which is equally fruitless in theory and in practice.

28. Translators' note: Alexander and Staub bring up sadism in their discussion of the response of the masses to the criminal justice system in an appendix to their book entitled "General Considerations of the Social Psychology of Punishment" (1956 [1928]: 209–23).

29. Translators' note: In the sense of "an eye for an eye."

30. The first "criminal code" that removed the concepts of "crime" and "punishment" theoretically and practically, replacing them with the concepts of "action dangerous to society" and "measures of social protection," is that of the Soviet Union (cf. N. Pasche-Oserski 1929).

31. Translators' note: Latin in the original, literally "of or from established law."

32. Translators' note: Latin in the original, literally "of law still to be made."

33. Translators' note: August Aichhorn (1878–1949) was a renowned Viennese educator who introduced new methods for the treatment of juvenile offenders confined in youth homes. As recounted in his classic 1925 book (translated into English a decade later),

Wayward Youth [a more accurate translation of the German title *Verwahrloste Jugend,* one which captures its tone of social critique, would be "Neglected Youth"], Aichhorn allowed unparalleled freedom and autonomy to his charges, a policy which had far better results than repression and harsh discipline. He applied these humanistic policies even to the most aggressive youths, dubbed "incorrigible" by the institutions. Unlike most others working in the field at this time, he felt, based on the treatment they had received from society, that the anger and hostility toward society of delinquent youth was usually justified. In 1922, after years of work with juveniles, he embraced psychoanalysis, after concluding that its perspectives coincided with his own experience. Aichhorn stayed in Vienna after the 1938 *Anschluss* with Nazi Germany, in part to remain close to his son, who was interned at Dachau. He worked quietly to keep psychoanalysis alive during that period. Then, in 1946, shortly before his death, he was instrumental in the reopening of the Vienna Psychoanalytical Society, soon renamed the August Aichhorn Society in his honor.

References Cited

Aichhorn, August. 1935 [1925]. *Wayward Youth.* New York. Viking Press.

Alexander, Franz. 1931. "Psychische Hygiene und Kriminalität." *Imago: Zeitschrift für Anwendung der Psychoanalyse auf die Natur- und Geisteswissenschaften* 17 (2): 145–73.

Alexander, Franz, and Hugo Staub. 1956 [1928]. *The Criminal, the Judge, and the Public: A Psychological Analysis.* Trans. Grigory Zilboorg. Glencoe, Ill.: Free Press.

Aschaffenburg, Gustav. 1913 [1903]. *Crime and Its Repression.* Trans. Adalbert Albrecht. Boston: Little, Brown.

———. 1923. *Das Verbrechen und seine Bekämpfung.* 3d ed. Heidelberg: Carl Winter Verlag.

Berg, Hermann. 1902. "Getreidepreise und Kriminalität in Deutschland seit 1882." *Abhandlungen des kriminalistischen Seminars Berlin,* vol. 2. Berlin: J. Guttentag.

Freud, Sigmund. 1961 [1925]. "The Resistances to Psychoanalysis." In *The Complete Psychological Works of Sigmund Freud, Standard Edition.* 24 vols. 19:211–22. London: Hogarth Press.

Fromm, Erich. 1930. "Der Staat als Erzieher: Zur Psychologie der Strafjustiz." *Zeitschrift für psychoanalytische Pädagogik.* 4 (1): 5–9. (English translation in this volume, pp. 123–28)

Fuld, L. 1881. *Der Einfluss der Lebensmittelpreise auf die Begehung der strafbaren Handlungen.* Mainz: Diemer Verlag.

Heindl, Robert. 1926. *Der Berufsverbrecher.* Berlin: Pan-Verlag Rolf Heise.

Herz, Hugo. 1905. "Die Verbrechensbewegung in Österreich in den letzten dreissig Jahren in ihrem Zusammenhang mit den wirtschaftlichen Verhältnissen." *Monatsschrift für Kriminalpsychologie und Strafrechtsreform.* Vol. 2.

Liszt, Franz von. 1905a. *Strafrechtliche Aufsätze und Vorträge,* vol. 2. Berlin: J. Guttentag.

———. 1905b [1893]. "Die deterministischen Gegner der Zweckstrafe." In Liszt 1905a: 25–74.

———. 1905c [1896]. "Die strafrechtliche Zurechnungsfähigkeit." In Liszt 1905a:214–29.

————. 1905d [1896]. "Die psychologischen Grundlagen der Kriminalpolitik." In Liszt 1905a:170–213.

————. 1905e [1898]. "Das Verbrechen als sozial-pathologische Erscheinung." In Liszt 1905a:230–50.

————. 1905f [1900]. "Das gewerbsmässige Verbrechen." In Liszt 1905a:308–30.

Müller, Heinrich. 1899. *Untersuchungen über die Bewegung der Kriminalität in ihrem Zusammenhang mit den wirtschaftlichen Verhältnissen.* Halle: Kämmerer Verlag.

Pasche-Oserski, N. 1929. *Strafe und Strafvollzug in der Sowjetunion.* Berlin: A. Baumeister.

Reik, Theodor. 1959 [1925]. *The Compulsion to Confess: On the Psychoanalysis of Crime and Punishment.* New York: Farrar, Straus, and Cuddahy.

Wittels, Fritz. 1928. *Die Welt ohne Zuchthaus.* Stuttgart: Hippokrates Verlag.

Selected Bibliography

Books by Erich Fromm

1941. *Escape from Freedom.* New York: Farrar and Rinehart.

1947. *Man for Himself: An Inquiry into the Psychology of Ethics.* New York: Rinehart.

1950. *Psychoanalysis and Religion.* New Haven: Yale University Press.

1951. *The Forgotten Language: An Introduction to the Understanding of Dreams, Fairy Tales And Myths.* New York: Rinehart.

1955. *The Sane Society.* New York: Rinehart and Winston.

1956. *The Art of Loving: An Inquiry into the Nature of Love.* New York: Harper and Row.

1959. *Sigmund Freud's Mission: An Analysis of His Personality and Influence.* New York: Harper and Row.

1960. (and D. T. Suzuki). *Zen Buddhism and Psychoanalysis.* New York: Harper and Row.

1961a. *May Man Prevail? An Inquiry into the Facts and Fictions of Foreign Policy.* New York: Doubleday.

1961b. *Marx's Concept of Man.* New York: Frederick Ungar Publishing Co.

1962. *Beyond the Chains of Illusion: My Encounter with Marx and Freud.* New York: Simon and Schuster.

1963. *The Dogma of Christ and Other Essays on Religion, Psychology and Culture.* New York: Holt, Rinehart and Winston.

1964. *The Heart of Man: Its Genius for Good and Evil.* New York: Harper and Row.

1965. *Socialist Humanism: An International Symposium.* Ed. Erich Fromm. New York: Doubleday.

1966. *You Shall Be As Gods: A Radical Interpretation of the Old Testament and Its Tradition.* New York: Holt, Rinehart and Winston.

1968a. *The Revolution of Hope: Toward a Humanized Technology.* New York: Harper and Row.

1968b. *The Nature of Man.* Ed. Erich Fromm and Ramón Xirau. New York: Macmillan.

1970. *The Crisis of Psychoanalysis: Essays on Freud, Marx and Social Psychology.* New York: Holt, Rinehart and Winston.

1970. (and Michael Maccoby). *Social Character in a Mexican Village: A Sociopsychoanalytic Study.* Englewood Cliffs, N.J.: Prentice Hall.

1973. *The Anatomy of Human Destructiveness.* New York: Holt, Rinehart and Winston.

1976. *To Have Or to Be?* New York: Harper and Row.

1979. *Greatness and Limitations of Freud's Thought.* New York: Harper and Row.

1981. *On Disobedience and Other Essays.* New York: Seabury Press.

1984. *The Working Class in Weimar Germany: A Psychological and Sociological Study.* Ed. Wolfgang Bonss. Cambridge, Mass.: Harvard University Press.

1986. *For the Love of Life.* Ed. Hans Jürgen Schultz. New York: Free Press.

1992. *The Revision of Psychoanalysis.* Ed. Rainer Funk. Boulder, Colo.: Westview Press.

1993. *The Art of Being.* Ed. Rainer Funk. New York: Continuum.

1994a. *The Erich Fromm Reader.* Ed. Rainer Funk, with a foreword by Joel Kovel. Atlantic Highlands, N.J.: Humanities Press.

1994b. *The Art of Listening.* Ed. Rainer Funk. New York: Continuum.

1994c. *On Being Human.* Ed. Rainer Funk. New York: Continuum.

1995. *The Essential Fromm: Life between Having and Being.* Ed. Rainer Funk. New York: Continuum.

1997. *Love, Sexuality and Matriarchy: About Gender.* Ed. Rainer Funk. New York: Fromm International.

Books on Erich Fromm in English

Burston, Daniel. 1991. *The Legacy of Erich Fromm.* Cambridge, Mass.: Harvard University Press.

Cortina, Mauricio, and Michael Maccoby, eds. 1996. *A Prophetic Analyst: Erich Fromm's Contribution to Psychoanalysis.* London: Jason Aronson.

Funk, Rainer. 1982. *Erich Fromm: The Courage to Be Human.* New York: Continuum.

Hausdorff, Don. 1972. *Erich Fromm.* New York: Twayne.

Knapp, Gerhard P. 1989. *The Art of Living: Erich Fromm's Life and Work.* New York: Peter Lang.

Landis, Bernard and Edward S. Tauber, eds. 1971. *In the Name of Life: Essays in Honor of Erich Fromm.* New York: Holt, Rinehart and Winston.

Lundgren, Svante. 1998. *Fight against Idols: Erich Fromm on Religion, Judaism, and the Bible.* New York: Peter Lang.

Schaar, John H. 1961. *Escape from Authority: The Perspectives of Erich Fromm.* New York: Harper and Row.

Selected Writings on Critical and Peacemaking Criminology

Anderson, Kevin. 1991. "Radical Criminology and the Overcoming of Alienation: Perspectives from Marxian and Gandhian Humanism." In *Criminology as Peacemaking.* Ed. Harold E. Pepinsky and Richard Quinney. 14–29. Bloomington: Indiana University Press.

Arrigo, Bruce A., ed. 1999. *Social Justice: The Maturation of Critical Theory in Law, Crime, and Deviance.* Belmont, Calif.: Wadsworth.

Barak, Gregg, ed. 1991. *Crimes by the Capitalistic State.* Albany, N.Y.: State University of New York Press.

Beirne, Piers. 1993. *Inventing Criminology.* Albany, N.Y.: State University of New York Press.

Bianchi, Herman, and René van Swaaningen, eds. 1986. *Abolitionism: Towards a Non-Repressive Approach to Crime.* Amsterdam: Free University Press.

Brownstein, Henry. 1992. "Making Peace in the War on Drugs." *Humanity and Society.* 16(2): 217–35.

Caulfield, Susan L. 1996. "Peacemaking Criminology: Introduction and Implications for Intersection of Race, Class, and Gender." In *Race, Class, and Gender in Criminology.* Ed. M. Schwartz and D. Milovanic. 91–103. New York: Garland.

Chancer, Lynn. 1992. *Sadomasochism and Everyday Life.* New Brunswick, N.J.: Rutgers University Press.

Chambliss, William and Robert J. Seidman. 1982. *Law, Order, and Power.* Second Edition. Reading, Mass.: Addison-Wesley.

Chesney-Lind, Meda and Randall G. Sheldon. 1992. *Girls, Delinquency, and Juvenile Justice.* Pacific Grove, Calif.: Brooks/Cole.

Christie, Nils. 1993. *Crime Control as Industry.* New York: Routledge.

Clear, Todd R. 1994. *Harm in American Penology.* Albany, N.Y.: State University of New York Press.

Currie, Elliott. 1985. *Confronting Crime: An American Challenge.* New York: Pantheon.

Daly, Kathleen and Russ Immarigeon. 1998. "The Past, Present, and Future of Restorative Justice: Some Critical Reflections," *Contemporary Justice Review.* 1(1): 21–45.

DeKeseredy, Walter S. and Martin S. Schwartz. 1996. *Contemporary Criminology.* Belmont, Calif.: Wadsworth.

Elias, Robert. 1986. *The Politics of Victims, Victimology, and Human Rights.* New York: Oxford University Press.

Friedrichs, David O. 1994. "Crime Wars and Peacemaking Criminology." *Peace Review* 6(2): 159–164.

Fuller, John R. 1998. *Criminal Justice: A Peacemaking Perspective.* Boston: Allyn and Bacon.

Galliher, John F. 1989. *Criminology: Human Rights, Criminal Law, and Crime.* Englewood Cliffs, N.J.: Prentice Hall.

Garland, David. 1990. *Punishment and Modern Society.* Chicago: University of Chicago Press.

Greenberg, David. ed. 1993. *Crime and Capitalism.* Palo Alto, Calif.: Mayfield.

Harris, Kay M. 1991. "Moving into the New Millennium: Toward a Feminist View of Justice." In *Criminology as Peacemaking.* Ed. Harold E. Pepinsky and Richard Quinney. 83–97. Bloomington: Indiana University Press.

Hartjen, Clayton A. 1978. *Crime and Criminalization.* Second Edition. New York: Praeger.

Lanier, Mark M. and Stuart Henry. 1998. *Essential Criminology.* Boulder, Colo.: Westview.

Lozoff, Bo and Michael Braswell. 1989. *Inner Corrections: Finding Peace and Peacemaking.* Cincinnati: Anderson.

MacLean, Brian D. and Dragan Milovanovic, eds. 1997. *Thinking Critically about Crime.* Vancouver: Collective Press.

McDermott, M. Joan. 1994. "Criminology as Peacemaking, Feminist Ethics and the Victimization of Women." *Women and Criminal Justice* 5(2): 21–44.

Michalowski, Raymond. 1985. *Order, Law and Crime.* New York: Random House.

Pepinsky. Harold E. 1991. *The Geometry of Violence and Democracy.* Bloomington: Indiana University Press.

————, and Richard Quinney, eds. 1991. *Criminology as Peacemaking.* Bloomington: Indiana University Press.

Quinney, Richard. 1980. *Class, State, and Crime.* Second edition. New York: Longman.

————, and John Wildeman. 1991. *The Problem of Crime: A Peace and Social Justice Perspective.* Mountain View, Calif.: Mayfield.

Reiman, Jeffrey. (1979) 1995. *The Rich Get Richer and the Poor Get Prison.* New York: John Wiley.

Rusche, Georg and Otto Kirchheimer. 1939. *Punishment and Social Structure.* New York: Columbia University Press.

Schwendinger, Herman and Julia Schwendinger. 1985. *Adolescent Subcultures and Delinquency.* New York: Praeger.

Thomas, Jim and Aogan O'Maolchatha. 1989. "Reassessing the Critical Metaphor: An Optimistic Revisionist View." *Justice Quarterly* 6(2): 143–72.

Tifft, Larry L. and Dennis Sullivan. 1980. *The Struggle to Be Human.* Sanday, Orkney, U.K.: Cienfuegos.

Van Ness, Daniel and Karen H. Strong. 1997. *Restoring Justice.* Cincinnati: Anderson.

Contributors

KEVIN ANDERSON, an associate professor of sociology at Northern Illinois University, has worked since the 1970s in philosophy and social theory as well as criminological theory. He is the author of *Lenin, Hegel, and Western Marxism: A Critical Study* (1995) and the coeditor of *Marx on Suicide* (1999). His articles on Marxism, Hegel, Critical Theory, Marxist humanism, and critical criminology have appeared in journals such as *Sociological Theory, Science and Society, Review of Radical Political Economics,* and *Justice Quarterly.* He has been awarded an American Council of Learned Societies Fellowship.

LYNN S. CHANCER is an assistant professor of sociology at Barnard College, Columbia University. She is the author of *Sadomasochism in Everyday Life* (1992), *Reconcilable Differences: Confronting Beauty, Pornography and the Future of Feminism* (1998), and articles in *Gender and Society* and other journals. She is completing a book manuscript tentatively entitled "Provoking Assaults: Gender, Race, and Class in High-Profile Crime Cases" (forthcoming, University of California Press).

RAINER FUNK, a practicing psychoanalyst in Tübingen, Germany, was Erich Fromm's last assistant in Locarno, Switzerland, and now serves as his literary executor, overseeing the Erich Fromm Archives in Tübingen. He is the author of *Erich Fromm: The Courage to Be Human* (1992) and other works on Fromm published in German. Since Fromm's death in 1980, he has edited two German editions of Fromm's writings: a ten-volume *Collected Works* and eight volumes of posthumously published writings. In his own work Funk is especially concerned with Fromm's contribution to psychoanalysis and social psychology.

HEINZ D. OSTERLE, professor emeritus of German at Northern Illinois University, is the editor of *Bilder von Amerika: Gespräche mit deutschen Schriftstellern*

(1987) and *Amerika! New Essays in German Literature* (1989). His work on German literature and Critical Theory has appeared in journals such as *PMLA, Monatshefte, German Quarterly, New German Critique,* and *German Studies Review.*

RICHARD QUINNEY, professor emeritus of Sociology at Northern Illinois University, has been developing a peacemaking criminology for several years. He was a Fulbright Professor in Ireland and has received the Edwin H. Sutherland Award from the American Society of Criminology. His books include *The Social Reality of Crime* (1970), *Critique of Legal Order* (1974), *Class, State, and Crime* (1977), *Providence* (1980), *Social Existence* (1982), and *Criminology as Peacemaking* (1991, with Harold E. Pepinsky). His autobiographical reflections can be found in *Journey to a Far Place* (1991) and *For the Time Being* (1998).

POLLY F. RADOSH is a professor of sociology and director of women's studies at Western Illinois University. The coauthor with Brendan Maguire of *The Past, Present, and Future of American Criminal Justice* (1996) and *Introduction to Criminology* (1999), she has also published theoretical and empirical articles on various issues related to women's crime in *Humanity and Society, Sociological Spectrum,* and the *Journal of Crime and Justice,* as well as book chapters in several edited volumes. In addition, she conducts research on and writes about the sociolegal status of women as unlicensed medical practitioners, such as midwives.

JOHN F. WOZNIAK is an associate professor of sociology and chair of the Department of Sociology and Anthropology at Western Illinois University. His research work in criminology has led to articles on the seriousness of crime, public attitudes toward crime, elderly offenders, correctional policy, stress and social supports among police, and rural police functions in journals such as *Criminology, Journal of Criminal Justice, Crime and Social Justice, Federal Probation,* and *Police Studies.*

Index

female crime: as challenge to cultural roles, 60–63, 67–68, 74–75; increase in, 60–61, *61, 62,* 67–69; motivations for, 66–69, 72–74, 78–79n11, 134–35; social character and, 66–69, 70–74; types of, 67, 78–79n11; understanding, 74–77
femininity, 35, 67–68
feminism: female crime and, 61, 68; on Freudianism, 88; goals of, 77
feminization of poverty, 69, 78n9
Ferenczi, Sándor, 7, 99
Ferri, Enrico, 114n1
Florence (Colo.), prison in, 38–39
football, male violence linked to, 66
Ford Company, crime of, 51–52
Foucault, Michel: as antihumanist, 113; on crime and punishment, 109–12; on Frankfurt School, 115n14; on institutionalization, 88. *See also* panopticon
Fox, Vernon, 48
France, economy and crime rate linked in, 86
Frankfurt am Main, 4
Frankfurter Zeitung (newspaper), 107
Frankfurt School: criminology contributions from, 83–84; Fromm at, 7, 12, 91–92; mass unconscious and, 42; as passé, 32; Rusche and, 106. *See also* Freudian Marxism
fraud, seasons and, 130, *131*
freedom, negative definition of, 33–35
Freeman, Annis, 13, 14
free will: accountability and, 140, 153–54n22; patriarchy's incorporation of, 71–72
French, Marilyn, 64, 65
Freud, Anna, 99
Freud, Sigmund: biography of, 128n6; on criminals with a sense of guilt, 89, 97; on death instinct, 115n7; debate on, 91; Fromm's interpretation of, 15, 92–97; on group psychology, 8; on murder case and Oedipus complex, 98–99; on resistance to psychoanalysis, 148; role of, 88, 92; works: *Beyond the Pleasure Principle,* 115n7; *Civilization and Its Discontents,* 93, 94, 115n7; *Group Psychology and the Analysis of the Ego,* 8
Freudian Marxism: development of, 83–84, 91–94; discussions of, 7; economic factors

and ideology in, 93–94; expanded to include crime, 99–106; Fromm's early, 91–97; as passé, 32
Freudian psychoanalysis: applied to crime, 87–90, 147–49; courtroom use of, 147–48; dialectical categories in, 91; feminist critique of, 88; Fromm influenced by, 6–7, 91, 95, 128n6; humanism applied to, 97; Marxism's implications for, 95–97; as materialistic, 93, 94; social approach to, 7–8, 92–97; as sole cure, 94; university status for, 92. *See also* Freudian Marxism; instinct theory; libido theory; Oedipus complex
Friedenberg, Edgar Z., 14
Friedländer (murderer), 123, 127n3
Friedrichs, David, 45, 47, 48
Fromm, Erich: background of, 3; characterization of, 43; criminal justice articles by, 97–106; influences on, 4–7, 10, 87–90, 91, 95, 103, 104, 106, 128n6, 149; literary legacy of, 14–16, 43, 83–84, 92–93; marriages of, 7, 13; political activities of, 13–14, 16, 27–28, 92; political context of, 96–97; psychoanalytic training of, 7; relevance of, 40–42, 112–14; religious influences on, 3–6, 14–16; sociological and psychoanalytic influences on, 7–12; teaching by, 12–13; terminology of, 11, 127–28n4; vision of, 53–55; works: *The Anatomy of Human Destructiveness,* 16, 115n7; *The Art of Loving,* 15, 24, 70–71; *The Crisis of Psychoanalysis,* 70, 121; "The Dogma of Christ," 14, 92; *The Forgotten Language,* 15; *To Have or to Be?,* 16, 23–24, 26; *Man for Himself,* 15; *Marx's Concept of Man,* 15; "The Method and Function of an Analytic Social Psychology," 94–95; "Politics and Psychoanalysis," 93; *Psychoanalysis and Religion,* 15; "Psychoanalysis and Sociology," 91–92; "Psychoanalysis and Zen Buddhism," 15–16; *Revolution of Hope,* 16; *Socialist Humanism,* 23–24, 27; "The Theory of Mother Right," 115n8; *You Shall Be as Gods,* 16. *See also* alienation; *Escape from Freedom* (Fromm); love; "Oedipus in Innsbruck" (Fromm); "On the Psychology of the Criminal and the Punitive Society" (Fromm); sadomasochism; *The Sane Society*

Typeset in 10.5/13 Adobe Garamond
with Futura Extra Bold display
Designed by Dennis Roberts
Composed by Celia Shapland
for the University of Illinois Press
Manufactured by Versa Press, Inc.

University of Illinois Press
1325 South Oak Street
Champaign, IL 61820-6903
www.press.uillinois.edu